Gather:
a celebration of
women's circles

A Womancraft Publishing Compendium

*Compiled, edited and with an introduction
by Lucy H. Pearce*

WOMANCRAFT PUBLISHING

Published by Womancraft Publishing, 2025

womancraftpublishing.com

ISBN 978-1-916672-15-4

Gather: a celebration of women's circles: A Womancraft Compendium is also available in ebook format: ISBN 978-1-916672-17-8

Womancraft Publishing is committed to sharing powerful new women's voices, through a collaborative publishing process. We are proud to midwife this work, however the story, the experiences and the words are the authors' alone. The views expressed by each contributor are solely their own and do not necessarily reflect the views of Womancraft Publishing.

A percentage of Womancraft Publishing profits are invested back into the environment reforesting the tropics (via TreeSisters) and forward into the community. 10% of the profits from this book are shared between For a Loving Future and The HOPE Foundation.

Contents

Introduction

Lucy H. Pearce

I learned the magic of the circle as a young child. I was a single child to a single mother who was following the threads of her own spirituality down many paths. I first learned the circle in my body through the silent communal worship of Quaker meetings, no priest, no hierarchy, just a group of people, gathered together in soul companionship to connect to the sacred within and to share that with those gathered. I am a Quaker at heart – not the Christian part, but the collective form of gathering and speaking when moved by spirit, that has always been there – weddings, funerals, Sunday services, even dinner parties, that ability to be moved by spirit to stand and speak. The lack of hierarchy or dogma. The absolute knowing that spirit can and does move through each of us, that each of us can be a channel, a vessel, to bring forth what others in the room need to hear. The courage to stand shaking, knowing that you are called to speak, but not knowing what is about to come through. Trusting the emergent, trusting your body and your voice to break the silence, to take up space, to speak your truth to listening silent ears of people who will not respond to what you say, bar a gentle nod of the head, a shy smile, the glisten of tears in the eyes. The space to speak aloud and be heard, not to have to fight for space to share. And the feeling of the space ebbing back into held sacred silence after what has come through you has been said. Breaking that tendency we have to respond, to share a story in response, to correct or make better. None of that happens in circle. It may happen afterwards, over coffee, but in that moment there is your voice, the spirit passing through you, the held space and the silence.

My other early experience of circles was that of circle dance. Again a group gathering, wordless, moving together, meditatively, the repeated actions taking one into a gentle trance state, that feeling of being one with the group, a living organism bigger than all the individuals who make it up, a giant sacred amoeba gently pulsating. It is a practice I have revisited many times in my adult life, including leading a giant circle dance of over a hundred people at a transformational women's event.

In my teens and young adulthood the circle held me still. I was a passionate drama student and later teacher, so theatre warm-up games were always done in circle: a transformative crucible for play and exploration.

The first women's circle I attended was the La Leche League breastfeeding circle, as a new mother. A discussion group, place of mutual support, we sat in a circle and shared our struggles, learning together, hearing the experiences of other women and feeling less alone.

At that time, I read the book *Circle of Stones* by Judith Duerk, a book that in its own gentle quiet way shifted my world on its axis for ever. A book I have returned to countless times over the years. A slim volume of reflections on history and women's culture, personal dreams and short poetic parts, she asks, insistently throughout – *how might your life be different if you had a circle of women?*

These words changed my life.

How might your life have been different if there had been a place for you…a place for you to go, a place of women to go, to be, to return to as a woman? … Where you were received and affirmed? A place where other women, perhaps somewhat older, had been affirmed before you, each in her time, affirmed, as she struggled to become more truly herself.

How might your life be different?

Judith Duerk

That shift in tense – from looking back with a sense of longing and loss – how might your life have been different – to the forward-looking invitation to vision and create a new way of life for yourself – how might your life BE different. No complaining, no regrets, the power is in your hands to make the world you wish to see for yourself. These were the seeds to a new life for me.

I printed out a quote and made a little invitation to the women I felt most connected to in the La Leche League group, inviting them to my home to start our own women's circle. We learned from there, partly from books, to get a starting blueprint, but it has evolved over the last seventeen years into something all of our own. Many women have come and gone but a core of us have remained. We have travelled so much individually – births and deaths, parent's aging, menopause, children struggling, mental health crises, family issues, separations, diagnoses, starting businesses, leaving jobs…and we have held each other through it all. Sometimes we meet for a walk, a swim or a meal, to watch a movie, drum or weave a Brigid's cross. But most often we gather in a little cabin, light a candle, have a cup of herbal tea and a slice of homemade cake and then settle ourselves into silence. One of us may share a poem or a song or a piece of music to shift the mood, to focus us. And then we check in, if we feel called. Speaking as long as we need to, without any response, we share what is real and true for us in the moment, often being surprised ourselves by what emerges. Then we ebb into silence, until the next sister is called to speak. Once each has spoken the conversation weaves between us on the themes that have emerged, tools or insights are offered if people are looking for these, but the option for no response, no further discussion is always there. We may do a short practice together, we might need a group hug. And then the meeting is brought to a close, each giving a brief check out and then off we go back to our individual homes and lives. It is something simple and sacred. We feel the lack of it when our lives are over-busy and we can't find a date that works for us all.

Our circle just is, whoever feels the need for a circle reaches out on our WhatsApp group, a couple of women who have the space tend to host them, and we each just know how it goes now, know ourselves and each other, and trust the process. There are no bells and whistles, no performance. It is like sinking into a warm bath of belonging: shedding your everyday clothes and masks and "everything's fine" and getting naked, metaphorically…and sometimes literally.

I have read many books on circles and been to many different sorts of circles. I have never trained as a circle leader. Although I initiated our circle and was the one most interested in the background and history of them because of my work, our circle is collective. At the beginning I definitely took on a leadership role. In part because that is what I do, and in part because I was the one researching them.

I was in my late-twenties when I entered a red tent for the first time, at an arts festival, and when I did, it felt like home. I wrote about them in my book, *Moon Time*, and worked with others to create one here where I live, which was open to the whole community. Some women travelled for over an hour to reach us, so hungry were they for the magic of circle, and how few there were at that time here.

My intention as I wove the material for this book together and commissioned pieces was that you get not only the theory and praxis and practical guidance from women deeply experienced in this field, but also the chance to peep inside the many different spaces that are usually kept private around the world. So you can be inspired by the diversity of practices, purposes and women who are making circles their own. To see that there is no one size fits all. No right way of doing it. There are things that work…and things that experience has taught us that tend not to. But there is so much possibility – from red tents, to menopause support groups, to spiritual circles, creativity circles, wisdom circles, grief circles and coming of age circles…

Each of our circles are different, they should be a reflection of the people that make them up. Some have leaders, some are collectively run and held. Some are paid and some are voluntary. Some are open to anyone and some are closed membership. Some have a range of ages and genders, others only have women at a specific life stage. Some are in ornately decorated spaces, others are not. They meet in living rooms, village halls, yurts in the wood, yoga rooms, gardens, community centres, classrooms, festivals and maybe around the corner from where you live.

What I hope I have communicated to you is the power of the circle that is more than the people involved – being in circle together, for the highest good of everyone there, with the desire to connect and learn and grow, with the willingness to be vulnerable, to be open to the emergent, to see what happens is a powerful thing. Something bigger is there too in that moment – whether you see that as your collective soul or spirit or Goddess. Something happens when we sit and speak and dance and sing and cry in circle. Something powerful.

But there is the shadow side of circle too, which tends to get less attention. First off, there is the danger that when we gather together we bring our baggage and relationship dynamics and unhealed trauma with us. I experienced this at the Red Tent I helped create. After that, I stepped back completely from circle leadership and public events, so deeply burned and hurt by the experience. This is why we have included contributions here on managing mental health and trauma in our circles, and the shadow side of sisterhood from Jaine Rose.

And then there are the stolen practices of circle practice and wisdom, where those of us who grew up without these technologies learn about them from Indigenous cultures and take on the practices as if they are our own. We may do so with the best of intentions, hungry for what we have been missing, and yet pain is caused, by the partiality of our understanding, by our monetisation of what is sacred to another culture, a culture that may have been punished, threatened and killed for using these practices that we borrow so lightly. We may not be aware of the pain and the anger that this causes these cultures we have so unthinkingly taken from. Until we are aware. Until we are made aware. Until we learn better. Once you see, you can't unsee.

Cultures have always borrowed from each other, adapted things to become their own, in food and music and fashion and dance and every other facet of culture. But it is hard to look face on at what has gone on in colonial cultures during the New Age, hippy and alternative cultural stealing of practices learned from Indigenous cultures without understanding, recompense or acknowledgement, all the while these cultures have been oppressed by our own. We discover that we have – perhaps consciously, perhaps unconsciously – continued the patterns of our forefathers, taking what is not ours as though it was. It is a topic that Amy Wilding, Shannon Cotterill and Sayra Pinto speak to passionately and powerfully.

And then there are those who are excluded – perhaps intentionally, perhaps unintentionally from circle. People who are different to us in different ways – perhaps culturally, perhaps by age or sexual orientation, disability or neurodivergence. And the thorny issue that has plagued many circles: the inclusion of transwomen. For circles, like ours, that are closed, meaning the same women go each time, this is not an issue. Ours was a mutual support group of breastfeeding mothers and budding friends who formalised our structure. But for groups like red tents or other open circles, the issue of who is made welcome is vital, and it is a topic that Coco Oya Cienna-Rey and the authors of *Red Tents* speak movingly to.

We find out more about how – and why – circles for certain groups of women – especially those experiencing major life transitions such as menarche and menopause can be so healing and necessary, providing places for sharing what our culture asks us to ignore, forging lasting bonds between women as they share resources and support.

We are blessed to have contributions from women who have dedicated three plus decades of their lives to women's work, founding mothers of women's circles from the US and Australia, ALisa Starkweather, founder of the Red Tent Temple movement and Jane Hardwicke Collings, creatrix of the School of Shamanic Womancraft. Then there are those of us in our mid years – Aisha Hannibal and Mary Ann Clements, founders of the Red Tent Directory, Amy Wilding founder of the Red Tent Louisville, Sayra Pinto of A Loving Future and myself at Womancraft Publishing, as well as many, many authors, both established and emerging in this field and women's circle facilitators and founders from North and South America and Europe. I am also delighted that we have representation from the next generation of women's circle leaders, in Macy-Doris, a sixteen-year-old circle guide…

This second Womancraft Compendium is called *Gather*, whilst the first focused on Weaving. Each Compendium seeks to reclaim the skills and qualities that have been the domain of women throughout cultures and history, and asks how we can apply them to our challenges today. How we can use these ancestral feminine skills to create a new more nourishing culture, one which truly meets the human needs of all of us? Creating circles, moving from lines to circles, from hierarchy to community is surely one of the most crucial steps and is one we can practice together not only in women's circles, but in our homes, our businesses, our places of worship and community action.

I hope this book will be first and foremost an inspiration, as you hear about the many forms of women's circles that are possible and vision your own. I intend for it to be a practical guide, sharing tools for facilitating and creating women's circles and poems and readings that you might want to share as a resource or discuss as a group.

I hope you find richness, variety, insight and healing as you read it. May it inspire you to start your own circle, or strengthen your practice, to make your group and yourselves more resilient and inclusive. Take what is of value to you now, and leave the rest. Revisit it in years to come, to see what speaks to you. Share the book around your circle. Start a book club and read it together. Gift it to your sister who is longing for something like this.

My dearest hope is that each copy of this book casts a ripples of circles around it. Circles reaching out to embrace all the people that long for safety, belonging, healing, growth and transformation in a world that rarely provides containers for these.

Let the wisdom of the circle and all that you learn there bless you and your community.

In sisterhood,

Lucy H. Pearce, Shanagarry, Ireland, May 2025

CIRCLES
AND LINES

'My Love for Her'
Jaine Rose

In the Beginning, the Circle

Lucy H. Pearce

In the beginning, the circle. One round opalescent sphere in the soft round depths of your mother's womb was fused with your father's seed, and life was born again in you.

Two tiny cells became four and then eight, until eventually you were a human body made up of billions. A constellation of life, beating to one heartbeat. Yours.

This was the first circle. You held in a bubble. Your body is still contained within its own bubble, your energy field. Your family are a larger circle that contains the bubble of you. Your community is another larger circle. All contained within the bubble of our earthly atmosphere. A blue green sphere spinning in space, orbited by a white moon, circling around a fiery spherical star.

Each has its own rhythms and cycles. Each one in constant motion. Just as your body has its own cycles of waking and sleeping, the in and out of your breath, the round of your menstrual cycle, the beating of your heart.

Now step back and see your whole lifetime before you. Each year a cycle, containing four seasons. Each season containing three months, each month itself a cycle of days. Each day has its own cycle, its own waxing and waning, its own rhythms of night and day. Each day marks a circle twice around the clock face. Each hour a cycle around the clock face, just as each minute is.

And now see all the circles connected with yours, each relationship you have, each project you start. Each is a world within a world. Each illness you experience, each stage of your life.

Welcome back to the wisdom of the circle.

Extract from *Full Circle Health,* Lucy H. Pearce, Womancraft Publishing (2017)

Spiral In

Cath Jevon

Spiral in

Follow the coiling snake

And the circling swan

Down to the land beneath the land.

Bones sinking deep through heart levels.

Join me in the wolf den

She's circled a nest for you

To cuddle up warm.

Limbs entwining

Roots finding

The optimum comfort

To rest

Recover

Receive.

In care

Compassion

Communion.

Stay

Sleep

Soften.

Our breath will rise

Our beauty materialise

Curling out

On murmurating wings.

Circles and Lines

Louise Allen

Have you noticed that life is defined by movement? From one task to another on a linear mission to get from A to B. This movement, a conditioned response directed unconsciously, has the destination as the prize. It misses the in-between spaces, ignores the journey. We race against time to get to somewhere, to achieve or complete something, only to find that the prize is elusive and the movement endless. Our minds race. Our bodies tire. From sunrise to sunset we list jobs, our minds already ten steps ahead, planning, thinking. We move in an upward trajectory, pushing harder and faster, in a society that is defined by a win-win mentality. We exist in a 'never-present' accelerating stasis. A contradiction in terms, we distract ourselves with 'busyness', while our lives pass us by.

Do you wonder why? Do you wonder how we got to this point?

Tim Ingolds' *Lines: A Brief History*, details how straight lines are upheld in western society as 'virtual icons of modernity, an index of the triumph of rational purposeful design over the vicissitudes of the natural world.'[*] He describes how the fixation between linearity and progress has defined our culture, mapping divides between our gender (male/female) and our moral condition, where anything other than a straight line is considered primal, untamed, animalistic. Ideologies, rooted in Cartesian and Spinozan[†] philosophy, perpetuated this human/nature divide, positioning man at the apex, holding dominion over life on earth. As Western society adopted these ideologies, linearity came to represent progress, reason, intellect, order, science and civilisation. The architect of modernism, Le Corbusier, famously wrote, 'the man of reason, walks in a straight line, because he has a goal and knows where he is going.'[‡] Today the life we experience is defined by a line that marches from birth, through childhood, to adulthood, to death. Within this linear trajectory, from our mid-twenties to

---

[*]   Ingold, Tim. *Lines: A Brief History*. London, Routledge, 2006. p.156

[†]   (Descartes 1973: VII, 81), from Plumwood, Val. *Feminism and the Mastery of Nature*, Taylor & Francis Group, 1994.

[‡]   Ingold, Tim. *Lines: A Brief History*. London, Routledge, 2006. p.157

forties there is a pinnacle of achievement often defined by youth, vigour, power, success. Past this point and our usefulness to society begins to decline. We witness this repeatedly in the ways that we treat our children and our elders.

For Indigenous cultures it is the circle that represents the cycle of life. In Ireland, there is a proliferation of examples: 'Crannóga were developed as a peculiar type of dwelling by Ireland's early inhabitants dating from the Mesolithic era through the Neolithic, Bronze & Iron Age.'[§] Our Neolithic burial tombs, Newgrange, Knowth and Dowth at Brú na Boinne, are cosmically aligned circular passage tombs.[¶] The remains of over 250 stone circles are dotted across the Irish landscape.

First Nations cultures see 'life not as a straight line from birth to death, but a circle where the young and the old hold hands at the door of the Great Mystery.'[**] In Indigenous societies children and elders are honoured respectively, for their close connection to the creator spirit in the early years of life, and for the accumulation of wisdom in later years.

In this world, the line could be seen as a metaphor for division. Reflecting a state of hyper-separation from the natural world, leading to the loss of meaning, a sense of being untethered, and ironically direction-less. Modern society, dominated by mechanised conveniences, has distanced itself from an embodied understanding of the elements and their interdependence with human life. Linearity promotes siloed relationships, removes context, and limits the potential for diverse, wide ranging and multi-faceted experience.

The negation of the cyclical nature of existence separates us from, rather than joining us to, each other. In confining our lives to a temporal existence, where progress is measured in linear terms, we have destabilised the foundations of our existence with profound societal and environmental consequences.

In stark contrast, a circle is whole. It epitomises balance, equality and community. A circle is not static, but dynamic, not exclusive but inclusive. Circles

---

§   "Crannóga." *Our Irish Heritage*, ouririshheritage.org/content/archive/topics/miscellaneous/irelands-crannoga.

¶   Prendergast, Frank. Research Report | Winter Solstice Phenomenon at Newgrange. Commissioned by Monuments Service of the Department of Housing, Local Government and Heritage, Ireland 2024.

**   Nerburn, Kent. *The Wolf at Twilight : An Indian Elder's Journey through a Land of Ghosts and Shadows.* New World Library, 2009. p.303

contain vortexes that expand and contract with boundless potential. Think of the sun. Think of the moon. We are related. In Ireland, we use the word 'deiseal' to denote moving 'sunwise'. To move sunwise is to walk with and not against the flow. We have forgotten how to walk. We have forgotten how to relate.

Druidic and Indigenous worldviews stress the interconnectedness of all life, viewing humanity as one part of a sacred circle rather than a hierarchy. This holistic perspective honours the balance between emotional, physical, mental, and spiritual aspects of existence, mirrored in the Celtic division of the year and the natural world.

Our ancestors understood that circles hold the current of our life-force in balance. They used circular structures and motifs to express unity, to honour the celestial bodies.

For centuries we have lived the story of the line. It has taken us on a long journey in evolutionary terms, perhaps a necessary one, but now we are at the tipping point. Imbalance is the norm. Fear is the norm. Enough is never enough. And we are almost 'never-present.' It might seem simplistic, but if we can shift ideologically from a linear mindset to an embodied circular philosophy, it could change everything.

All of life exists within this circle, that is our planet. We must start again, by encircling the square. We must create spaces for circles to re-emerge. Sharing circles, talking circles, drawing circles, dancing circles, wisdom circles, teaching circles, story circles, life circles, women's circles. We must remember that,

> *'Stories go in circles. They don't go in straight lines. It helps if*
> *you listen in circles because there are stories inside and between*
> *stories, and finding your way through them is as easy and as*
> *hard as finding your way home. Part of finding is getting lost,*
> *and when you are lost you start to open up and listen'.*[*]

Remember, it is the journey that holds the magic and it is this journey that is my story, your story, our stories to tell. It is time now, to find your way home. To open up, to rejoin the circle.

---

[*]   Wilson, Shawn. *Research Is Ceremony: Indigenous Research Methods.* Fernwood Pub, 2008. Ref. Tafoya, 1995 p12

The Circle Holds Infinite Variability

A Lisa Starkweather

The circle is an ever-present thing. It's the center from which you come, and back from where you go.

Joseph Campbell

Our Birth Stories Originate with the Mother and the Circle

All humans were conceived from an egg grown within an amniotic ocean matrix of a circle. Well okay, more like a sphere. But still our mother's round bellies protruded. Most of us, in our birth stories, emerged from the cylindrical cervix and yoni, albeit stretched to the max. Or we were lifted out of our native womb home into the earth-realm; a planet, astonishingly smooth and round, orbiting with other planets circling around a ball of starfire. When you step back and take that in, we all begin life with the circle and mother as central to our origin stories.

When we discover a choice that Mother and Circle awakens in our memory cord, a major reconstruction of beliefs and the building of new cultural foundations become possible. We allow ourselves to see and experience a wondrous spiritual geography holding a profound ancient truth when we shift focus on She with a Circular origin. We return to a concealed knowing of what was once buried in the rubble of patriarchy and forgotten histories. The circle, in innumerable creative endeavors, often ceremonially and community fed, opens a portal. This portal is one that many hearts have deeply sought and when it is held and tended and cared for, it is for many like drinking from the holy and experienced as recognizable homecoming.

The Circle as a Portal

What is at the root of its power? That we are together and we are held. That we hear, see, listen, know and respect one another with each of our stories, where our bodies are given room to take up space and where we have a place that is uniquely ours. Depending on direction and intention with what is known as a container (that which this holds), when supported by strong and rooted guidance with pre-determined agreements, there can be both safe and brave openings for truth telling and for healing where there was once trauma and trapped emotional expression and never before shared stories. When we learn the practices of not shaming, not fixing, not interfering or judging and instead become holders of not only the pain as it rises up and out from where the body stored the memories, but also witnesses to the shifts and openings that are made possible, we allow things that have been long hidden to both surface and dissipate. The circle as we have intimately known it has not always been calm or peaceful or civil but can also resound with rage, grief, trembling fear and palpable changes of heart and reclamation. And though it may be one individual, our collective memory, our shared stories, our well of empathy, rises to meet this one's heart as our own heart. We recognize similar feelings, dilemmas and even traumas running through our ancestral lineages and when this happens people feel less alone. It becomes a natural balm to loneliness and also feeds the deep hunger to belong and be known and held.

Naming the Many Circles of the One

The formation of the life of circles hold infinite creative variability. Circle may illicit an understanding of one kind in particular with strict and long held teachings that come from ancient practices taught by Indigenous elders and those who were directly mentored and guided by them. As our conversations and understandings about cultural appropriation deepen, the lineage of these particular circle teachings requires our respect in how they are brought forward with permission and rootedness to their ancestral roots.

In the decades of my lived experiences among dozens of subcultural communities, many variations of transformational circle experiences were co-created and enacted. In name only, here are some of the various kinds of circles that have brought great healing to the people: grief circles, all night fire circles, restorative justice circles, opening and closing circles, fish bowl circles, rites of passage and menarche circles, croning circles, healing circles, Red Tent circles, dream circles, breathwork circles, appreciation and honoring circles, sacred dance circles, plant medicine circles, council circle, ceremonial circles gathered round the labyrinth, the fire, the altar, the spiral that is laid down with candles and evergreens, the mandalas of human bodies with intersecting moving circles in both movement and emotion, drumming circles, the circle that gathers round the grandmother tree, the carpet work of Shadow Work circles within the archetypes realms, the circle gathered on the mountain or around the cauldron filled with native herbs. I even remember by age three, my pre-school circle and learning my place within it.

Over time, through bringing my visions to life, I brought forward with others the Re-Virginizing Circle, the Sacred Feminine Mandala circles, the Bones Check Ins, the Sword Circle, a Healing Circle that was a body of work around grief which was not influenced by Sonbonfu Some but original to womb work from the Women's Belly and Womb Conferences, a Figure 8 Yin Yang Circle Between the Feminine and Masculine Energies, a High Priestess Labyrinth Circle and myriads of other rituals that regularly took place within this context. What is possible then? So much than what most have imagined of the circle which heals human hearts.

Dream a Circle Within a Circle

For me, with forty years of my lifeforce and commitment to bring the Sacred Feminine to the forefront, most of my work when I am at home takes place within a twenty-four-foot diameter round space, our yurt. One enters the circle itself. There is no recounting all we have witnessed and felt from the profound depths of our lives being sourced from these practices and experiences together or the learnings which include failures as well as heightened moments of bliss and gratitude.

What I can share is to listen to your dreams. That is where my first circle ceremony was revealed. It asked of me to enact the vision I received with the people for our healing. I was twenty-six years old and I had been praying for a very long time to be of service to humanity's healing before the dream became real. In this ever-changing creative matrix, go to the source from which we came and weave. Always enter here with respect, gratitude, reverence from all the circle has given to our hearts. Allow the circle to reconnect you with who you are, where you have come from and where you will return to. We each are kin and belong in this precious circle of life and the gift it brings is to help us remember who we each are in our core and to give thanks for the beauty of being alive. Thank you for being in circle together. Blessed Be.

"We are a circle
Within a circle

With no beginning
And never ending."

The Circle of Women

Suzanne L. West

All over the Earth the women watch and wait

For the cracks that appear between the oppressive slabs

Of the patriarchal sidewalk

We lean over tenderly, listening for the seeds

Laying long dormant in the exposed bits of soil

Waiting for conditions to be right

Always finding their way to the light

No matter how long it takes

We trust the seeds to know when it's time to grow and flourish

We are patient even when the world is aflame

We hold the space for the Sacred Feminine to reemerge

Not as in matriarchal myths of old

But as something new and precious and filled with radiant power

Stepping off that rigid sidewalk

We welcome Her into our wise and wild feminine meander

Our Dearest Mother, responding to the needs of this moment

Watered with our tears and lighted by our love

Her seeds take root in our hearts

And we, the Circle of Women

Sing Her once more into the fullness of Being

*   Lyrics by Rick Hamouris

Alchemy Of Sisterhood: Unveiling the Magick of Women's Sacred Gatherings

Gillian White

Once a month, as the moon swells to her fullest, the woods come alive with whispers of anticipation. Deep within the heart of the forest, nestled beneath the canopy of ancient trees, lies a round tent aglow with the ethereal light of the moon. The air hums with magick, carrying the faint strains of celestial melodies and the crackling warmth of fire.

The women begin to gather; their laughter intertwines with the songs of the night creatures – the rustle of leaves, the hoots of owls, and the distant calls of coyotes. Each sound is a thread woven into the fabric of their shared experience. It's a time of celebration, connection, and rediscovering the ancient bonds that tie them together.

In this sacred circle, they are more than mere individuals; they are sisters, bound by a common thread of resilience and grace. They are a tribe united in purpose and spirit. They are family, chosen not by blood but by the resonance of their souls.

They call it many names – sisterhood, camaraderie, kinship – but its essence remains unchanged: a circle of healing and empowerment where each woman finds solace in the embrace of her spiritual family.

As the moon casts her luminous gaze upon the gathering, she softly calls to all who dare to listen: Open your heart and feel the presence of your sisters. For in this circle of womanhood lies a power unlike any other – an energy born from the depths of love, unity, and the timeless magick of the feminine soul.

As you approach the threshold of this sacred space, a resonance stirs within your bones, echoing the ancient whispers of your lineage. It beckons, drawing you into its embrace with a familiarity that transcends time.

The round house's wooden door swings open, calling you inside. As you step over the threshold, it envelops you in a wave of comforting warmth – a womb-like haven cradling your spirit.

Though the faces around you may be unfamiliar, there is a knowing deep within your soul that this is where you belong. As you accept a cup of tea and find your place among the circle, a sense of home washes over you, grounding you in the collective energy of sisterhood.

Hands interlocked, the circle is cast, each sister meeting the gaze of another with unwavering trust and love. With each declaration, the energy within the space swells, thickening the air with the presence of elemental beings, ancestral guides, and guardians of the four directions. The already full roundhouse expands, accommodating the vastness of their collective presence.

The passing of the Rattle of Truth heralds the priestess's proclamation: "Speak your truth, for it is the most potent tool you possess." Yet, before the words can flow outward, they must first be heard within – a symphony of whispers that resonate from the depths of one's soul.

Close your eyes, she urges, and listen. Listen to the subtle cadence of your truth, the gentle murmurings that guide you along the path of self-discovery. In the silence, revelations may bloom, answers may emerge, and clarity may dawn like the first light of morn.

Within this circle of trust, sisters become sacred truth-bearers, guardians of each other's vulnerabilities. Here, in this safe haven, you are invited to share your truth, unravel the layers of your being and lay bare the essence of your soul.

For in the sharing, there is healing. In the listening, there is understanding. And in the embrace of sisterhood, there is the alchemy of transformation – where truth becomes the cornerstone of empowerment, and love becomes the catalyst for growth.

In the sacred space, our words intertwine with tears, laughter dances freely, and even anger finds its voice as spells are woven with the power of our spoken word. Together, we burn away barriers, release burdens, and hold space for healing our souls.

As the night air exhales, softly celebrating the profound healing that has unfolded, it whispers its gentle approval. "Well done, dear sisters," it seems to say, signalling that it is time to draw our gathering to a close.

Standing united, we offer our gratitude for the blessings exchanged and the deep healing received. With hands drawing the energy back unto ourselves, we collectively raise our arms, lifting the gifts of our experience skyward, releasing it like beautiful stars of hope to inspire, bless, and strengthen all the sisters worldwide who may feel lost and alone.

Though the circle dissolves, its essence remains unbroken, woven into the very fabric of sisterhood. With a whispered "merry meet, merry part, merry meet again," we honour the cyclical nature of our journey, embracing the eternal dance of connection and separation.

Stepping through the threshold, we traverse the sacred portal once more, emerging from the womb of the tent reborn. Though outwardly unchanged, something profound has shifted within us. We are the same, yet different – deeper, healed, transformed by the alchemy of sisterhood and the magick of our shared experience.

*

This tale shares one of the countless gatherings I've hosted in my yurt. It began humbly in the warmth of my living room, where a small group of six, sometimes fewer, convened monthly. Yet, whether our numbers were grand or intimate, the power of our gathering remained potent.

Life, as we know, is a labyrinth of challenges – mental, spiritual, and emotional. Amidst these complexities, seeking support for our well-being is as vital as tending to our physical health. I've learned that having a nurturing tribe, however small or large, where one feels safe and heard is essential. It's about cultivating a circle of souls who see and value you, standing as pillars of support in times of need. In gathering together, women reclaim their voices and heal the wounds of patriarchy. Through sisterhood and solidarity, we forge a path towards empowerment and liberation. Let us continue to nurture our circles, for in our unity lies the strength to break free from the bonds of patriarchy.

She Who Remembers

Raven S Hunter

This is a tale of an ancient one who came to me in my dreams
she circled round me and whispered my name
and said do you remember me?

Do you remember the sacred groves
where we danced in the night through the trees?
Do you remember the standing stones
where we gathered in the hills by the sea?

Now the mist is fading the veils grow thin
The sweet memories come floating in
The dreams remind us of who we were
and now we're remembering again
we're dancing and remembering again
we're remembering our powers again

She who remembers
She who remembers
Whispers your magic name

Do you remember dancing round
and jumping the fire and the flames?
Do you remember the sacred chants
the visions the stories the dreams?
We were the healers and sages then
and now we remember again
we're remembering our magic again

She who remembers
She who remembers
Whispers your magic name
And now we remember again.

WHAT IS A
CIRCLE

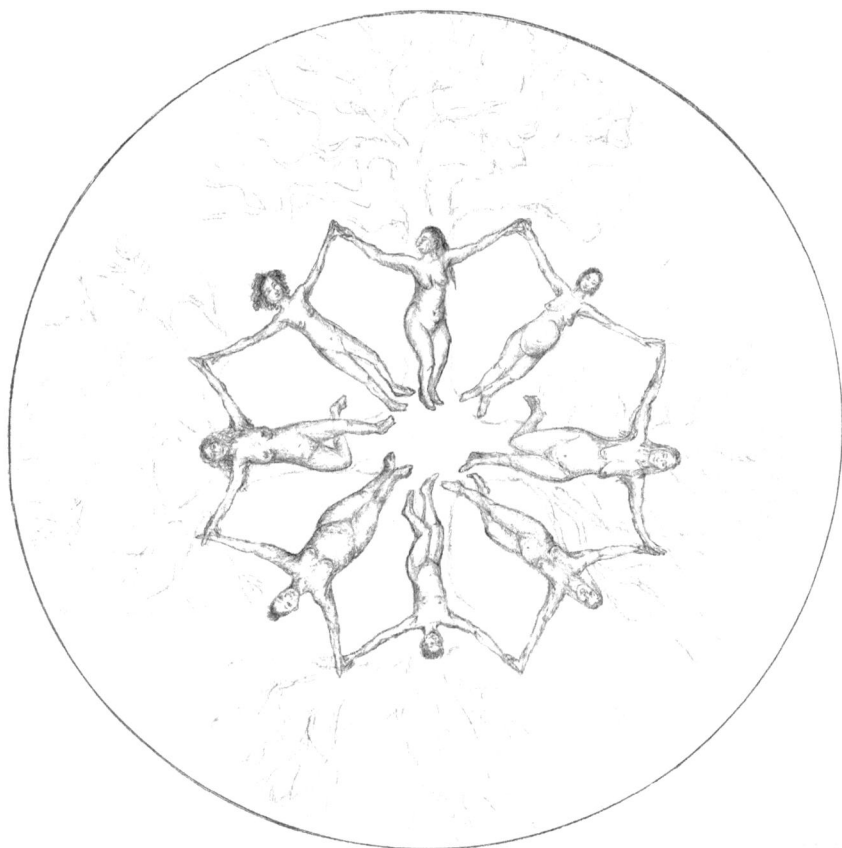

'Connected'

Rosalie Kohler

Women in Circle

Jennifer Miller

A cloth is spread on a coffee table, which serves as a temporary altar holding a candle, flowers, a goddess statue, incense, and symbols of the four directions. It is the beginning of a new lunar cycle. The air buzzes and crackles with potential. What happens in this space instigates change for the women who have gathered here. What happens in this space is so powerful, in fact, that it can transform the community and the world.

Something we need all of our lives, but especially in midlife, is a circle. Sisterhood may feel like a slippery, elusive thing to grasp at this age. There are the hurts and betrayals to overcome, for we've all felt friendships detonate. We've pulled the shrapnel from our backs. We've run our hands over the scars, remembering. There is also the fear of rejection or of being inadequate somehow, as ghosts from the school yard come around to test our self-esteem. And there are more practical reasons as well. There is the lack of time when so many demands come knocking on the door and, for some, there may be a lack of energy from chronic pain or illness.

Still, so many of us desire community. We desire it enough to seek it out or build it from scratch. And why? Why are we pulled so strongly to the shape and the idea of a circle?

Because when it is right, it heals. Because nature gave us this blueprint to follow in the roundness of bird nests, sunflowers, celestial bodies, and tree rings. Because we know that sitting in rows made us competitive, not cooperative, and we are through with that model of hierarchy and control.

When women sit together in sacred circles, a common theme is how much of our power we've given away. It's crucial to have space for processing our accumulated grief and rage, so often unallowed or dismissed by society. We welcome the magnificent elephant into the room. We dive into the ditchwater to find some treasure. Every story is a need for love and acceptance, which wasn't met by others, and so we finally learn to give that to ourselves. Power and sovereignty return like a dove healing from an injured wing and taking flight, and it is a glorious thing to witness and to feel.

We spiral through our transformations, celebrating our highs and holding the reins through our lows. We unlearn what we've been taught about a woman's worth. We shed ideas about power over and embrace power with. We do not try to fix each other, for we know that healing is an individual journey, but we can say, "I see you, sister. I hear you." And that is like a balm for the spirit, the simplicity of being acknowledged, of being received. How often does that happen for a woman out in the world?

I have known so many who do not feel heard, not even by their own partners or their families. All women have dreams they dare not express anywhere else, hands shaking and tears streaming as they give voice to what they desire, testing how the words sound, letting them fly around in a space where they will not be judged as ridiculous or impossible.

Women hold space for the impossible. We know how. We've been training for it all our lives.

When I think back to my experiences of being in a circle during my early 30s, the main benefit I received was having a space to explore what I actually wanted and needed. With two unfulfilling, disastrous marriages behind me, I was in the process of reclaiming myself and becoming the authority of my own life. All of us were, in our own ways, deconditioning from patriarchy and leaning more into female selfhood. Sometimes we raged. Sometimes we cried. Sometimes we made art to express our inner selves. Sometimes we invoked the Goddess, danced around fires, and made magic under the moon.

Twenty years later, now in midlife, a circle means something a bit different to me. I know exactly what I want and need, and I claim it. I have a surer sense of who I am as a woman and as a writer after walking through the labyrinths of therapy and spirituality. I still show up with openness and vulnerability, but I feel that the circle is also a place where my midlife wisdom is valued. I do not feel passed over, unseen, or pushed out to the margins, which is what Western culture does to women who are past childbearing age.

In the circle, what I've lived through counts. It has been distilled into a potent elixir. And the same is true of the sisters who join me there, each adding their own powerful medicine to the brew. We walk away refreshed and recharged, ready and able to carry on with the soul work we came here to do in this life. And I believe the most essential part of that work is to keep transcending patriarchal norms, to carve out new pathways for ourselves and all the generations to come. Every women's circle is linked energetically to the Goddess and to the greater circle of humankind. Together in our living rooms, back yards, red tents, forest clearings, yoga studios, and healing spaces, we are raising power, raising hope, raising love, raising change. May it be so.

The Lost Sorority

Aisling Henrard

There is a theme currently playing out in my life. A dream catcher is pulling together, with no specific pattern and composed of many different strands. The dream is our world and the strands are one-off connections made by female friends, woven together in a collective search for the lost sorority.

The interrogation around sorority and its absence in my life started to make an appearance a few years ago. I was reminiscing with my husband and his friends, let's call one of them Rachel, about the birth of my daughter. We were relating experiences and Rachel commented on how strange she found my disappearance from the lives of my husband and my older adopted son following my daughter's birth. She elaborated on the pain I had caused my husband by disappearing at the moment when he most needed me. In a way, she was right. Reflecting on that moment, I realise that in an attempt to deal with the life-changing impact of a newborn child, I had retreated into an inaccessible cocoon where my only concern was keeping her alive. In Rachel's critique, she was simply recounting the situation as she observed it; experiencing my husband's pain at the time, being his friend, not mine. Her comments though, relayed with curiosity rather than maliciousness, cut me to my core. She touched on a deep, old wound, first experienced years before when I navigated the treacherous waters of teenage friendships. My husband's friend, in ignoring my postpartum depression, my neurotic over-protection of a child born after years of gruelling IVF, and survival instincts that saved my mental health after the birth, unwittingly raised an entirely different issue when accusing me of abandoning my husband and son following the birth – the lost sorority.

I'm writing as a forty-one year old woman, on the edge of the millennial age group. We grew up watching the movies *Mean Girls, Carrie, Clueless, The Craft, Cruel Intentions* and others. Movies where the conflict and/or competition between women was the main plot driver and was presented as normal and rudimentary. The concept that women had nothing to gain from trusting other women was deeply embedded in our 1990s and 2000s culture. Today, we watch *Real Housewives of Beverly Hills* and consider it entertainment to watch adult women betray each other on camera. There is no equivalent show for men. Men were learning other challenging traits from pop culture – toxic masculinity for one – but this competitive friendship was unique to women. Recently rewatching *The Devil Wears Prada* for nostalgia's sake, I was struck, not only by the fact that early 2000s fashion has not aged well, but how the story only became interesting in the desperate choice the protagonist had to make – whether or not to go to Paris in the place of her colleague. *It's you or her, kid!* These women are told to save themselves at the cost of other women. Also, there was not one single scene in the movie in which Miranda, the devil herself, suggested that following her success she might send the elevator back down for younger women. Of course, these are just movies, you might argue. But as the first generation with unlimited access to popular entertainment via MTV and Blockbuster video rental, we were learning to navigate the subconscious messaging in film, as these new media exploded. Psychologically, there was no way our parents, our mothers, could have known to prepare us for that. Critical thinking was limited to academia and not applied to popular culture.

We soon grew up and moved out. I was of the first Irish generation for whom university wasn't a hope but an obligation. We were expected to depart *en masse* for regional cities, removed from the traditional environment of the encompassing, matriarchal family. We were thrown into navigating the challenges presented by our new circumstances with no established sisterhood on site when we arrived. And all of that we navigated with barely post-pubescent minds, when the notion of the self was a highly malleable concept, changing and adapting in response to the needs of each new social situation, in a simple act of survival. We took what we learned from television and magazines and quickly formed superficial relationships that looked meaningful from the outside, but could turn on a whim. We gathered information about each other, and then we used this information to make sure that every one of us stayed in our place and never got ahead of ourselves with foreign "notions."

My husband's friend, in exposing me in front of our partners, revisited two of the many false narratives of the patriarchy. Firstly, calling out each other's women's weaknesses in a public forum, presenting competition over support. "How could you have done that, I never would." And secondly, the availability of a woman at all times to everyone who may need her, especially her husband. I have never before or since experienced such a visceral and urgent need to leave a place immediately.

Unwittingly, she touched a gaping wound I believed had long closed, if not healed. My teenage friendships were tight-knit. They were formed in my toddler years and grew through school as my gang, and I followed similar paths in life. At one point, I realised that my path was perhaps not exactly what my friends had in mind for themselves. I was often the outlier in the group. Not an outsider, I had enough self-preservation to not break too many of the myriad rules of female friendship, but I had different ideas about who I wanted to be. I dated the popular boys (or at least I longed for dates with them) because that's what our gang expected of me, but when left to my own devices in a nightclub, I'd end the night kissing whoever had made me laugh the most. Often that was the "fat" or "ugly" boy and I remember being ridiculed for these errors of judgement in the piss-taking way of the Irish. I went home confused, having had a great night out laughing with some lad who was not "our type," and feeling crappy for it. I also found myself on the wrong end of the piss-taking stick for some of my more unusual clothing choices. I had a sewing machine and wasn't afraid of doctoring a t-shirt or a pair of jeans to make them more silly, fun, creative... Mine. But these were my best friends, right? They'd known me forever, so of course they were right. I should stay in my lane.

The culmination of all these identity-shaking tremors came out of the blue in my first year in university. Three close friends appeared at the door of my parents' house and asked to talk to me privately. They proceeded to explain to me their concern for a developing behaviour they had noticed. It had come to their attention that I was too promiscuous. I was sleeping around and this was not approved of. I had recently shared the concern that I might have picked up an STI (I hadn't, thank Jeeves!) and I imagine this was the rationale for the intervention. The reckoning was for my own good, but however well-intentioned it was, my experience of the incident was that of being trapped in a very small room while the women closest to me, who knew me most intimately, poured shame on my suddenly burning self. Their accusations were no word of a lie – I was wonderfully promiscuous in university, fully exploring my sexuality after years in the barren wasteland of rural Ireland. I had discovered the pure, sweet joy of an enlightened approach to sex and love, and was taking to this new way of life with the appetite of a thirsty traveller coming across a desert oasis. But none of this was permitted in Catholic Ireland. And my sisterhood, the women who I depended on to reflect back to me the ideas that I held about myself, were determined that the right thing to do was to put me firmly back in my place as the Good Girl.

The incident completely and utterly destroyed me. My mother came into my room following their departure to find me inconsolable. She did her best to comfort me, but following that incident I was changed for a long time. I was cowed. What a wonderful word. Cowed. I was transformed into a domesticated, permissive, unintelligent beast of the yard. Terrified of losing the friendships by which I defined myself, I set about playing my assigned role with renewed vigour.

It didn't last long, of course. Blood will out! I was soon back to my old (new!) tricks and laying waste to the university population of men and women alike. Fully exploring my sexuality, I was delighted with the cornucopia of human bodies afforded by an Irish university full of formerly repressed teenagers! Despite my renewed joy in exploring the human form, it took a long time for the sense of shame to fade. I'm not sure it ever fully disappeared. It took longer still for those friendships to heal. They were never quite the same again, though we all pretended. I took to the road, went travelling at the end of my first year at university, and eventually left Ireland completely thirteen years ago, but I still seek out these friendships when I go back. A few years after that moment, when we had matured somewhat, we tried to talk through what had happened but I don't think I ever felt safe enough, or even fully understood what had happened, to truly let go. So, we agreed to move on. Today we connect on a different level and though it's nice and familiar, I'm cautious.

If this all sounds a bit too much like a movie for teenagers, that's because this is what we were watching at the time. Magazines such as *Seventeen*, *Teen* and *Cosmo Girl* taught us that other women were rivals for attention. That we each had an assigned place and must stay put and within that space we had to work on ourselves to draw the most attention; that we had to shine the brightest, to be the most interesting. For whom? Well, ostensibly, for boys, or so we were led to believe. But in the end, it really was for each other. To show our rivals how strong we are. Even today, when I dress nice, I don't dress to attract men's attention. This is merely a pleasant side-effect of my efforts. I dress for women. So other women will want to see me, want to be me, as I see and want to be them. I'm envious of that coat, those shoes, that perfect hair. The sense of competition is pervasive.

The most profound damage resulting from all of this teenage determination of self and value juggling was the destruction of my faith in the sorority. I felt shamed by my sisters. The same way I felt shamed when my husband's friend, someone who I was on the way to considering a sister in my new country, called me out as a bad wife and mother.

I could ask what pushes women to do this, to call out one of their own instead of championing them. But we know the answer. We believe we are helping our sisters; setting them on the correct path to being a successful woman (under whatever specific terms). Instead, we have the opposite effect. We uphold the needs of a patriarchal society, and ignore the needs of our sisters. A woman shamed as a slut, as a bad wife, a bad mother, a workaholic, too smart, too loud, too vibrant, too successful, too anything, is a woman back in her place. Unthreatening. Upholding the status quo. A sexually liberated woman might wake up one day and realise she doesn't need to marry a man to have lifelong companionship. A successful businesswoman may start to ask awkward questions about wage equality and bias in promotional hierarchy. It suits the status quo if women don't ask these questions. It suits even better if we are women telling each other not to ask these kinds of questions.

The last few months, this review of old memories and the question of the lost sorority have come to me unprovoked. A recommendation for a podcast here, a shared article there, a meme, a comment, a project idea shared. Collectively, and unknown to themselves, women are asking for the reimagining of a life with sororities. Reaching out to one other, in a shy, tentative, unspoken way, asking, *Will you be my friend?*

In asking this question, we are also asking each other, *Will you hold me when I'm hurt? Will you champion my successes? Will you help me raise my kids? Will you share my anxieties? Will you allow me to fail, with no shame? Will you help me live a life of no regrets?*

Will you know me, truly know me, and love me for who I am?

Since I moved to Brussels thirteen years ago, I have been searching for my sisterhood. It wasn't an intentional search – I didn't sit down one day and tell myself, *Ok, now I need to gather my girls around me!* I launched various projects which always resulted in pulling a small posse together for a while, but just at the point when we should develop intimate ties to each other, life pulled us apart. A capital city with a constantly churning population is a hard place to try to build one's tribe. And yet, unknown to myself, I kept trying. My therapist recently pointed out that I managed to pull myself through an incredibly difficult moment in life, due in part to the profoundly deep one-to-one relationships I've formed with female friends in Brussels. Having left my blood sorority at home in Ireland, I set about, if not replacing them (my close sisters are irreplaceable…) then replicating what I have with them, within my new physical reality. I found wonderful women and with intention and care, drew them to myself, forming a powerful shield which protects me and raises me up: ex-colleagues, current colleagues, club friends, creative project partners, friends of friends; I identified women who understand that the root of a powerful female friendship is a total lack of judgement, and I built a new life with them.

The next logical step is to bring them all together to form a group, a sisterhood. But how? What is the vehicle for this? Traditional community vehicles have disappeared, for the most part intentionally destroyed. A colleague (another soul sister who I am intentionally pulling into my fold) recently recommended I listen to the brilliant BBC podcast, *Witch*, presented by India Rakusen. The recommendation was yet another sign of our generation of women reaching out to each other in an attempt to address the absence of sisterhoods. The podcast is a revelation. Among many other things, Rakusen explores historical female bonds and the reasons for their rupture. I was quieted to learn that the word 'gossip' is complimentary in its root. It was originally used by women to refer to their closest female friends. By giving the word negative connotations, we give those relationships negative connotations by proxy. And so we break down female bonds, one word at a time. I listened with envy to groups of women – self-styled sisterhoods and covens – describe the bonds of their relationship and how the group cares for each member; this is exactly what I have unwittingly been trying to build since moving to Brussels.

A friend recently joined a dating group for women who want to make friends with other women of our age. Her first foray was successful, and she has been on a number of lovely "dates" with a woman from the same city. Myself and our other friends follow the development of this new friendship with hope! It is amazing to me that the relational constructs of our society are so broken, so lacking, that we have to go in search of female friendship online. Where are our women's circles? Where are our covens? How can we rebuild the lost sorority, when our cultural mirror – television, movies and social media – has utterly undermined the concept? When our youthful experience has left us hurt, vulnerable and wary of ever forming multiple close bonds with other women, where do we turn?

As I see it, the first step has already begun. That unspoken reaching out towards one another by sharing sisterhood-themed treasures found amongst the trash of contemporary culture is active in each of us. The next step is the hard one – the question spoken aloud. *Will you be my friend?*

What is a Sacred Circle? The Key Ingredients

Melia Keeton-Digby

The circle is everyday ceremony: the invention of our most ancient godmothers, who, upon witnessing the myriad ways nature exalted this humble shape, claimed it as the spiritual center of their communities. Held by the simple rituals of opening and completion, honoring and appreciation, the circle acts as a vehicle for both storytelling and transcending our stories. In circle, we are conversing with the Divine.

Baraka Elihu

On the surface, a sacred circle of women looks simply like a group of sisters, gathered in a living room or other discrete place, to discuss a shared topic. On the surface there is talking, listening, laughing. But look closer and there's crying, witnessing, mirroring, deepening, role-modeling, grieving, drawing upon experience, and sharing the wisdom of experience. And then, below the surface of all of that goodness lie even more riches: a swell of healing, blessing and unmistakable transformation occurs.

There are some fundamental, key ingredients required for any sacred circle to be healthy and effective. My mother-daughter circle, The Heroines Club, is based on these crucial components, and it is important that you keep these intentions at the forefront of your heart as you develop and maintain your own circle.

Sanctity

Circle time is meant to be sacred. As we enter circle, we step away from our everyday routine and enter a place of healing, blessing and replenishing. There is an agreement, both spoken and unspoken, to hold each other and the gathering itself as sacred. Even the youngest of daughters will recognize and appreciate the reverent aspects of circling. When we enter circle, we come with love, consciousness, honor, and respect, setting the intention for a soulful, bonding, and heart-opening experience.

Safety

Trust is paramount. For deep sharing, learning, and personal growth to germinate, mothers and daughters must know that their expressions are safe and will be protected with the strictest confidence. In circle, we trust that our personal stories will be kept confidential. While we are certainly encouraged to talk about our *own* experiences in circle, we do not share the words, information, or stories of another with anyone outside of the circle.

Witnessing

Bearing witness is a sacred act and a profound honor. Witnessing between women deepens and fortifies the soul of both the woman sharing and the woman bearing witness. To be a sacred witness means to simply hold space for what is. In concrete terms, this means that when a mother or daughter shares a check-in or responds to a discussion question, we listen with our full heart and mind; we give her our full attention. When she finishes speaking, we do not respond with any cross talk, advice, fixing, "what I would do is," referrals, or feedback. With acceptance and honor we simply say, "Thank you for sharing your heart/ wisdom/ experience/ story/ thoughts with us." We offer gratitude for her process, trusting that each woman (and girl) already has all the answers she needs *within* herself and that, like a flower growing toward the sunlight, she *naturally* bends toward healing. We do not have to "do" anything to affect positive change in our sisters' lives; as quantum physics teaches us, the simple (and profound) act of observation can literally change reality. Listening is loving.

Authenticity

On the stone pathway to the gathering place of the original Heroines Club at the Mother-Daughter Nest rests a sign that reads: "just show up." Authenticity is letting what we are experiencing on the inside "show up" on the outside. Authenticity is courageously uncovering and expressing how we deeply feel. Our deeper, tender feelings are a large part of what makes us human, and circle holds space for this authentic sharing. In circle, we practice pausing, going inside, taking a breath and noticing how we feel in our body before we speak, so we are more likely to find words that reflect an earnestness that connects us in a more fulfilling way to ourselves and others. Circle says, "Come, show up and be exactly who you are, exactly where you are in your life, at this very moment." Feeling the unconditional love and acceptance of circle, mothers and daughters feel safe enough to remove any social masks and remember the beautiful truth of who they really are.

Silence

Silence has energy to it like no other source. By recognizing the silences within our circle discussion and embracing those soft spaces, we connect more deeply with ourselves. In circle, silence is valued for allowing us to digest what was said and discover what will be given voice to next as it emerges in the present moment. Silence offers an opportunity to unearth the mysteries and lessons that exist within and allows for individuals to integrate their experience, staying grounded and engaged. When a woman or girl honors the voice of her silence and the power to *not* speak by "passing" the talking stick, we thank her in the same manner as when she shares from her heart with words. Welcoming silence requires practice because many of us instinctively feel uneasy when encountering pauses or interruptions in flow and we often feel an impetus to fill the perceived void. In circle, we know this is not necessary and we resist the habit of filling silent gaps with superficial talk. Silence, as the old saying goes, is indeed, golden.

Ritual

A sacred circle includes some form of ritual. For many people today, the idea of ritual is associated with exotic religions or the occult. Others may believe that rituals are something only ordained priests or ministers can access and create. The truth is *anyone* – from any religious path or belief system – can participate in and benefit from the act of ritual. Ritual is simply any action taken with the intention to remember our connection to the Divine (God, Goddess, Highest Self, etc.) and the grand plan of Life. At The Heroines Club, a simple candle-light ritual carries the circle into the sacred realm, potentiating and elevating the experience for all.

Co-Creation

Just as we co-create our experience of life, we co-create our experience of circle. There is no hierarchy in circle and all participants including one or two facilitators have a precisely equal role in the process. Circle allows that everyone and every expression within the circle are equal. Each circle co-creates its own powerful synergy, which would not be possible without each woman's specific participation and unique offerings. As we say in The Heroines Club, *"We are all the teachers, and we are all the taught."*

Conscious Community Building

The Heroines Club creates a circuit of energy with other mothers that magnifies the love, nurturing, grace, and empowerment we offer our daughters. From this experience, a community is born based in love and support, giving and receiving. Belonging to this conscious community offers a sense of identity, helping us understand who we are and knowing we are a part of something larger than ourselves.

"And may all mothers know that they are loved,
And may all sisters know that they are strong,
And may all daughters know that they are powerful,
That the circle of women may live on."

From *Circle of Women*, by Mica Ella

Extract from *The Heroines Club*, Melia Keeton-Digby, Womancraft Publishing (2016)

Woman Circle

Carly Mountain

Circles of women shedding skin

Circles of women awakening

Circles of women unshackling

Circles of women holding

Circles of women resurrecting

Circles of women stepping back into their skin

Circles of women feeling in

Circles of women breathing

Circles of women coming home to the body they live in

Dancing, cries and unveiling the lies

Dancing, stirring and feeling alive

Dancing, singing and being in the hive

of the pollen filled, rich yolky home of woman.

Evolving In Women's Circles – Stepping In, Up and Out

Hazel Evans

Let's dance and sing, and share our stories, wide and far and deep,
For the wisdom of our sacred landscapes is here for us to meet.
Let me be seen through the eyes of you, and you through eyes of me,
As we weave the timelines of ancient ways for one and all to see.

The first time I sat in a women's circle, I stepped into the great unknown, and my life changed forever. I moved away from casual gatherings with friends, left behind tea parties where everyone was "just fine," discussing the weather and last night's TV shows. I stepped beyond my bloodlines of daughter, sister and mother, and into a realm where I could experience myself through the eyes of every woman.

Women became soul sisters, ancient and new, each a portal to another existence. A vast library of women's wisdom in a circle of life. Through these gatherings, new timelines opened and time as I knew it dissolved, revealing how our souls had journeyed together before. I witnessed past lives, unearthed ancient wisdom, and opened to the deeper meaning of our connections in this lifetime.

Triggers, admiration, resistance, overwhelm, honouring, challenges, love, all these and more arose as I witnessed myself in the eyes of other sisters, learning the truth of ourselves. In doing so, I practised becoming a clear vessel for growth and transformation.

My journey has evolved over the last fifteen years, leading me through a spiral of experiences in many different types of women's circles, some open, some private, and across several countries. Each held a distinct energy and purpose, deepening my connection to inner wisdom as I surrendered to the gifts of exponential growth found in these sacred, ceremonial spaces.

Early in my journey, I was drawn to step up and study sacred practices and initiated as a Priestess of Rhiannon, devoting to the path of love and sacred sexuality. Within a private circle, I learned how to hold sacred space from a deep remembrance of the ancient temples and rites of passage. I reclaimed the pure life force of my body, sacred sexual energy, becoming a vessel of creation.

Recalling the presence of my Indigenous heritage, I pulled lost wisdom back through my blood and bones, rediscovering it through deep sharing, ritual, ceremony and shamanic journeying. As sisters, we witnessed each other's processes of evolution, often through sacred acts of creation: dance, performance, writing, drawing, and I brought in any medium I could to channel energy and to further awaken my innate gifts as an artist.

As we sat in circle, our gifts and stories intertwined. Our eyes met, and we offered tears as a sacrifice to the old ways. In this safe and sacred space, we could finally shed karmic skins, end outdated contracts, and emerge anew. Ready to walk this earth as the women we were always meant to be.

This is the profound potential of women's circles: a journey of transformation that begins the moment you step in with the full YES of your heart, womb, and soul.

Over the years, I transitioned from participant to leader, learning to call in aligned energies, create safe containers, and invoke the necessary forces for deep transformation in women's circles and ceremonies. It was intense, wild and liberating.

I stepped in. I stepped up. And then, one day I stepped out.

A new journey called, one I had to take alone, without the comfort of sisterhood. I was growing, and I could grow no further if I remained. So I stepped out. I didn't know how long it would take, but I trusted that by leaving, I may one day find a way to step back in. That journey took another four years.

It became a quest for divine union. To understand why the rising feminine was not fully meeting the pure masculine. It was a deep investigation, and I needed to work directly with men, just as I had with women, to heal, bridge the gap, and discover a path of authentic harmony and balance. I longed to be met in my deepest feminine essence by a sacred masculine counterpart. Through this, I came to see myself as a mirror, reflecting both the feminine and the masculine.

Now, renewed and aligned, I am weaving myself into a new web of creation, ready for the next cycle of evolution.

Even a lone wolf has her place by the ancestors' fire, sharing her stories. There comes a time when the outcast returns to the homeland to find a warm cup of soup waiting on the hearth; when the wandering Priestess is welcomed back to her tribe, bringing the wisdom and courage of her solitary initiations. Even a trailblazer needs a hug sometimes.

Every woman carries inspiration and unique gifts. Each holds wisdom within her sacred body, consciousness and experience. Some tend the hearth, some raise children, and some walk the wilderness. Every role is vital in the ecosystem of circles. The spiral of life supports us all, guiding our evolution.

Whether you feel at home in your sisterhood or are called to step into the unknown, trust the journey. Do not fear outgrowing the comfort of what you know. A new circle will always be waiting on the other side of your pilgrimage, soul mission or fierce path. The most important thing is to follow the voice of your heart, womb and soul.

You will know when the time is right to step in, step up and perhaps even step out.

Women's circles, like the women who create them, are spirals of evolution – of life, death and rebirth. We choose how we participate, navigating our growth and transformation.

Each circle is a wellspring of wisdom, a sacred source from which we may drink. If you dare to venture deeper into your own sacred inner landscapes, lean in and witness the divine reflections around you. The mirror of each woman will show you the way – but never stop holding and shining your own light.

Honour what feels right so the spirals of evolution may continue. As you step out, another steps in; as you step up, you inspire others to do the same. May the evolution of ancient women's wisdom support your journey to exponential growth.

Introducing Red Tents

Aisha Hannibal and Mary Ann Clements

A Red Tent is a place where women gather to rest, renew, and often share deep and powerful stories about their lives. The Red Tent is many things to many people. It is a womb-like red fabric space, it is a place where women gather, it is an icon and it is a state of mind.

Isadora Leidenfrost, PhD and ALisa Starkweather, *The Red Tent Movement: A Historical Perspective*

Each Red Tent is a unique reflection of the community of women who create it. But these varied spaces all share something in common: the longing for connection and belonging; the sharing of how we are feeling and who we are in our lives at this time; the nourishment of ourselves and each other; the slowing down, changing the pace for rest and replenishment; the simple act of sharing time and space with a group of women; the opportunity to let go of the other responsibilities in our lives: When women come together, magic happens. We know this to be true from our own experience. We have also seen that when these Red Tent communities grow, they can become a beacon to others. This is our hope, our vision, our dream – Red Tents as liberatory community spaces for women around the world.

When we first heard about Red Tents we discovered a loose, diverse and largely uncoordinated movement of women meeting in similar ways. Many we connected to were drawing inspiration from the best-selling novel *The Red Tent* by Anita Diamant, which was first published in 1997. The story spread to a wider audience, in 2014 when a TV mini-series was made based on the book. *The Red Tent* is a fictional retelling of a biblical story set in Old Testament times, in which Diamant paints a picture of a Red Tent where women gather, connect and support one another during their menstruation, pregnancy and childbirth. The evocative portrayal of intergenerational sisterhood spoke of being guided and supported through life as part of a community and marking rites of passage through celebration and ritual. As Isadora Leidenfrost, PhD and ALisa Starkweather say in their book *The Red Tent Movement: A Historical Perspective*, "For many, the story resonated deeply and caused us to question if there (could be) …a place like this in our society."

Though Anita Diamant wrote a work of fiction, the ideas she included in it drew from what she knew of and had read about women's menstrual rituals and gatherings in Indigenous cultures around the world. In the Lakota Native American tradition, for example, there are moon lodges, which are a creative place where women go for respite when they are bleeding and where elder women give teachings. These are a vital part of the Red Tent lineage. Whilst Diamant's book has given its name to today's women's spaces and inspired many women, it is not in itself the origin of these ideas but rather a particular format through which they have been communicated. It seems to speak about a shared but hidden longing: for women's space, for ritual, for community. All of which are sorely lacking in many contemporary cultures where patriarchy and whiteness are valued. These types of traditions held by women to support one another have been deliberately devalued and largely erased. We remember them in large part because many Black and Indigenous women have continued to remember and practice them and have held sacred traditions that affirm women's culture and relationship to one another. There is a long history especially in white and colonised cultures of seeking to wipe out Indigenous and women's rituals and traditions as a means of exerting power and control. For example, prior to the American Indian Religious Freedom Act of 1978, many Native American traditions, customs and rituals were prohibited by law in the US. And in the United Kingdom, where we write from, people thought to be witches, mainly poor or elderly women, accused of practicing magic were violently executed well into the eighteenth century.

And so in some ways Red Tents are, as ALisa Starkweather and Isadora Leidenfrost, PhD call them, 'reclamation work' helping us connect to lineages and traditions that our cultures have lost, to the practices of our ancestors. As Madeleine Castro points out, there are also in Red Tents "echoes of consciousness-raising groups that emerged [...] during second wave feminism" and we like to think of these groups and the women who created them as part of the lineage of Red Tents also. Like Red Tents, these were groups in which women could sit together, share their struggles and challenges and learn from one another.

For us, Red Tents are not spaces reserved solely for those who menstruate. However, the idea of a menstrual retreat or refuge is part of the lineage of the Red Tent and so we want to explore it briefly here. In many cultures, including our own, taboos have developed around menstruation. In some parts of the world this has led to segregation and neglect. In our own, we are still fighting for an acceptance of menstruation and the conversation about it. In their book, Isadora Leidenfrost, PhD and ALisa Starkweather chart the history of menstrual gatherings as both a blessing and a source of nourishment, as is depicted in the novel, and also as a curse and a means of ostracisation. It is important to note that not all traditions associated with menstruation and other life traditions are empowering and supportive for women. However, we know that there have been places and times in human history where women's cycles and fertility have been more positively honoured and embraced. There are many communities of women who have remembered this and have traditions of honouring their bleeding time. Maisie Hill puts it well in her book *Period Power* when she says, "At best a menstrual retreat can provide respite from chores and responsibilities and create time to share in female company, but at worst they are detrimental towards physical and mental health and can risk death. Let's be clear in distinguishing that removing oneself from daily activities to enjoy female company is inherently different from enforced segregation and neglect that is violent and oppressive and based on the belief that women are impure or dangerous."

Camilla Power, an evolutionary anthropologist who looks at early human societies in her work, believes that ancient menstrual rituals may have been part of what enabled them to evolve. She thinks that monthly rituals celebrating bleeding existed in early human groups alongside the lack of overt physical symbols of either ovulation or menstruation, and that this made it difficult to determine when an individual woman was actually bleeding. Communal rituals that took place when it was a full moon and the skies were bright didn't indicate that female cycles are all aligned and predictable but instead honoured the power of menstruation in general, celebrating it as a rite while keeping the precise timing of menstruation in each individual woman a secret. This served to limit the success of the 'alpha males' who triumphed in our close relatives, gorillas, who procreated and then disappeared. Instead in humans, it was those males who were willing to stick around, who successfully procreated and prospered. And it was they who she believes helped feed their young and thereby supported the necessary brain development in humans as we evolved. Menstrual rituals may therefore in fact be the oldest tradition with which Red Tents share something in common: they celebrated the female-of-centre experience without needing it to be uniform and were a foundational building block of communal human life.

We first heard about Red Tents from ALisa Starkweather, who is our inspiration in this work. This book would not be here without ALisa and the wisdom and stories she shared with us and many others that have helped seed this movement. ALisa's vision for the Red Tent Temple Movement came to the UK through Women in Power (WIP), a transformational women's initiation programme of which she is a founder. A group of women in the UK, including Nicola Kurk, who is also a WIP founder and inspirational sister of ours, committed in 2009 to holding a Red Tent each month, taking forward ALisa's vision in England. Mary Ann was involved in that commitment, and during that year some new longer-term Red Tents were born. ALisa's vision was of there being a Red Tent in every village and town. She calls these spaces Red Tent Temples. Like other women who have contributed to an increase in Red Tents, such as DeAnna L'am who advocates for a Red Tent in every neighbourhood, ALisa saw how they could become part of the fabric of our communities. Like her, we think of them as "a place for us where we can meet each other and at the very same time take care of ourselves and one another." This was – and continues to be – our starting point: that Red Tents are an accessible, community-based initiative for women, supporting them to connect with and take better care of one another. Another important aspect of the vision that ALisa shared with us was that Red Tents were about being rather than doing: a place to slow down, to honour the cycles of our lives, connect with the wisdom of other women and share our journeys. These central ideas remain important to us and our vision for Red Tents to this day. From ALisa we learnt to see that in the simple practice of creating time to listen to one another, journal, share our healing skills and creativity, we were inviting a culture of supportive sharing and connecting amongst women that our cultures so often devalue and disrespect. She also invited us to think about these spaces not just as supportive, fun and replenishing but also as something we desperately needed and which had a role in shifting culture.

By creating these spaces and honouring our deep connection we were offering and practicing an alternative to critique and competition between women. We were practicing a way to be in connection and collective care for ourselves and each other. Part and parcel of this was the invitation to stop and be, to breathe, to be in the body and to let go of the busyness and constant doing: to feel and sense, rather than know and judge.

We think of Red Tents as community-held spaces where women can come to connect with each other in ways that aren't necessarily common or familiar to us. And we think of the practice of doing this, of meeting each other monthly to share, and rest, as something that allows us to connect to one another in a different kind of way from what we might be used to. Connecting by intentionally listening and deliberately seeking not to 'fix' or critique. Doing this we think can be a liberatory practice that helps support change in our lives and in our world.

Extract from *Red Tents: Unravelling Our Past and Weaving a Shared Future*, Mary Ann Clements and Aisha Hannibal, Womancraft Publishing (2021)

Womb Spaces

A Lisa Starkweather

In a time of growing polarities and divisions there is a lot to refute but there is a truth that we can agree on at least for now; every single one of us held by the root of our placenta, gestated in the womb. The womb place is the home of our common origin for all human beings. In 2006, I founded the Red Tent Temple Movement and among other things, envisioned the Red Tent as an archetypal symbol of a womb space. There were many reasons for this. Before we delve into why, please let me begin by acknowledging the trigger that the word womb can bring up for the women born without wombs, for those who want or do not want wombs, for those whose wombs have been removed, for those who have been in the heartbreak of infertility, for those who grieve abortions, adoptions, sexual assaults, challenging birth stories, for those who ceased to bleed and those who never did and those who do not want their gender to be defined by any of this. Conversations of the womb can bring up a spectrum of emotions and politics too. It turns out, so can the Red Tent.

There is no mistaking that Anita Diamant's novel, *The Red Tent*, carried many of us deeper than mere imagination. We remembered home and sisterhood. It evoked a bone memory of a place and a time where women were mentored by other women, where the children were cared for, where we gathered with the rhythms of the earth and moon, where we honored rites of passage in our bleeding, our birthing, our dying, where songs and stories were passed on and images of women as sacred were taught and tended to as part of the culture. Though her book was not based on historical references because she created The Red Tent in her own mind, Ms. Diamant also recognizes the ancient and modern practices of menstrual huts and traditions worldwide. For those whose culture preserved menstrual practices or had years of experiences with women as powerful allies, this story was as an affirmation versus a revelation. But if any of our lives were being lived out in separation, aloneness, bereft of eldering or any semblance of honoring of our bodies, this memory was jarring and called attention to what had been missing, or worse, forgotten.

There was recognition that even having lived our entire lives without ever having experienced what a just and loving world might look like because of the oppression of our bodies, our voices, our power, our visions, our very lives, we still held nostalgia, a longing for a home, that we each carried in our hearts. Where did this come from? Why do we search for this, even without knowing what it means to be held, to be cared for, to be nourished and tended to? Or could it be that this place reminds us of sanctuary, a place to grow our children and ourselves within, a place of homecoming, a womb place of sorts? For many the Red Tent is a homecoming.

Before reading *The Red Tent* novel I was influenced by another book, *Circle of Stones: Woman's Journey to Herself* by Judith Duerk posing her many questions of "How would your life be different if…?" Each question brought to form a possibility, a place, an experience that could redefine our culture if we brought this to life. Since 1998 I had been facilitating the Women's Belly and Womb Conferences, and not having read Ms. Diamant's book yet, I was already busy creating red cloth circular womb spaces in order to evoke the plethora of stories about our relationships to our bodies, minds and souls. Every woman was sung into this space – "You were born from a woman. Your mother had a name. No matter what your story with her, we honor the womb from where you came."

My first Red Tents that I attended were in 2004, where I felt the power and the grace this space held for women to gather. In 2005, in an online group and in person, I was mentoring women how to take this from a mere concept into the reality of making physical Red Tents and how to raise them up for large gatherings. In 2006 I wrote an email to Anita Diamant expressing that I wanted to start a worldwide grassroots movement. When her answer returned my best guess from a legal and ethical stand of not wanting to associate herself, she did not mention any context of my email and only wrote back a short message, "I bless your empowerment work with women," which for all I know was what she wrote back to many of her fans.

Some months later a joyous cry went out on the stage of the Northeast Women's Herbal Conference where I was teaching when I asked if we were ready to raise up a Red Tent in every village, city and town. Five hundred women answered with a resounding yes. Our first call had representatives from five countries and the grassroots were seeded in fertile soil.

For well over a decade, I held monthly global support calls and raised up Red Tent Temples everywhere I traveled, learning from experience what happens while holding this space. It offers many valuable lessons. I was clear that we needed to build a more woman-honoring culture, and there was not yet a sacred space that I knew of in modern times where it was made easy for women to gather in community regularly that was specifically for this and also stood outside of the dominant patriarchal culture. In choosing the Red Tent as womb space, we could do this without the confines of something that we culturally appropriated from, because I believed that it was rooted from fiction even as we recognized the deeper influences. (This premise was later challenged by women from various cultures and backgrounds, most especially from Black and Brown Indigenous women whose histories are not often seen or known. I respectfully listen and learn so that we can continue to see past best intentions into truer contributions of women's collective histories because dismantling work is an essential part of where we are now.) In the Red Tent we could discover for ourselves what it had to teach us. We could freely share our stories, bring soup and tea and share our experiences and resources. It would not be governed by religious or corporate influences, but rather by us living out the experiment of what we would learn from raising it up for ourselves in basements, living rooms, healing centers and yurts and generously hosting them for others over time.

I placed the word "temple" in the title, which at times I regret. It was originally to honor the temple of our bodies and to acknowledge that we had lost in most of our modern cultures (not all) a temple to gather with sacred feminine principles. I also strategized that although there were many isolated Red Tents with various ideas, that to bring a Red Tent Temple meant that you could see us moving together as a collective movement and that some of what was envisioned would hold some continuity in form even as it progressed in its own evolutions.

Over time I met many other passionate women leaders who were devoted to other forms and styles of the Red Tent. Some protocols I advocated for were for those hosting Red Tent Temples to be as open as possible so that whoever entered felt respected, that we would meet on or near the new moons (and for some full moons), that it was recognized as a woman-led space, that it would not be a franchise or to be profited from, that people could learn and grow here, that we would share our stories in circle and that we would share what was important to us rather than anchoring a set form of rituals which could risk confusing people because of the many diverse beliefs systems of participants. My hope for what the Red Tent Temples consisted of was to keep the door open so that people could find their own relationship to what was inside – as is often true for archetypal spaces where people find meaning – and to learn what was there for them in their own healing.

In 2012 Dr Isadora Leidenfrost further lifted the global conversation with her award-winning documentary film, *Things We Don't Talk About: Women's Stories from the Red Tent,* which has been viewed over a million times worldwide. The Red Tent, as a loose grassroots phenomenon, often with no ties with the Red Tent Temple Movement, was finding resonance with many people. And it was also creating dissonance with some too: Was it culturally appropriated? Did it welcome the trans communities? Dogmas were anchoring where only bleeding women or woman-born could enter. And never men. Was it a safe place for women of color or did it further marginalize and not address systematic racism? Could children be inside? Was it a fun party place or did it hold more substance? And what to do when you had conflict with a woman who was coming?

You may know of Red Tents that hold different set of values, a different idea of what they are and I respect this. There may be some with more dogma and therefore less welcoming. They may be harboring a magnificent vision that is anchored in beauty and love from leadership devoted to Red Tents over time, even if it is different than what you learned. As the planter of the seeds for the Red Tent Temple Movement, I saw the Red Tent as an archetypal landscape that would find resonance from its association with women's issues and connection with womb space as experimental for modern times. With so many ways that it can be held in our communities as a useful container, I advocate it as a tool for reclamation and even reconciliation.

My Red Tent is a yurt on our land. When our local reporter visited, I invited him to come in with me. Just as I had experienced with women, he was over-come with tears when entering, remembering his mother from Columbia and sensing that he had entered a rare women's domain which he remembered as a child. This idea of a womb space is useful, and on rare occasions – with women's leadership and permission – some of us have facilitated men in healing ceremonies to connect with their own connection to the mother's womb. We have a great deal of issues with misogyny, so I think this is a good thing and something that I would like more of in the overall culture. For me, the Red Tent can be experienced as a place where we can learn skills, applicability and share stories that can connect us, while being held by a symbol that is loving to us all. Can it be a place to build bridges, foster compassion and bring us together? I hope that you are appreciating that we are making it up as we go. Red Tents are an experiential idea that is in evolution. And some people in their passion have made sacrosanct lines that cannot be crossed if it is to be a "true Red Tent". Maybe the womb has room for twins and triplets in how multiple visions emerge? We shall see. My prayer is that we remain respectful of one another and what we bring to this sacred space.

More than a concept, the Red Tent is practice ground for us to learn how to get along. Our lives and communities are facing vast changes and we need tools and skills to support our ability to adapt most especially in times of crisis. What may help you open the door is to find what is helpful to raise a Red Tent that is right for you and to find what can be put to good use, not as an ideology but as a repertoire of skills and tools for healing.

Amidst our present global cultural landscapes, we see the importance and the challenge of holding containers where it is all here – women's empowerment, racial justice work, transgender politics, non-binary gender inclusion and a whole lot of ideas of what the Red Tent is, ought to be, could be, or never will be. We get to choose how we live the story.

Once I heard an elder say wisely, "Be careful how you tell the story, because how you tell the story can become the story." What will be our story to tell of the Red Tents? To delve, requires openness and curiosity to the many conversations that are needed at this time for humanity's healing. How do we make this a safe and brave container that can nourish our souls, hold our hearts and expand our abilities to embrace respectfully the many stories and concerns so that those who participate feel seen, heard and held? It will take labor, thoughtfulness, tolerance and commitment to outcome.

How, you may ask, does the Red Tent evoke memories and emotions and more than that, a sense of homecoming? Out of so many deep and moving stories that could be shared, I choose two. Years ago, down a long path in the woods, my sole intent was to dust the cobwebs, sweep away the signs of mice and construct a beautiful Red Tent. After laying down the rugs, putting up the red cloth in every direction and placing the flowers on the table, I opened the door to whoever might find it. It was not on any map of the conference and I left little signage, yet women still found their way once they heard rumors that it was off the beaten path somewhere in the forest.

One woman who was impelled to find it shared her personal experience with me through her tears. She entered the space to find herself alone. Opening the veils of a red cloth canopy she nestled on the pillows below and while she slowly began to rock rhythmically, she found herself humming softly. Back and forth, back and forth arose this haunting melody repeated, and every single note evoked emotion for her. Where was all this grief coming from? With a gasp of recognition, she sourced its origins. She was three years old when her mother died and what she found herself singing was the long-forgotten lullaby her mother used to rock her to sleep with. Something about this place called her home and returned her mother's song as if she was waiting for her daughter to come through those doors and remember.

Another story was shared with me about this Red Tent waiting in the woods. In the late hours of that same night, several women quietly sat in the near darkness when another entered well past midnight. She had never set foot into a Red Tent and yet her body felt the safety and the sacredness of this moment of being somewhere that she always longed for and never yet knew. Without thought, or preconceived notion, she fell to the floor and began weeping. Years before she had experienced a brutal sexual attack and had hidden her grief and rage so deep inside that no one ever knew what she had endured. Now her body was speaking and releasing this trauma memory in the dark of the quiet forest in the Red Tent made for her. The women who had been in there did not speak. Instead, they slowly circled themselves around her and with her permission held her close until the last of her cries were heard.

A Red Tent will be different each and every time if you choose to enter the portal, if you choose to hold this space for yourself and others. It is a reservation of time for our inner worlds and listening to our collective stories. Sometimes it will exhaust us as we witness the pain we are all holding. Sometimes it will lighten our loads. Sometimes you will feel safe and other times let down. We keep making the story even when that means you are beginning to come through the door or you are leaving for a while.

Take a moment to ask: what has brought you to the door of the Red Tent? What is your deep longing that you are hoping can meet you? What is your life's journey that has you at this passageway? Have you lived the vision of what may be or are you wondering if such a reality can even exist? Are you here in support or are you here in a critical mindset of what may be missing in the narratives?

Are you seeking a new story or are you questing for one that may have been lost and is returning? All points of view and perspectives are welcome, especially if anything of relevance is to be gleaned from this now diverse worldwide grass-roots movement. Please know that you are welcome to find your way with us, even as we are finding our way with what we bring alive in this continuous story. We are going to make mistakes and from them we can learn how to fail forward. Mostly, if you find value and see good use, please enter. If you find further suffering, close the door and open another that may be more useful. Trust yourself to know.

Wherever we call home together, may we continue to foster empathy, connection, equity and healing for all. May we take the risks required to tell a new story together – one that brings us more alive and able to count on one another as siblings.

The Red Thread

Andrea Gonzalez

In the years that I lived, certain things looked different. Connection felt different, it was more potent and present. The red thread united us, rather than separated us. It brought us back into ourselves, instead of disconnecting us from who we truly were.

It was that thread that held us up, while we navigated the uncharted waters of early womanhood. It was the whispers of our grandmothers that guided the way and calmed us down, when our minds would go as unsteady as a river after a heavy rainfall.

It was the hands of my sisters that weave the threads of life together with me, as we learned what to weave, what to leave behind and what needed untangling.

It was the hands of our aunties, which showed us how to untangle the knots.

It was the laughter of us all, while we celebrated how sacred it was to be a lifegiver, that brought us life.

And then somehow the sacred red thread was beginning to snap. In some places the tension was just too much, in others it was snapped intentionally by other hands; and in some places it became shameful to celebrate this thread, to love it, to hold it sacred. And slowly it was forgotten.

Some lost it completely, some others hid it away until the time was right. And the bravest souls, the strongest threads kept on going, uniting, connecting and weaving together.

And then a turning point came. Our souls were calling, singing and chanting for its return, longing to find it.

We, keepers of life, need this thread, the weaves of wisdom passed down to us, as we move through the cycles of life. The world needs this understanding, this sacredness, this trust.

The ones that had held onto it were strong and prepared, the ones that hid it were ready to dig it out, the ones that had been stripped from it were craving to have it back, the ones that had forgotten were starting to remember, and the ones that never knew its sacredness were the ones that found them and pulled the threads back together!

This is you, my dear, the one calling us back together. You have found the sacredness of the red thread that unites us all.

And it is we, your grandmothers, the ones that have held onto it for you, so that you can once more step into the power of becoming a lifegiver.

Through tears, laughter, songs, flowers, symbols and time, we have been singing to you, holding you all until the time was right.

I am the mother of all mothers, I am the voice that sings in the wind, I am the spirit that holds you and all lifegivers sacred, I am all that which is around you and within you. I am the thread.

I am your tears, fear and dreams. I am holding your hand every step of the way. And through these cards, this mere tangible object we call a game, I give back to you all that is yours. So together we can give it back to all the bodies that bleed this sacred blood.

As you roll, flow with love and find the jewels of your soul, and let your true colors shine into the world, without fear, for you are a beacon my dear!

Through the stories we connect,

Through the songs we remember

With our voice, we speak the truth

We learn to flow and surrender,

We are here to grow, we are here to shine together.

This sacred blood connects us all

To the very spark of creation.

The ones that have been before you,

your ancient mothers.

CIRCLE
PRACTICE

'Sacred Rage'

Eva Živa Blažková

Side by Side

Georg Cook

Shoulder to shoulder

Hand in hand

Voices in chorus

Rooted in unison

A song carried

From the past

Into the future

Contained in the

Hearts of women

The Five Sacred Elements of Women's Circle Leadership

Amy Wilding

They say well-behaved women rarely make history, and the patriarchy is *counting on us all being well-behaved.* If the patriarchy weren't so terrified of us, would women's bodies be more regulated than assault rifles?

If there is one thing I know, it is that women together are POWERFUL. My method of pushing back against this system of misogyny and toxic masculinity has, for nearly two decades, been to gather the women. In circle, we awaken and reclaim the power and agency and sisterhood that is our birthright.

Perhaps you have heard stories of the magic and the power of women gathering together for support and encouragement and know that the women in your life – and you yourself – are deeply hungry for this type of community. Perhaps you have sat in a sacred women's circle and have felt your own inner flame of inspiration and passion ignited and know that it is your path to share your light with other women. Perhaps you have a daughter whom you wish to raise within the empowering fold of other mothers and daughters, together intentionally navigating both the challenges and gifts of being female in the twenty-first century. Or perhaps you are called to contribute to the growing sisterhood of women whose passion is coalescing to form a great wave of cultural change, and you sense the transformational power and healing potential of women's circles.

If you are holding this book, no doubt you have heard the unmistakable call to gather the women, to come together and make space for truth-telling and healing and growth. More than just a whim or fleeting "what if...," your heart knows that your unique gifts are needed in the world right at this very moment, and that you have something valuable to offer your community. The call to lead women's circles is not a coincidence – it's a message from the Universe.

If you feel drawn to this path, it is because your unique medicine is needed now.

And yet you may still feel something holding you back. You feel a deep calling to lead women's circles, but...

You wonder if you're "qualified enough" to step into leadership.

You have imposter syndrome – who are you to guide others?

You fear you don't have enough experience, knowledge, or wisdom.

You worry about what people will think if you take up space.

You feel overwhelmed by the logistics of actually leading a circle.

You know you are meant for this work but need a clear path forward.

The most common reason women hesitate to step into leadership? They don't feel "worthy" enough. But let me be clear: You don't need permission to lead.

You don't need more credentials, more experience, or a stamp of approval.

Our patriarchal culture has conditioned us to believe that leadership is hierarchical, that stepping into our power is ego-driven, and that we should defer to "experts" rather than trust our own inner knowing. But women's circles are not hierarchical. They are rooted in collaboration, not domination; in intuition, not ego.

You already hold the wisdom within you.

You are already the leader you've been waiting for.

You do not need permission to tap into your own innate power and wisdom.

The blueprint for women's circles is in your DNA.

When we gather in sacred circle, we reawaken something deep and ancient within us – the truth that we have always been the keepers of wisdom, connection, and transformation. In a world that tries to diminish and silence us, circles are a radical act of reclamation.

As the facilitator of a thriving circle community in Louisville, Kentucky, women reach out to me regularly to share their desire and inspiration to lead women's gatherings, and while they themselves are quite diverse in terms of their personal paths and backgrounds, what they seek is invariably the same:

They want to be told *exactly* what to do in order to create a successful circle.

They long for a clear path. A guide. A map through the mystery.

They want me to confer upon them the *right* to step into leadership and the legitimacy to gather the women.

But I can't do this for them. No one can.

Perhaps this is the result of being the inhabitants of a culture that values conformity over creativity; perhaps we all have a certain level of uncertainty when stepping into uncharted territory. But I think it's also the result of being raised female in a culture that systematically disconnects us from other women, both physically and emotionally – just as it disconnects us from our own intuition and inner wisdom.

This was most certainly true for me. I first began gathering women for support and sisterhood when I was pregnant with my first child, twenty years ago. It was completely intuitive; I have no biological sisters, and my mother is not present in my life. I knew I needed sisterhood.

For many years, I continued to circle casually with women – my friends, their friends, and those who felt called to share in this healing and liberating experience. As I witnessed and experienced for myself the power of creating a safe and sacred container for our growth and empowerment, I began to feel passionate about creating a space for others to join us – not just our friends or those already in our orbit, but the women of our wider community. From this spark, Red Tent Louisville was born.

With that shift, something shifted inside of me as well. I started to feel like, probably there is *a right way* to do circle, and I need to figure out what it is! I watched others; I learned from others, and (inevitably, right?) I imitated others. I borrowed ceremonies, I echoed words. I collected clothing that seemed to lend an air of spiritual gravitas. I appointed my red tent sanctuary with the accoutrements that I thought would make me appear official. An expert. To be worthy of this kind of leadership, this kind of *being seen*, I would of course need to be an *official expert*. Or so I thought.

While I did have others to help illuminate the path of leadership ahead of me – and for them, I am deeply grateful – the most powerful lesson of leadership took time to reveal itself: I had to root into circle leadership wholly as *myself*. Unarmored. Unpolished. Unapologetically real. It wasn't until I shed the accumulated accessories and the borrowed beliefs that I could finally return home to the truth of my own leadership – authentic, vulnerable, fallibly human. By giving myself permission to stop looking outside myself for guidance and validation, I came full-circle back to where it had all begun: my intuition.

From that place, I found an authentic rhythm – one that allowed women and girls to step into the circles I offered and leave carrying something sacred: the connection, the learning, the healing, the sisterhood that is nothing short of life-changing. I became both more comfortable and more confident, trusting myself to navigate the flow of each gathering with ease and grace. I showed up as my real self in each circle – one time choosing to wear literal pajamas to a gathering that coincided with my heaviest, most energy-sapping day of my cycle – and in doing so, the women who circled with me felt that they too could show up with complete authenticity. That is its own kind of magic.

As my circles (and my experience) grew, others began to ask for guidance – specifically, how to lead circles the way *I* lead circles. I was honored to support them, to hold the lantern on their path toward leadership. But first…I had to figure out how to do that. I knew I couldn't teach other women how to *be* me, or how to plan and lead circle exactly as I do. What I could do – what I *had* to do, I realized – was guide women to lead from *their own center*. To step fully into their authenticity and bring forth the unique magic that only they carry.

With that realization, the framework revealed itself all at once – like a tapestry coming into focus only when you step back from the individual threads. Having long worked with the four sacred elements – earth, air, fire, and water – in both my personal spiritual practice and in the crafting of healing rituals for others, I felt the distinct hum of everything coming together. The sacred symbols of my Irish, English, and German heritage rose to meet me – ancestral threads returning, weaving themselves into the perfect circular vessel for this transformational journey.

But there was still one piece missing: The center of the circle, the leader. The woman. The one who calls in and channels the sacred, the one whose passion and purpose radiate outward to answer the calling and create the container. The fifth sacred element was not just necessary, but crucial. Spirit.

What arose from that insight was not a one-size-fits-all template for women's circle leadership training, but rather a deeply personal exploration of what it means to lead, hold space, and cultivate life-changing circles. I began to see how the sacred elements themselves could guide this journey – each one offering a distinct yet interconnected aspect of circle leadership. With the five sacred elements in place, I was ready to alchemize: passion and purpose into action and reawakening.

EARTH
Creating a Strong and Sacred Container

The element of Earth invites us to create the safe and sacred container that serves as the foundation of our gatherings. At times supple and pliable, at times solid and immovable, Earth allows us to find and maintain the edges of our circle – both literally and figuratively. Earth brings the energy of grounding and stillness, providing a sense of safe homecoming to all who attend.

The first step on your journey of circle leadership is to invoke the wisdom of Earth: to follow the example of Mother Gaia and cultivate with intention an environment whose purpose is to both nurture and support. Perhaps more than the other elements, the work of calling in the power of Earth requires a certain finesse; a base made of quicksand cannot hold the weight of a community, but a base of iron may be too immutable to provide a sense of nurturing and warmth. A container with undefined edges does not have the strength to provide a sense of safety and purpose, but rigid walls do not allow for growth and expansion. Finding the delicate harmony between solid boundaries and gentle welcoming is the alchemy of Earth.

Contemplating the questions and calling forth your own ancient wisdom as you find the answers will prepare you to create the safe and sacred container for your gatherings.

- Where will your circles be located?

- Who will attend?

- Will your circles be the same group of women each time, or open to all?

- What will be the investment of the participants – financial or otherwise?

- How often will you gather, and for how long?

- How will you create a safe container for your community?

- What tenets/covenants/contracts will your participants commit to?

- Will you have a social media presence? On what platform?

- How will you navigate drama-seekers, conflict, gossip, "fixing" etc.?

- How will the women in your circle co-create with you?

- What leadership responsibilities will be shared?

- What will help to bring the circle back on course if something goes awry?

- How will you open and close your circle gatherings?

- What can you bring into your circle space as a representation of the element of Earth?

AIR
Finding Our Voices

Once the safe container has been created, we may begin to hold space for women and girls to find their voices. The sacred element of Air invites us to connect with our personal authenticity and speak the stories of our lives. This is the energy of truth-telling – of exhaling what has been held in silence. Air supports us in naming what is real, what is remembered, what is ready to be released. As many poets and wisdom-keepers have noted, speaking one's truth and truly being heard is, in itself, a form of healing.

Air is associated with the direction of East, the place of new beginnings. Here, the rising sun shines its first light into the shadowy places within us, offering energy for rebirth and renewal. In circle, Air brings the breath of clarity and the wind of transformation. It connects us with the healing power of storytelling – the ancient medicine of words carried on breath, witnessed in sacred space.

This element is personified by the archetype of the Teacher, reminding us that every woman carries wisdom, and that all of us – facilitators included – are both teachers and learners within community. To lead from Air is to guide with presence and curiosity. It is to listen as much as speak. When we center the element of Air in our circles, we invite truth to rise, voices to soften and strengthen, and stories to become bridges between us.

With truth and authenticity as our guiding principle, we consider the following aspects of circle manifestation and leadership:

- What is the primary message of your community?

- What fundamental truths will be upheld?

- How will you support women in finding and expressing their truth?

- How will you uphold and model sacred witnessing in your community?

- How will you demonstrate and encourage authenticity and vulnerability?

- What helps *you* feel safe enough to speak your truth? How can you recreate that safety for others?

- How will you hold space for women whose truths differ from or challenge your own?

- What is your relationship to your voice – literal and metaphorical? Where has it been silenced, and where does it want to rise?

- How will you navigate moments when silence says more than words?

- How will you mirror or acknowledge what has been shared by each woman?

- How will you acknowledge and work with shadow energy as it is illuminated?

What can you bring into your circle space as a representation of the element of Air?

FIRE
Fanning the Flames of Transformation

The sacred element of Fire invites us into the heart of transformation. It asks us to remember our inherent wildness – the raw, radiant power that lives within each of us. Just as wildfire clears the forest floor to make space for new growth, Fire urges us to burn away what no longer serves. It calls forth passion, courage, and the will to act. When we attune to this element in circle, we ignite not only our personal power but also the collective flame of change.

Our inner flame compels us toward movement, toward boldness. It is the spark of truth that cannot be silenced, the sacred discomfort that pushes us beyond our edges. Fire reminds us that transformation is not always gentle – it can be fierce, even consuming – but it is always sacred. As we stoke the flames of our own stories, griefs, and desires, we become more alive, more awake, more ready to step into the fullness of who we are.

Fire is the realm of the Visionary – the archetype who sees beyond what is, into what *could be*. It illuminates our sense of purpose, fans the flames of inspiration, and connects us to our limitless potential. In circle, Fire asks: What are you willing to release? What do you long to create? What do you burn for? It is the element of becoming – transforming passion into power, and power into purpose.

With transformation and wild wisdom as our guiding principles, we consider the following aspects of circle manifestation and leadership:

• What is *your* vision for this circle?

• What women's issues are you passionate about?

• What ignites your flame of inspiration?

• How will this circle help women identify and harness their potential?

• How will your passion be channeled through this circle?

• How will you promote personal and global transformation through your circles?

• How will your circle ignite the passionate fire of women in your community?

• How will your circle invite women to fuel their inner wildfire?

• How will your circle invite women to reclaim their wild wisdom?

• How will this community encourage growth and evolution?

• What transformational experiences are possible within this community?

• What can you bring into your circle space that represents the element of Fire?

WATER
The Rhythm of Circle

Water is the sacred current that moves beneath the surface of every circle. It represents the emotional body of the sisterhood, inviting us to ebb and flow with grace, to soften into feeling, and to trust the movement of healing as it rises and recedes. Water teaches us that there is no straight line through emotion – only waves. When we create space for those waves to move freely, a natural rhythm emerges. This rhythm is not forced or dictated by the leader – it is discovered, like a tide that reveals its pattern over time.

In circle, Water supports the release of stored pain and unprocessed grief. It holds space for endings, transitions, and the slow work of letting go. Through its invitation to feel deeply and to move honestly with what arises, Water becomes a conduit for emotional alchemy. It asks us to notice the cycles we carry – the patterns passed down, the wounds we've woven into wisdom – and to honor our capacity to change. When tears are welcomed, when silence is honored, when laughter bubbles up unexpectedly – this is Water at work.

The archetype of the Healer lives in this element. But to lead from Water is not to have all the answers – it is to stay present through emotional weather, both your own and others'. A circle that invites the element of Water allows for flow rather than rigidity, feeling rather than performance. The facilitator becomes a vessel: sensitive to undercurrents, responsive to energy shifts, willing to follow rather than always lead. In this way, the leader does not control the rhythm of the circle – she attunes to it, becomes part of it. Water asks: Can you soften? Can you listen without fixing? Can you trust what is moving through you and let it move through the room?

With rhythm as our guiding principle, we consider the following aspects of circle leadership:

- What healing would you like to welcome and facilitate in your circle?

- What rhythms and cycles will your circle honor?

- How will you as a facilitator create a safe space for emotional processing?

- How will you prepare yourself to witness and potentially guide women in their intense emotions, such as grief, loss, fear, shame, or recovery?

- How will you hold space for uplifting emotions such as joy, love, enlightenment, peace, and connection?

- What is your relationship with your own emotions? How do you tend to them, and how do they move through you?

- When emotions rise unexpectedly in circle, how will you anchor yourself?

- In what ways can your circle ritualize emotional transitions – endings, thresholds, initiations?

- How will you model emotional authenticity while maintaining energetic integrity?

- How can you embody *fluidity* – the ability to shift, adapt, and stay present in the unknown?

- What symbolic or literal forms of Water could you include in your circle to support emotional movement?

SPIRIT
Holding the Sacred Center

YOU, sister, are the center of your circle, and the living embodiment of the sacred element Spirit. Your commitment to holding space for other women is not just logistical or emotional – it is energetic. You are the hearth, the anchor, the heart. From your centerpoint, every other element – Earth, Air, Fire, and Water – radiates. It is your presence, your intention, and your willingness to serve that gives the circle its pulse.

As the Spirit of your circle, you are called to offer your unique medicine – not as performance, but as presence. Just as breath moves in and out, so too does this role invite both giving and receiving. You may, and must, allow yourself to be nourished in return. You cannot hold the Center from a place of depletion or obligation.

To lead from Spirit is to trust that your intuition, your story, your sacred knowing are not just *enough* – they are essential. Like a ripple on still water, your inner truth will carry outward and touch every woman in the circle. It does not need to be loud to be powerful. It only needs to be true.

The Center is held by the archetype of the Channel – one who opens herself to receive wisdom from the Sacred Feminine and translates it into form. You are not expected to be perfect, or always clear. But you are invited to stay open. To listen inward. To follow the invisible thread. Spirit reminds us that circle leadership is a devotional act, a spiritual offering, a remembering. And at the very center of it all…is you.

With the guiding principle of the Sacred Center in mind, we contemplate the following aspects of Circle leadership:

- What call from the Universe are you answering?

- What is your unique, personal magic?

- What ancestral heritage can you call upon for inspiration?

- What intimidates you most about holding the center of the circle?

- What parts of your story want to be seen and shared as medicine?

- Are you coming to leadership from a place of service, or a place of need?

- How can you continue to keep your channel clear and open as a vessel for the Sacred Feminine?

- How can you best serve the purpose and intention of your community?

- How will you ensure your own boundaries are seen and honored?

- Have you given yourself permission to step into your sovereignty as a facilitator?

- Have you given yourself permission to be open to *receiving* from this group as well?

- What rituals, practices, or daily devotions help you reconnect to your spiritual center?

- What energy do you want women to feel when they step into your circle?

- What can you bring into your circle space to represent the element of Spirit?

Circle leadership is not a fixed role – it is an alchemical process and a living journey; it is a process of transmutation that evolves with you, breathes with you, and asks you to return, again and again, to your own deep knowing. There is no certification that can bestow what you already carry. There is no authority greater than your own intuition. The call to gather the women is not about mastering a method. It is about remembering who you are, trusting what you hold, and offering it with devotion.

As you walk this path, you will be changed. You, along with the women in your circle, will be transformed – by the stories you witness, the courage you cultivate, the healing that unfolds in your presence. You will deepen your capacity to feel, to trust, to lead with both strength and softness. You will come to understand that the sacred container you create for others is also a sacred mirror for yourself. You will feel the indescribable power and magic that arises when women are gathered.

Let the five elements guide you, not as rules but as invitations. Let your leadership emerge as an expression of your essence. Let your circle be a sanctuary where magic lives, truth is spoken, and lives are changed – starting with your own. When you choose to lead with authenticity, to gather others in sisterhood, and to hold space for transformation, you change the world.

'Holding Hope'

Rosalie Kohler

Tending the Circle

ALisa Starkweather

One enters the sacred, when one bows her head to the presence of mystery and what is hidden in the unknown, yet to be seen. Before we arrive, to any mantle of responsibility, it is best to pray and to ask to be a vessel – an instrument for healing and for service. Strip yourself at this gateway of uninvited worry or pride or pretentiousness, and instead infuse oneself with wholehearted willingness to meet grace with humility and fierce love.

Here, on the holy precipice, let go of expectations while holding to the highest possible outcome that can be collectively experienced. As facilitator, be the composer, be the conductor and the music too as you open your veins like attentive ears to the song that wants to be sung. Give this spaciousness, which holds not only the sweet note, but silence, rest, breath and rising wonder.

When you first speak to the circle, steep yourself in deep presence, taking in with all your senses who has gathered. Ask yourself: How do you ready, prepare and anchor energy together? What infinite possibilities are ready to awaken? There is a ledge between the mundane and the numinous. It crackles and speaks when the split opens between the two. Everyone comes into attention. It is here you all hope to arrive and begin, though many did not even imagine it possible, many having never known this portal existed. Later, no one will be able to capture this felt sense in words, though songs will be sung of what lives now in bones.

The HOW in the Gathering

First, we gather. It is good to sing, to move, to drum, to attune in the place that says we are here and we are ready. This is a place that can be opened ritually with strong medicine songs and holders who are ready to call us into presence. In the Women's Belly and Womb Conferences women dressed in red came up through a symbolic birth canal into a ritual womb space. In the cacophony of women's voices, drums, rattles and beautiful imagery, greeters with evergreen boughs dipped in ocean water sprinkled each emerging crown in welcome. My chant opened the way:

You were born from a woman
Your mother has a name
No matter what your story with her
We honor the womb from where you came.

Opening circles hold a great deal of excitement and also potential fear for those arriving with underlying expectations of what is possible. It is a moment to build trust. This is a good place to start to name. By naming, you are saying that you are not going to assume that we are all the same or that every person can find resonance with those whom they do not know. This is what naming sounds like.

Naming the Unnamed

"You are welcome here. You are welcome here even in your discomfort, your nervousness, with your thoughts of feeling different or even feeling that you may not belong. All your feelings are welcome here, even your judgments and all the ways you protect yourself. You are welcome here with your own unique self that may include introversion or neuro-divergence or any feelings that have you watchful. You are taking care of yourself. You are welcome here with your curiosity, your openness, your excitement of what this time may be. You do not need to be a certain way as we begin. You do not need to dance or move unless you choose to. We ask that you do your best not to compare yourself to others but to let yourself be comfortable with any choice you are to make. You are welcome to be yourself and to give yourself all the time you need to choose for yourself how you will participate and what you will share. Make good boundaries for yourself and know that you can take your space. You belong here, just as you are. Welcome.

Take a moment now to invite yourself to take your place in our circle. If there was something not spoken or not named that you wish you could hear right now, please take the time to hear this from the inside or say it quietly on the outside. Be welcomed.

There may be things that are spoken that have you wonder whether they fit with your beliefs or not. No one here is required to adhere to the same beliefs. Honor your own. And know that you are respected. At the same time, we invite you to keep an open mind as you learn what is alive and present for those who hold this space. You are free to ask questions of us later if you want to know more or learn more of our reference places. Keep what serves you and leave what does not.

Take care of your body, your boundaries, your heart. Transformational spaces can bring up a lot of feelings. They are natural and they are welcome and only you know what is best for you in the speed you choose to meet your own emotions. We are here to support you if needed.

This place is not therapy. It is not intended for our hardest stories and traumas to be laid out in specific detail during shares because they might be too much for people to digest. You can however bring forward something that is ready to be shed at the core of your story and something that you want to name for yourself. The circle can be a place of reclaiming and letting go and remembering. The circle also welcomes laughter and tears, rage, fear and grief. If you can, let them move without attempting to push them down. We are not perfection, a utopia or a performance. We learn as we go and we do our best to be accountable. All that is real in you, vulnerable in you, precious in you, is welcomed."

Building the Container

The container is what holds the vision and the experiences and the agreements that build trust. If you want people to lean in with less vigilance which is constantly tracking personal and group safety *(from all the times no one took care of that in the family nor the culture)* then be sure to set the container with what is expected and what boundaries are in place.

Before we list some possible agreements, however, let's discuss the problem with making rules. Once a "rule" is in place, there is the possibility of something happening that causes an interruption or an exception. To be watchful of every rule can also be a form of control. And once "a rule" is communicated and then broken, you risk breaking trust.

What is more true and helpful, is to remind us that we head into the mystery and that we may need to "re-contract" an agreement if there is a change in plans needed. One of our best skills is to learn to go with the flow and even to go at times out of the boundaries of time. There is a quote (sometimes attributed to Eisenhower), "Planning is essential. Plans are useless." In this way, choose communications wisely and give assistance to those who need help with both feeling structure while also yielding to flow that is not always within the boundaries of time and space and rigidity.

So, you might start with something like: we will do our best with these agreements and sometimes there will be unexpected or needed changes that arise. When this happens please do your best to go with the flow and we will do our best to acknowledge and communicate necessary changes.

- Do your best not to interrupt others. (Sometimes an exception might be a facilitator who is in support when needed, or a timekeeper if a share is being timed or a special situation.)

- We will plan on beginning and ending on time and there may be time adjustments needed.

- We will listen without side-talking while we are in circle.

- We will be respectful towards one another even if we do not agree.

- We will not attempt to fix another person.

- We will do our best to be conscious not to use the language of blame, shame or judgment.

- We will not comment on another person's sharing unless it is relevant for what we ourselves are going to share or unless we have permission.

- We agree to keep confidentiality where asked.

- We understand that power and what we have learned about authority figures has us trained to obey. Please take care of your needs. If you need to go the bathroom for instance, you can leave and take care of yourself. If you need to stretch or move, please feel free to do so. We only ask that you be considerate of the space and do so with least disruption.

- If there is emotional work here, you know yourself best. Please do not venture further than what you know is safe for yourself at this time. This is true even if a facilitator encourages you. Only you know what is best and no explanation is needed. You are free to choose and to make boundaries that are best for your participation.

- Please ask for support if you need it.

Note: There may be agreements asked for prior to arriving as well. Be sure to give best instructions for people so that what is asked for is not a surprise. Example of this follows.

- Please refrain from scents, essential oils, perfumes or scented deodorants during this event. This includes bringing scented candles.

- Please plan on arriving on time.

- The space is shoeless so bring good slippers or warm socks.

- Parking may take some time to manage. Give yourself time.

With this you may also want to add what I call a bring list. Each one will be different with the event. If food is asked to be brought, do specify any restrictions in advance.

Bring List
- Journal and pen

- Warm clothes and layers

- Water bottle

- Pillow and/or pad

- A symbol for the altar

- Food to share that is vegetarian, or gluten free, or dairy free or organic

- Optional: drums, rattles.

Weaving Our Hearts

After the welcoming, one has a thousand doors to create with, yet at the core of this moment is connection. This is what most people miss. We are so inside of a performer/audience mindset that we can leave out the most important step – the weaving of our hearts. We need to adopt best practices of how we inter-relate and to also get behind our why collectively. This gives purpose to our coming together and helps us to see that we have all come for a common goal. If our lifeforce and time are precious, then when we choose to bring what lives here forward with our consciousness together, the circle can open with wonder and deep gratitude for being present to such an experience.

Separation comes when we see ourselves apart from others. Can you come in with your senses and feel those you are with? Slow things down even if the space or the silence may feel uncomfortable. Allow a settling to happen and in this a deeper arrival. This is where you may share prayers, a dance, an invocation or intention of your why. This is where you may have the circle make smaller circles to greet and talk even if it is in pairs. Or you can use the middle of the circle to identify who is here and why by calling various situations and having those who feel strongly about that come in and see each other while the larger circle witnesses.

It may sound like
Come forward if you …
Come forward if you are here for…
Come forward if you have experienced…
You may want to end this with finding something you can all agree to such as:
Come forward if you are happy to be here right now…
One of my favorite things to tell people when we begin is this. No matter what is going on here, imagine that you are having a dream. If you woke up from this same dream, you would say to yourself, "I just had the most amazing dream!" Yet when you are in this dream, you sometimes don't take it in or pay attention to just how miraculous and beautiful the dream is.

The other challenging situation in sacred space is to be ever mindful of being inclusive of humor as well as seriousness. This is not church or a library. Laughter creates bonding between women. Whatever you can do to bring levity as you bring depth is key to a strong container. To do this sometimes we need to punch a hole through the thick membrane of somber topics and also find our way in our ability to be light as well. It is a balancing act.

There are many, many ways to be in circle together and where you will go from here. If you name what needs naming, set your agreements, invoke your purpose, pay attention to connecting hearts and giving levity to what lives in the deep of our traumas that transformational spaces can illuminate, you are off to a start where people can settle more deeply into the power of what your time will hold. Please do not be afraid of stepping into the mystery, of moving one's body or to lifting one's voices in unison. By doing so, someone among you will leave this time knowing their lives will never be the same again. You have prepared the circle for whatever is ahead.

The Importance of Closure and Integration

Closure is just as important as your opening because likely you have moved a great deal of physical and emotional energies. Like a cauldron, you have stirred up the waters and likely rearranged stories, ideas and insights. Please take as much time at the end of a circle as you did to begin with and remind people of what it might feel like to transition from this space to home. We call this part integration. Many times, we close by each person having a chance to check out and to voice how they are. If we are not able to do that, we may ask for a word from each person to also track how an individual is feeling. Each person is unique and just as you did a naming in the beginning you may want to remind them of how to have closure too. List all the ways they can care for themselves that works best for them to digest. Always leave the circle with an offering, be it a blessing, a song, a prayer or a laying of hands on the earth and then opening to the heavens.

Woman, Woman
Thank you for showing up
Thank you for sharing, your sweet love and truth
We are so grateful, for your holy presence in all that we do.
And though we may not see you, in your heart let this circle remain
Then the power of our loving you, goes on and on, long after we're gone.

Every Block, Every Neighborhood, Every City, Everywhere Needs Herstory

Jeanne Teleia

"On every block, in every neighborhood, in every town, in every city, in every state, and in every country!" That was the motto of one of my first real women's circles – that to change the world and have a life well lived, women needed to have their own circle in one of these places. It still rings true today nearly forty years later.

I first attended a circle with only women in my early twenties when I joined an anti-racism/oppression training group in Washington, DC. While I had already identified myself as a feminist by then and refused to be called a 'girl', I got an eye-opening experience about what white privilege had been like in my life thus far. But it was also the first time I'd been in woman-only spaces. It was a revelation of how alike we all were with our common experience of being women.

Some years later through a Unitarian Universalist community, I attended my first class about the herstory of the Goddess. I was incensed that I had never learned any of this. It turned my conception of traditional history on its head. I became a seeker and sponged up everything I could about Goddess cultures. I even went through a year-long process of changing my name to reflect the names and energies of Goddesses and real women from my life that I wanted to call upon.

I continued to gain more experience and confidence through a newly formed 'Moon Hut' in Boulder, Colorado where women-only spaces were being created. I joined a women's circle, and we created the rituals from scratch – one or two women took turns leading the circle by picking a theme and creating activities around it whether it be with music, art, movement, sharing about a topic (often a taboo one) or our real lives, or picking some readings to share and discuss. We incorporated practices from other cultures (out of ignorance) like smudging and clearing energy and read together books like *Women Who Run with the Wolves*. We all contributed to creating a 'center circle' or altar which usually ended up being incredibly beautiful. Anyone that could was encouraged to host the circle at their homes.

In most of my circles, we didn't have a closed circle, so women came and went but there ended up being a core group of us who nurtured the group. Some of us became friends and saw each other outside circle time but we strove to create a strong sense of our own identity each month as a group. Sometimes, it was all any of us had that supported our path as a woman in this world.

Picking a focus...or not?

Since then, I continued to create and develop Full Moon or New Moon (or both) circles for women, and mostly because I needed them myself. I needed to be seen, heard and understood from a woman's perspective, and being validated in this way really helped in a world of gaslighting of our concerns and struggles.

I incorporated learnings about the moon cycles in parallel to our own cycles and got more in touch with nature by holding some circles outside and singing (or howling!) at the moon. Often our focus is based on the wheel of the year – again focused on Earth-centered or Nature-based traditions from which many Goddess cultures came or had as central to their beliefs. Caring for the Earth is a basic premise for women – as she cares for us, we must care for her in return.

Most of my circles have some educational component because I want other women to have the knowledge that I didn't have about our REAL herstory – the Goddess cultures, the archeological evidence of how present and important we were in so many cultures throughout history, and how we weren't always communities of violent oppressors, but that did in fact live in matrifocal, matrilineal, or matriarchal societies that were much more peaceful. It was important to share pivotal books and information from other women scholars who were rewriting history to incorporate herstory. I reveled in seeing women's eyes hunger for more.

I sometimes led a group based on the 'Rise Up and Call Her Name' curriculum – a thirteen-session deeper dive into various Goddess cultures around the world including art, music, dance, ritual, readings and other creative activities to really connect with that herstory. I especially encouraged white women not to just adopt practices and beliefs of other cultures (as I had seen too many doing and rejecting their own culture) because inevitably if they dug back long enough, they would find that their ancestry did in fact include all the same nature-based respect and woman-affirming elements.

We all need to feel proud of our true herstory in order to learn how to bring that ancient wisdom into our current lives and societies. We all also needed to learn what the Burning Times were really all about and how it has been our Holocaust that no one talks about. Women are still persecuted today, and the patriarchy encourages a lack of connection with our ancestry and each other.

Practicalities

Deciding on when the group should become closed and perhaps another created in another neighborhood is essential and based on the needs of the six to eight core members. That is a good number of people so there is enough time for everyone to share. Circles last for about two hours with some time for socializing before or after.

There are always people who you don't exactly like or think you'd get along with outside of circle but inside, a sacred space of listening and finding common ground is held sacrosanct.

You need one or two people to take care of a mailing list – emails or now even a text group, and that responsibility could and should be rotated so everyone has buy-in but doesn't get burned out. That's what I see the most – one or two women holding too much responsibility for planning and keeping the group alive as volunteers and then getting sick of it or not feeling appreciated when people don't show up or communicate.

Getting women to buy into the running of the group by asking them to be responsible for even small parts of it is essential AND it builds life and professional skills too. As time goes on, other women can take on leadership roles as they grow in confidence.

Singing and some form of movement and creativity are essential elements in my women's circles. I went to multiple women's camps and learned from other women about all the Goddess and Earth-centered/honoring songs and simple dances that have been around forever. I learned from Wiccan priestesses, Earth mamas, hippies and scholars. Singing, chants, prayers, dancing, storytelling, art and more were all incorporated into some form of ritual – for fun and as time-honored healing and bonding rituals.

After so many years in circles, the power of the talking stick never ceases to amaze me. It is also essential to have group agreements around confidentiality ('what is said in group, stays in group') and how things like the talking stick work. I have found it best to have agreements like being aware of the time you are using so that all have a chance, no cross talk, being allowed to have the stick, take up space and be silent. I also encourage women to get together socially outside of group. My goal is always to create a real community where you have someone you can call on at 2 a.m.

We encourage times where women talk about their professional as well as their personal lives. Sometimes, people will network this way or receive services from another they have met in the group, but this has to be carefully managed if they are personal services like therapy or coaching lest a dual relationship be created or conflicts arise.

When one or two people are consistently creating, leading and facilitating the group, I have found it necessary and validating to ask for donations or a fee. It takes a lot of time, energy and supplies to run a group and that should be acknowledged. As the group forms and gels and others take on leadership roles, the circle can be donation-based for new people or anyone not running the circle that month.

The laughter and tears – these are a given and a necessity in any group. Life can be hard, but we must find joy. We can be raunchy, funny, irreverent and un-stoppable so the laughter comes, sometimes right alongside the tears. Sometimes those tears are from the deeply felt loss of never having had a connection like this circle in your life – no women ancestors who taught you to love your body or your cycles, to fight for your space and not 'just be nice' instead of being kind by being assertive. We feel this loss keenly at some point, only when we finally have it.

Challenges and Opportunities

I believe women-centered leadership should be less hierarchical/patriarchal and more fluid because every woman has something to contribute, not just those that 'know' certain things about herstory. One of the reasons I didn't like most women-centered entrepreneurial groups or non-profit leadership is that they inevitably used 'Robert's rules of order' or something which felt very male oriented or based on a hierarchy. It just wasn't fun to be in these groups which were too goal oriented and not interested in forming true relationships with each other.

In fact, that is always where I saw more conflicts and the stereotyped women's wounded behavior showing up.

As a mental health professional, I am sensitive to women's groups not becoming a therapy circle as it is not appropriate for that level of need. Leaders must be able to intervene with someone who is either dominating group or needs some outside intervention. Women are too easily pulled into the 'helping' mode and not getting their own needs met in the circle without some parameters around every woman having time and space.

Conflicts are a given and normalizing this should be done right up front. Women will usually not speak up about something they are unhappy about and leave the group if they are not encouraged to deal with it, or the group will splinter when divides are allowed to fester. One of our greatest challenges is how to be in conflict and resolve it without worrying about hurting someone else's feelings or being reactive to our own. This is where good leadership is essential and a commitment to growing our emotional intelligence is vital. Everyone should be made aware that they are responsible for their own reactions and feelings. Conflicts can be managed if we role model and demonstrate it to newer women in the circle. That sometimes means two leaders talking things out either outside or during the circle time.

Most women come from some level of trauma or loss and this too is acknowledged in group – to be heard, sometimes held, is to start or keep the healing going. Again, good leadership will know when to intervene if it's getting too much like therapy, but there is a fine line there and often not easy to navigate.

No matter what, we want to know each other, who is important to us, what is important to us, what we yearn for, what we dream of, our struggles, challenges, and our successes. We want each participant to feel known, cared for, accepted, validated and important. In addition, learning our true herstory in our circles is central to our own empowerment.

Every block, every neighborhood…start one today!

follow your own pathway

Sue Johnson

first work out the direction you wish to travel
this is your journey
the final destination will be yours alone

prepare well before you take that first step
visualise where you wish to be at the end
use all the senses to achieve this

ignore those who insist you will fail
or say you should follow a tried and tested trail
let them do as they wish

gather spiritual armour to sustain you
on days that are difficult and fogbound
give thanks always for any help given

step confidently towards your chosen goal
it doesn't matter if the steps are small
keep going and the end will be in sight

help others along the way if you are able
as they in their turn will help you
avoid those who are vain and bitter

or any who do not share your vision
you do not need that kind of negativity
wrap them in red thread and move on

rejoice when you reach each staging post
reward yourself for the work you have done
rest in peace at the end of each day

MAKING SPACE, TAKING UP SPACE

'She Moves Mountains'

Jennifer Margulis

Circles and Cultural Appropriation

Sayra Pinto

Cultural appropriation is what happens when people with personal, interpersonal, and institutional power in a racialized society adopt, adapt, claim ownership, and rob people of their traditional cultural practices, cultural adaptations, and innovations to gain personal, reputational, monetary, and institutional advantages within that racialized society.

We believe that this is what has been done with the Indigenous circle process by many in the restorative, transformative, and healing justice movements. Over the past twenty-five years, our communities have witnessed in disbelief as [certain white people] have been held up by academics, restorative justice advocates and knowledge makers to the extent of providing funding, publishing opportunities and reputational support while Indigenous people and people of color are marginally involved or even welcomed.

Many people ask what it takes to be trained and have permission to do circles. We at For a Loving Future do not believe training is possible. We believe that the idea of training is actually counterproductive to the practice of circles. We are encountering people who have spent time, money, and used their relationships to become circle keepers who actually have very little idea of what circles are and what they are for, and consequently, continue to carry harmful behaviors and attitudes about power, difference, and the meaning of community. We are saddened by their sense of loss and confusion when they are actually in the presence of the practice. We think what has been done to them is irresponsible and harmful.

There are some *key impulses* that fuel the cultural appropriation of Indigenous ways of being, seeing the world and building community. These impulses come from the settler colonial project. They are:

1. Accessing something of value without permission from the people to whom that something belongs because doing so makes someone feel better;

2. Claiming belonging to a tribe because it is difficult to own one's belonging in the settler colonial project;

3. Practicing Indigenous ways because it makes someone feel special and more important than others;

4. Running towards indigeneity out of a sense of not belonging anywhere; and

5. Feeling a right to something that belongs to Indigenous peoples because somehow one or two individuals have said someone could have that thing.

"…But it feels so good and so right."

Many people currently doing circle work in the restorative, transformative and healing justice spaces feel entitled to the circles themselves because they see immense value to the people they are about when they are implemented.

Indigenous peoples connected to the land they come from should have a moral and ethical role, and a protagonist role, in creating opportunities for those processes to be held. Their voices and ways of thinking should feature in a central manner in the creation of those spaces. In the end, circles are about communities. They cannot flourish in the hands of individuals. They should emerge first from Indigenous communities from the lands where they exist or where there is a desire for them to exist and the rest of us should assist at the request of First Nations members.

The right role for non-tribal Indigenous peoples is to be *for* and *about* the wellbeing of tribal communities in connection with our own work on our own communities. It means we have to be OK with being exactly who we are, where we are, and who we are with. The past is not coming back, the future is the result of our present, and in the present time we can model solidarity with tribal nations, and we can bring our non-tribal communities closer to health and wellbeing by working with these communities to get them there.

The Mechanics of Circle Process

Much like the Medicine Wheel, which is layered, circle process is also layered. The first layer of circle is the long-term process of building relationships. The person hosting the circle minds the long term process of building relationships and also creates opportunities to tend to those relationships.

This means that people ought to come together to practice being together and so that this relationship building process can take hold. We often describe hosting very much like hosting people over at our house. When people come over your house, one should work to make sure everyone feels comfortable, welcomed, and invited into the space.

Hosting Circles

We encourage people who are interested in creating circle processes to think of their role as hosts, not as facilitators. Hosting is an art form that requires self-awareness, self-discipline, and an ethic of generosity directed at the community.

Here are a few important added tips for implementation:

1. **It is really important to seek the opportunity to be a learner of circles.** This is so because the practice stems from Indigenous ways of understanding the world. It is premised on the practice of Indigenous ontologies, ways of seeing the world. Because we live in a culture that is very different from the practice of such ways, it is important that we exercise humility and seek always the opportunity to learn, reflect, and change our behavior to support the implementation of this practice. The journey of circles is endless for the practitioner because we constantly have to grapple with a dominant culture that does not support this practice. We have to build communities of our own that can support this process. In order to do great work in circles, it is imperative that practitioners sit in circles as too, without the added layer of responsibility of hosting.

2. **Practitioners cannot control the process.** The process of preparing for the circle determines the quality of experience in a circle. We cannot mandate what happens in a circle, we can only invite and prepare. This is another way in which this practice requires an ethic of humility.

3. **Values are important.** Circles are "no-rule" spaces. Unlike traditional facilitation where a facilitator may name the rules or guidelines that people are expected to abide to during meetings, circles operate from a place of shared leadership and agreement. Generally, the more diverse a group that comes together to be in circle is, the more important it is to take time to generate what we call agreements – a grouping of agreed upon ways of being together. A great question to begin the process of generating agreements is, "What do you need from yourself and from others in this group to bring your best self here?" And then follow up it with, "Do we want to try to give ourselves and others what we need to bring our best selves here?" We often use the metaphor of baseball in that we ask people if it is remotely possible to become a Major League Baseball player by reading the rules of baseball.

People always say no. Then we explain that implementing group agreements is like baseball in the sense that you can read what you are supposed to do but what you actually need is practice.

4. **Trust the talking piece.** When introducing the talking piece, explain that one always has the choice to share, be in silence, and pass the talking piece when holding it. When one does not have the talking piece, the invitation is to listen deeply for what the other person is trying to convey, not for what demonstrates what we think to be true about the person speaking or what we think they are saying before they are even done saying it. The opportunity is to be fully present to witness someone else's choice in the group. Given the vast philosophical differences between the practice of facilitation and the practice of hosting circles, it can become very tempting to interrupt the use of the talking piece. Don't. Model trust in the process you are inviting people into. It is important in our view to create a sense of predictability in the way in which the talking piece moves. Also, in keeping with Indigenous ways of how energy moves in a group and in the universe, the talking piece is generally passed from right to left or in clockwise direction. At times, when one is south of the Equator, the talking piece is passed from left to right. This has to do with building a sense of connection with how energy moves – the direction of the Earth's rotation and of the Milky Way in order to evoke a sense of connection with all that is in the universe. This understanding is important because the energy in a circle does change when you send the talking piece the other way around.

5. **Modeling is central in circle process.** Make sure you model first when you invite everyone in the circle to participate. For example, if you are beginning a check in round, make sure you go first so that everyone can see what you are inviting them to do. This is not to create norms or expectations of good behavior. People always do what they need to do in the circle. However, modeling supports the understanding that everyone is good enough to participate even if participation just means being present in the circle.

Previously published on lovingfuture.org

Cultural Appropriation

Amy Wilding

If you close your eyes and imagine a women's circle, it's likely that some specific images will come to mind…a gathering space around a circle, some candles, comfy rugs or pillows, a talking stick, and perhaps a sage or palo santo smudge stick for cleansing the space and welcoming attendees.

If you had been present at one of my Red Tent women's circles for the first several years of my offerings, that is in fact what you would have seen.

I, like so many others who feel called to gather the women, took as my examples and role models myriad other women who had been offering circles before me. Some were my direct guides, while others were women I had admired from afar. It did not occur to me during that time to question the appropriateness of their (or my) use of specific ceremonial objects as a white American woman, and it would take me years to understand, and stand in full accountability for, the practices I utilized during that time. I simply did not know what I didn't know.

Cultural appropriation is a term that has risen in the common vernacular over recent years, and you may have heard it in reference to women's spirituality and circle practices such as the use of white sage, palo santo, talking sticks, some aspects of yoga, belly dance, and cacao ceremonies, to name a few. Although we may be familiar with the general concept of cultural appropriation, it can be a bit slippery to truly understand the full meaning – and its implications for us as circle leaders.

Cultural appropriation is defined as "the unacknowledged or inappropriate adoption of the customs, practices, ideas, etc. of one people or society by members of another and typically more dominant people or society."

There's a lot to unpack there.

For the purposes of understanding cultural appropriation as it relates to women's circles, we can paraphrase this definition by saying that when we as white women co-opt a practice or use objects or items that are sacred or ceremonial within the cultural heritage of BIPOC communities, for our own benefit and/or to lend ourselves an air of spiritual gravitas or credibility, we are participating in cultural appropriation. Add to this the frequent commodification of these objects or practices by white people, and we compound the problem exponentially. In short, if we are taking something that does not belong to us via our own ancestral lineage and using it for social or material gain, it is likely cultural appropriation.

I know this can be a hard pill to swallow. To be completely transparent, I will admit that I struggled with this myself when the issue was illuminated for me. Because this was the way of circle that was both intentionally and tacitly modeled for me, most often by other white women, I had a difficult time accepting that I had any personal responsibility related to this issue. Didn't these practices transcend race or culture, I wondered, and offer magic and meaning for *all* women in circle?

It is fair to say that women's circles have become something of their own culture over the past decade or two, owing in large part to the visibility of the Red Tent movement following the publication of Anita Diamant's book, as well as the legacy of consciousness raising groups during the 1960s and 70s in the United States. Given that the cultural transmission of circle practices, ceremonies, and rituals is in large part passed from one woman or community to another, it is easy to see how certain potentially problematic practices may proliferate through time and across communities. We freely and lovingly share and integrate ideas, practices, and customs that inspire or move us, often times without understanding or acknowledging their origins.

The practice of "smudging" with white sage and palo santo is one example that I can draw upon personally when considering the unintentional but very real spread of cultural appropriation. White sage (*Salvia Apiana*) is native to the Southwestern United States, southern California, and Northern Mexico and has been not only a staple food, but also a sacred plant ally to multiple Indigenous communities such as the Cahuilla, Kumeyaay, Chumash, and Luiseno for thousands of years. Because the practice of smudging with white sage specifically has been co-opted by the spiritual community at large, this plant is now overharvested (and even poached) to the point that it is in decline with threat of becoming endangered, making it more and more difficult for the legitimate heirs of this ancestral practice to use.

Similarly, the use of palo santo to cleanse and balance energy has become very on trend in the US despite its South American origins. First used by the Inca hundreds of years ago during their religious rites, palo santo ("holy wood") was also harvested for medicinal purposes. The appropriation of this sacred plant has turned it into a mere commercial product, the over-harvesting of which has led to significant deforestation in and around Ecuador.

Talking sticks have also become a widely visible feature in many women's circles, including my own in the past. A talking stick is a ceremonial tool traditionally used by several Indigenous peoples of North America, particularly among the Haudenosaunee (Iroquois), Cherokee, and nations of the Pacific Northwest Coast such as the Tlingit, Haida, and Coast Salish. In its original cultural context, the talking stick was used during council gatherings as a sacred object to facilitate respectful and egalitarian communication. The person holding the stick had the sole right to speak, while others listened with full attention – ensuring every voice was heard and no one was interrupted. The stick itself was often carved with meaningful spiritual symbols and treated with reverence, sometimes passed down through generations. In recent decades, this practice has been widely appropriated in white-dominant spiritual and wellness spaces, often divorced from its cultural roots and used without acknowledgment or relationship. While the intention to create sacred space for sharing is important, using a talking stick without cultural understanding or permission can contribute to the commodification and erasure of Indigenous traditions.

As a white woman with no ancestral connection to Native American or Indigenous Central American culture, why did I adopt these practices as part of my own circle's ceremony and ritual? Mainly, because it is what I saw other women do. Not knowing their ancestral lineage, it is impossible for me to say whether their use of these items was an example of cultural appropriation or not. I can say with certainty, however, that as a member of "a more dominant culture" – a white descendant of white colonizers – my use of sacred objects belonging to the ceremonial practices of Indigenous people, on colonized land, was both unacknowledged and inappropriate.

When it comes to cultural appropriation in ceremony and ritual in women's circles, I understand why it happens. Quite simply, we hunger for meaning. When using sacred plants or objects in circle, we feel connected to a lineage and history – though in most cases, it is not our own. That does not mean, however, that certain objects or practices cannot feel inspiring and sacred and meaningful to us; indeed they can and do. And that can make it even harder to look at our own adopted spirituality, and to understand the importance of accountability.

It's an odd thing, being an American; we are so generally disconnected from any sense of significant ancestral lineage and connection to place that we truly long for the depth of history that is lent by the use of the sacred objects and practices of ancient cultures. Ceremony transcends place and lineage, and that feels *good* when we feel so culturally adrift, but it is also our responsibility to be accountable for the unethical practices that we participate in and perpetuate.

Being aware of and sensitive to the sacred lineage of other cultures does not mean that we must lead circles devoid of ritual and ceremony, however. The recent accessibility of DNA testing now allows us the opportunity to see beyond the two to three generations that most of us have direct access to, and view our heritage through the long lens of history. Many of us Americans are cultural mutts, so to speak, white Americans often have a predominantly European lineage that we now have access to. In connecting to the thread of our own ancestry, we begin to claim the gifts of our people and feel the sense of meaning and belonging that we have been seeking.

Coming to this place of understanding in my own spiritual journey has led me to a beautiful new path of exploring the sacred traditions of my own Irish, English, and German ancestral lineage. It has been deeply nourishing and inspiring for me to learn more about Celtic women's spirituality, traditional ceremonial and medicinal plants native to the land of my ancestors, sacred drumming, German Wise Women traditions, the symbolism of Northern European folklore, and more. Regardless of each person's individual ancestral heritage, there is a wealth of meaning and tradition to explore.

Indeed, when I work with women in my Women's Circle Leadership certification program, one of the tasks I assign each participant is the exploration of her lineage and the identification of sacred rituals, objects, plants, rites-of-passage, etc. specific to her ancestry (and depending on the diversity of her heritage, this may be quite a deep dive!). The goal of this exploration is not necessarily to copy or reproduce these practices, but to begin to develop *her own relationship* with the spiritual practices of her people and to create meaningful ceremony with that as her foundation.

As you consider your ceremonial practices in this new light, and are unsure as to whether you are participating in cultural appropriation or merely expressing inspiration and appreciation for other cultures, there are some important questions you may ask yourself.

1. Where did I observe or learn about this object/practice?

2. Was I invited to learn about and given instruction on the use of this object/ practice by a member of its community of origin?

3. When using this object/practice, do I offer acknowledgment to its culture of origin?

4. What messages have traditional communities expressed about the use of this object/practice by those outside of their culture?

5. Does the commodification of this object lead to disruption and/or oppression of local economies or ecosystems?

6. Does the object/practice originate in a culture that has been historically oppressed by colonizers?

7. Has the use of this object/practice by white spiritual practitioners led to the loss of sacredness and/or accessibility for the community of origin?

8. Am I using this object/practice to enhance the image of my spiritual credibility or authority?

If you find that your answers to these questions lead you to consider the practices in your circle and shift away from the possibility of participating in cultural appropriation, you may have many feelings and perhaps even more questions. I encourage you to continue your exploration by reading about ceremonial practices and sacred objects that you have used in your gatherings, by having conversations with other circle leaders, and most importantly, by listening to BIPOC individuals when they address this topic.

The transition from cultural appropriation to ancestral alignment may feel daunting at first, but can be accomplished with small steps, such as replacing your practice of smudging with white sage or palo santo by offering smoke cleansing, or creating an essential oil blend, using traditional herbs and plants from your lineage – perhaps that you even grow yourself. Rather than using a talking stick, you can maintain the respectful flow of sharing during circle by passing a ball of red yarn (symbolizing the red thread of menstruation) from woman to woman, as we do in my circles; as each woman takes her turn to share, she loops the yarn around her wrist three or four times, thus creating a bracelet with which we are all interconnected. At the end of circle, we raise our "web" of yarn, marveling at how we are not just physically but spiritually woven together, and then cut the yarn and tie the loops around each woman's wrist.

Another important facet of my leadership training process is recognizing the fact that we *all* have the ability to create meaningful rituals and ceremonies. We can literally just make them up! The word ritual is derived from the Sanskrit word *rtu*, which means "an act of magic toward a purpose." I just love that. The word 'ritual' is also related to the word for menses, and some scholars believe that the earliest rituals ever developed were connected to women's monthly bleeding. With that fact alone, we have access to the very genesis of ritual. Although it can feel intimidating to imagine creating your own ritual or ceremony for your women's circle, I can say with certainty that these carry just as much meaning, magic, and healing as any that we may inherit or adopt – and in fact, this is the final assignment for women in my leadership training program. We need only the intention and inspiration to craft something new – and powerful – for our community.

The purpose of this discussion is not to call anyone out or create shame around the use of practices that are meaningful within the circle experience, but rather to inspire awareness and growth in women's circle leaders. I offer the grace of someone who has been there myself as I invite you to consider whether your circle, and the BIPOC communities of the world, may be best served by releasing practices and/or objects that are not components of your ancestral lineage and instead recrafting your offerings to reflect your connection to your heritage, and your respect for the heritage of others.

Ultimately, the work of becoming an aligned and ethical circle leader is not about perfection – it is about awareness, humility, and devotion to truth, to growth, to honoring the sacred in a way that uplifts rather than appropriates. When we root ourselves in the lineage of our own people, we are not limiting our spiritual expression – we are deepening it. We are choosing integrity over image, connection over convenience, and reverence over replication. This is how we create circles that not only transform lives, but also honor the lives and legacies of those who came before. And that, too, is sacred.

A Sense of Belonging

Shannon Cotterill

I was born in Sydney, Australia, in 1979. My mother landed here from Scotland as a teen with her family as 'ten-pound poms' and went on to marry my father at the tender age of twenty. My Dad is as 'Aussie' as they come, but his Grandparents were Irish and Scottish immigrants from Belfast and Glasgow.

I have called the Central Coast home since I was four, a beautiful spot nestled between Sydney and Newcastle. I love this land and the coastline where I live. Miles and miles of beaches, secluded coves and scenic bushland to explore. Some of my favourite moments here are the scent of the earth after rain, the bright coloured birds that call our garden home, vast blue skies, vivid sunsets over the mountains, and searing heat followed by summer thunderstorms.

I know how fortunate I am to live in a country that is a safe haven, with freedom to be whoever you wish to be – especially as a woman.

Australia is the 'lucky country' filled with abundance and opportunity, but it was brutally colonised in 1788 by the British. The original custodians were stripped of their connection to Country, community, language and spirit. In just over two centuries 65,000+ years of rich culture and wisdom dramatically changed forever. Understandably this wound is very raw for the First Nations people of this land.

Even though my star fell here (as my dear Indigenous friend Ned told me during one of our deep conversations around this subject), I didn't realise just how much guilt I hold, and how displaced I feel from the lands of my ancestors. I'm sure I'm not alone in these feelings.

I am Australian, yet at the same time I have always yearned for the mother land. I have been to Scotland several times visiting my Mum's hometown of Stirling, and my soul remembers this place. Walking the cobblestone streets where generations upon generations of my ancestors have walked, I felt that sense of home so acutely my heart ached. Perhaps it's the fact that my ancestors' bones and stories reside there?

At the same time when on Australian soil I know I'm also a part of this land, this unique energy. When hear the distinctive cry of the black cockatoo then see her unmistakable form glide overhead there is an undeniable stirring within my body – an electric energy – a soaring sign from spirit.

My body and bones are formed from this land. The wild earth, salty sea and eucalyptus…

But within my blood, there is the pulse of ancestral threads and ancient stories.

My soul yearns for a touchstone, an anchor, for a place where I truly belong. For connections that run deep and ancient. I have felt envious at times of my Indigenous friends whose connection to their culture and Country is so deep, beautiful and meaningful…but then quickly felt shame when remembering how much pain and suffering their people have been through, and just how much has been stolen.

Perhaps these feelings are why I was so drawn to attending my first ever women's circle in 2019 when invited by a friend. At the time I was desperately seeking connection to something bigger, something with more meaning than the daily hum drum and routines of life (especially as a busy mother of three!).

The ritual was to be held not far from my home in a sweet beach house with views over the Pacific Ocean. I met the circle facilitator and my future mentor, Kate Reed, and to begin our time together she guided us through the process of introducing ourselves to the land – something that had never crossed my mind to do.

We were asked to walk barefoot outside to the garden or beach, to a spot that we felt intuitively drawn to. Once there, connecting our energy to the land by placing our hands upon the earth, then stating out loud and 'introducing' ourselves and our lineage from parents to grandparents and beyond if you could remember.

I wandered quietly down to the water's edge to the tideline and felt called to a particular spot far away from the other women. I stood with my feet firmly grounded in the sand, feeling the gentle sea breeze on my skin and my energy calming…crouching down I placed my hands on the earth and closed my eyes.

"I am Shannon, daughter of Alison and Shane, Granddaughter of Monica and Alexander, Rosemary and Mervyn, Great Granddaughter of Mary and Andrew, Alison and James, Marion and John, Lily and Samuel. I come here with love, respect, and ask for your blessing to be here on this sacred land."

As I went through this process, I experienced an overwhelming sense of being held. I kept hearing in my mind, "You are welcome, you are safe, you are loved," over and over again. This moment was so profound it brought me to my knees, tears streaming down my face. The relief, the acceptance, the belonging.

I am a child of the stars after all.

Once I felt the energy dissipate and I composed myself, I cleansed my hands in the salt water and walked back to the house. I entered circle with a deep sense of gratitude and a new-found respect for our great Mother Earth, for all that she holds and supports.

Since that day I have made it a ritual of mine to introduce myself to the land wherever I go. Whether it's just a local bush walk, staying in a new town or visiting a different country. Would you just walk into someone's home un-announced? When we barge into a new location that's essentially what we are doing to the ancestors and guardian spirits of that place. This perspective shifted so much for me in regard to respecting the land you reside on, its history, its people and its ancestors.

I encourage you wherever you are to go ahead, introduce yourself, and then pause. What do you feel? Are you welcome? Or should you perhaps leave this place undisturbed (yes, I have received a 'no' before and swiftly turned around!).

Believe me, you will know.

This experience inspired me to go on and train to become a Sister Circles facilitator, it has turned out to be one of the most rewarding aspects of my life. Holding circle is a way to weave the sacred back into our lives, to connect with others soul to soul regardless of age or background.

Some of my most memorable circles have been attended by women ranging from seventeen to seventy years of age – we all have wisdom to share from our unique life experiences and perspectives. Humans are meant to be in commu-nity with each other, connected to the land under their feet and the cycles and seasons that swirl around them.

Circle has brought me home to myself, and to a deep sense of belonging.

Mother Nature. In her glory, she is not shy.

She blooms in the most outrageous colours, she shows us her mood through the sky. Rolling pastel fairy floss clouds, sweet warm floral scents in the air...or cracking thunder and howling wind, searing her way over the surface of the earth. Shaking, trembling, angry.

She does not hide. She is raw, real and all powerful.

The changing seasons, the cycles of earth and womb.
Mother Nature knows that there is a time for everything.
A time to rise and a time to lay dormant…

She asks you to honour where you are right now.

Women's Circles: the magic, the undertow, the tides

Jaine Rose

Women's circles have long been spaces of profound growth, healing, and connection. I know this personally; I have had the joy of being in many. I have circled with women over and over in woodlands, roundhouses, moors, cottages, by open fires, rivers, and tucked up on a multitude of soft, welcoming sofas. They are places where we gather to share stories, honour our journeys, and witness one another in our fullest truth. In a world that often thrives on competition and isolation, these circles offer a powerful counterbalance – a model of community grounded in collaboration, empathy, and shared wisdom.

Being with sisters can be the most incredibly moving and heart-expanding experience as we hear each other's words, as we live through starbursts of joy, terrors that numb us, bone-deep grief, and all the days of life and love that are in between. We drum, sing, swing our hips together, stamp our feet, howl at real or imagined moons, and even descend into wild and fabulous madness and uncontrolled laughter. These are our sisters; we are bonded by tears, woven together in solidarity and deep and authentic care.

Women's circles matter, they always have. We conspire together, that is, we breathe with one another – conspirare – and midwife each other through the very many chapters we live through, as twisty and turny as they almost certainly will be. To be truly seen and understood kindly and in our full selves, is one of the most healing and beautiful gifts we women can receive from each other.

These circles are all the more important as women's experience and the body politic are still substantially different from men, and a safe space is needed to navigate ways together through intersections of patriarchy, capitalism, and white supremacy. As women, we are brought up to expect predatory aggression, insults, and constant messaging that we're not good enough. We are trained to be pitched against each other, to be small, and to fit in at any cost. So meeting with women in circles, we have a chance to reframe, unlearn all that we were told. We understand that there is a strong need to begin to shape new cultures, new narratives.

So far so good, but as well as this hallowed space we women create, what of the undertow, tides, and currents that we may have to swim against?

The experience for many women in women's circles and groups is that after a sweet time of togetherness, cracks appear, difficult behaviours can start to arise, and often the circle implodes, breaks down, and replicates the very same oppressive structures that we're culturally trying to escape from in the first place.

So how is it that things can go wrong, and how do we find a way through?

Why do some groups work beautifully well, and other groups flounder? How do 'difficult' people integrate in our circles?

Women's circles can be romanticised ideals of what we'd love sisterhood to be, without the recognition that we are pre-formed and moulded in a trauma culture. Sometimes a binary narrative is wrapped around women being good, and men bad. We can hold the naive belief that either conflict won't happen, or that if it does, we are all reasonable and nice enough to find a way through it. Women can be silenced with emotional bypassing, in a 'we all need to love each other' narration, a form of toxic peacekeeping that will quietly erode from the inside outwards. We appease too quickly, rather than speaking plainly about what we see happening. We swallow down our discomfort yet again, because this is what we've learnt to do, to be safe. Each time we do this, each time we don't give voice to our worry and distress, everything that follows will be a little less honest. We begin to pull away. Or perhaps we do speak out and are met with dismay, judgement, and a shutting down of our voice. We are on our own and in a wilderness we do not understand or know how to get out of.

What we can fail to recognise is that we are not all equal in terms of our capacity, needs, and privilege. We can lack an understanding of neurodivergence and trauma, and the tools to navigate gender questioning. We don't have enough trauma-informed awareness to hold us safely in groups. We're hungry to get together, but we don't know how to do that well, and healthily.

At a time when we need our circles to be truly resourceful, we perhaps don't recognise that we are operating within parameters of white feminism, which has traditionally copied patriarchal, top-down power structures. Many of us have experienced the woman who strongly needs her vision to be adhered to, at any cost. The woman who started the circle, or who owns the house or land where the women meet. This all feeds into unequal power dynamics. When dysfunctional behaviours arise, to stand and call out women is to be exiled.

Finding a healthy way through conflict is not about persuading each other that we're right but about embracing the idea that we hold different values, emotional language, and capacities. Can we compassionately seek to understand each woman present in the circle? When our nervous systems are on high alert, how do we stay safe?

One way would be to move towards a flat model, where each woman holds equal status, or sociocracy – where consent and safety are sought, or consensus circles where each voice is heard. All these are helpful, but not always possible. The alternative to unhealthy leadership can often result in groups having no structure, no leadership, which could free-fall into chaos and dysregulation. The group can then lack clarity, and the woman who does perhaps have a vision and the organisational skills to implement it gets disempowered. Rejecting the old power paradigms will be a positive thing, but then what? We need to bring our full attention and robust skill of relating to the models of being in circle with each other.

Miki Kashtan, in her groundbreaking and visionary work in non-violent convergent facilitation, invites us to focus on willingness and stretching towards each other to find a place where we can meet comfortably and with open hearts. Rather than fleeing from what is contentious and troublesome, or shutting down, she invites dissent. She welcomes failures and sees the value in deeply listening to the outliers. Traditionally we have been discouraged from expressing anger or addressing conflict directly, but when women can take shared ownership of the conflict and potential wounding, we become stewards of the circle. Inviting dissent helps us let go of the pressure to agree to something that we feel inside doesn't sit well with us. It makes it safe to speak what feels true to us then, even if we are the lone voice in the group. Suddenly we are not seen as the problem but as the gift bearer.

So perhaps if we unlearn all we think we know about women and conflict, all we've been trained to subjugate within ourselves and the wider group, we can begin the work of rebuilding healthier circles. We lead with bravery and resilience, but most of all with heart and kindness. We begin to expand our tolerance for sitting with what is deeply uncomfortable, without judgement. We hold outlier sisters in compassionate resonance, knowing that they hold treasure for the whole group. When we understand the landscape of what is most painful, we can move towards a willingness to find solutions that all the women in the circle can feel good about and give consent to.

We understand that within the sacred spaces of our beautiful women's circles, the echoes of collective and individual wounds will arise. This is not the problem – how we journey through this pain though, is everything. We know that these dynamics can sometimes be fragile; we know we fall, but that we can pick ourselves up and try again. It can ultimately be healing, empowering, and an act of wild rebellion to find new, strong ways of being together. And that we can do this in a difficult, quickly changing world that seeks to destabilise women at every turn. We stand upright in our collective sovereignty, hands at each other's backs. When we commit to this work, we not only strengthen our circles but also transform them into sanctuaries of authentic connection, power, and integrity – wonder filled and magical cauldrons where every voice is valued, and every wound has the potential to heal.

Black Sisters – Taking up Space – What Your Presence Brings

Coco Oya Cienna-Rey

It is the principle of love that brings us to liberation.

bell hooks

I have been sitting in sister circles of one form or another for over twenty years. Small and intimate affairs where friendships and bonds were formed. Throughout that time, I have often been the only black woman in the space. Yet it never really occurred to me that that was the case: I had blinded myself to that fact. Possibly because I have lived that reality throughout my life since childhood living in a predominately white country. However, this was brought to the forefront of my reality in August 2024 whist attending an event for over two hundred women. It was the first time I became acutely aware of being the only black woman in a space and having an overwhelming feeling of unsafety in my body.

Maybe it was because of the sea of unfamiliar faces. Or it could have been the spirits making themselves known in the room. Or the history of the building I was sensing, one steeped in slavery dressed up as philanthropy. Or it could have been that it was just my time to step more into the wise woman archetype, the theme of the day. Or because that month in the UK race was high on everyone's agenda and there had been riots on the streets. Whatever it was, it was a melting pot of energies. I could feel the ancestors in the room and I was being called to clear the lingering shadows. To address the intertwining stories of the space.

It soon became apparent that the day would unfold through a set of divinely ordained steps where I was greeted by the exact people who could assist the process of deepening into the understanding of what was taking place. The pivotal point being when one of the facilitators found me in the gardens and listened to what was taking place and then said these words – 'I am so sorry for the harm my ancestors have caused yours.' It wasn't asked for yet it was needed. To be seen, to be heard was healing for both of us. Together we removed a layer of history that was no longer true. We enabled true connection to come in across time and space. There was no blame or shame, no guarded hearts. Just a knowing that if we are feeling it, then it was up to us to heal it. That it was our work to do. And that the work could be that simple.

During this time in humanity, as separation is rising to be seen and loved back into wholeness, there is a whole new level of connection waiting to be invited in. Amidst all of the chaos in the world, we are being asked to deepen into our embodied being. And we are being asked to look at where there is disconnect as well as connection in our circles. We know there is sisterly love yet somehow it isn't creating the level of connection we would wish to see. This is evidenced in the lack of diversity that is right before our eyes. It takes work and a concerted effort to make spaces more diverse and inclusive. To zoom out and see the whole picture of what is going on with race in our circles. We may be moving towards a state of oneness but we are not there yet. Therefore, we must tend to what is being presented as we hold the vision for oneness during our circle time. We do not live in those escalades of idealism yet and to ignore that as a fact is a privilege we as black women will never know.

We are creatures of belonging: we want communities and we want them to be diverse. Yet we can't have that until we define who we are in relationship to diversity. This takes opening deeper into the ways we communicate our truths about it and it takes being more vulnerable with our interactions. It takes moving out of habitual ways of being together. And it takes being honest about how we are showing up and how we may be colour blind and biased in our spaces. It takes examining what we are holding internally when it comes to race. This is how outer systems change, by feeling and shifting from the inside out.

If that day in August taught me anything, it is that magic can happen when we show up in our vulnerability as our real, raw and radiant selves. On that day I felt the spectrum between power and powerlessness. The power of knowing that the ancestors had been waiting for someone to give voice to the fact that black and brown sisters don't always feel part of the space when it is predominately white. And I felt disempowered from being the only one there at the time to feel it. It was up to me to bring forward the language that says – *I am here and I am taking up space beyond the fluffy words of solidarity as I moved beyond the thoughts that I may get cancelled for speaking out.* For making the invisible visible thus unearthing the subtle layers of silence and revealing the heaviness that has been carried in order to survive – *I know you see me – but do you really see me? Do you really stand beside me in solidarity? Can you truly be an ally if you ignore the facts of our experiences, or will you leave the emotional labour of communicating what's hidden in plain sight to the black or brown women that come to these spaces to deal with it?*

Since the race riots across the world in 2020 when George Floyd's death triggered a series of events and Black Lives Matter went viral, I thought more change would have taken place. Race and inclusion in women's circles is still one area that needs addressing in a bigger way. There have been small waves of people speaking up in spiritual communities, but nothing of real significance has happened and no real change has been made. The numbers of black and brown sisters have remained relatively the same in our circles as it was twenty years ago. There are however more waves of people speaking up about their experiences as black and brown women who are bringing awareness as educators of how to make them more inclusive environments. The wisdom to do so is there, you just have to choose it. This is for our collective and ancestral healing, not just individual ones.

*

As wise women, we came to the earth at this time for a reason. To highlight the imbalances in the world. To bring order to chaos. To bring union to separation. Therefore, let's stop shying away from the necessary raising of the issues around race or covering them up with platitudes. I can guarantee that as black women if we are doing the work of clearing our lineage concerning race and slavery and all the threads that came with that, then there is work to be done on the opposite spectrum from our white sisters and it is work that now needs to be done in community, together. Let's get brave and open the doors that have been closed for way too long. Doors that ultimately lead to deeper long-lasting healing.

The responsibility of my white sisters isn't to upskill about the black experience, but to acknowledge and speak about what it is to be white in your circles. To understand how it is for you to be in a position that could be viewed as powerful or privileged. Instead of putting blackness on the table, it is time to centre whiteness and ask are you looking at where you could be being biased in your spaces because of it? This is about understanding and getting a grasp of where you sit on the map of race and how are you going to utilise that information to make a change. Not just with the women you feel comfortable being around but in our wider community. And this doesn't just mean inviting us into your spaces as a token of diversity and inclusion, because if we are being invited but it doesn't feel inviting, then is the invitation worth taking up? Or is there need for some deeper work to be done first? Especially when it can be detrimental to our bodies to do so. Our bodies carry the memories of our ancestry in buildings and places where it would not have been safe for us to enter. In places where we would have been hung, drawn and quartered or expected to serve. Where we would not be a part of the conversation or even have a seat at the table. We are recognising the emotional toll it takes for us to even get to the table and take a seat.

There is a sense of not wanting to rock the boat. Of not wanting to be the one that brings these things to light. Being asked as black women or brown women to fill in the gaps when it comes to race is a blind spot and negates the fullness of our experience. It can be exhausting. We have to go beyond the limited labels and narratives of race and start talking more openly and factoring in deep nourishing self-care when we do. Dear black sisters, find your courage to speak up if you sense something is out of balance and my dear white sisters, please support us when we do. Support us in the naming of what's in the room, even when we can't yet fully articulate it. What we are feeling is real and backing us in articulating these pieces is foundational in bringing about change. Backing shifts the energetics in our circles and bring forward something new and innovative, especially when we examine how we have internalised the concepts of division in order to survive.

When we back one another, we move beyond the well-oiled formulas when it comes to us holding circles. We admit that our circles are not as inclusive as we'd wish them to be; yet the tools of those we exclude are being used regularly. We understand that to change the dynamics of what we create when it comes to diversity, we have to be willing to open to new ways of connecting and take down the invisible barriers of division. We have to let go of the notion that we are doing it because we want to be seen as good. Or that we have a specific goal in mind. Or that there is some box of inclusion that needs to be ticked. All expectations have to be removed. It has to be done from the pure raw sense of self-reflection and exploration. We have to get curious about what arises when we let go of doing it for a specified outcome and instead drop into true vulnerability, so that we are seen in our full naked truth, enabling us to open up to new avenues of connection.

*

The important lesson for my black sisters here is that we cannot negate our very human experiences that have occurred whilst living in societies and cultural realities that see us in a very different light and give us the labels of minority. Even if we do not wear that as an identity, our bodies pick up the energetics of those narratives. We are not victims to these circumstances but we have all worn the robes of victimhood when the truth is, that on some level, we have been diminished and have diminished our own experiences because other people's perspectives have categorised us as a minority. We get to share through our lens of reality and it gets to inform the narrative and guide a new way of being.

So, take up space. Know that if these kinds of stories, feeling, sensations and intuitive hits are rising in you then it's time to come forward and speak. It is time to share the reality of what it like to continually go into spaces and not feel represented. It's time to speak out about how it feels to see the tools of your ancestors used in a way that may not be fully honouring of you being in those spaces. We can tell the stories of what it's like to bring our bodies into circle and how we feel the unsaid things in the room. We can be the ones that spark a new generation to bravely confront the truth. We can honour the distortions of those in our bloodline who didn't get to speak about them and confront them on their behalf.

This is our work to do. To bring it forward in circle. To know it is beyond just saying we can let it go by ourselves. These are stories stored in our collective subconscious memory that have been passed down to us and we are the ones we have been waiting for in order to set the records straight. We know the difference between airing the story and wearing the story. The difference between retraumatising self by retelling the stories and not telling the stories to transmute the other. The difference between wallowing in them and diving deep in order to rewrite them. We are alchemists here ready to transform and forge new territory.

We have to feel it to heal it. To do the real boots on the ground work to move beyond the surface. It is beyond just cutting of cord or throwing our ills in the fire or singing and chanting to make it go away. We are going deeper inward. This is work that can only be done through the body, it is in our flesh and bones. This is us growing into our ancestral wisdom. We can no longer walk away from that which we are being called to acknowledge. The heaviness of carrying it has been wearing. We may feel that this is bigger than us. But know as we uproot the past, the rage and emotions that run through the waters of our being get to leave. And we get to feel freedom and liberation in our being. We get to be the transmitters of light and insight.

*

What can you bring to white spaces as black women? Your full radiant self. Stand loud and proud in who you are as a being. No more shrinking to fit in or dampening your language or behaviour to be understood. You have a job to do. To transmit yourself as a remembrance that you were born in the image of 'Original Woman'. So why on earth are you hiding yourself? Black, beautiful sisters, what can you bring to spaces? Your knowing, your feeling, your presence, your gift of grace, your willingness to be held and seen. And your willingness to remember that there was a time when God was a black woman and that sense of divinity still lives in you. You can bring the knowing that the whole of the human race sprang forth from the motherland of Africa and you all carry that DNA in your blood and bones. Bring yourself and know that your pain and sorrow will be seen. And trust that you will be held lovingly as together we tend to and shed the distortions we inherited collectively.

Our vulnerability plays a key part in this process. I would never have gotten to these realisations without speaking the vulnerable truth of how painful it can be when we place our black bodies in white spaces. Where the truth of who we are is often overlooked. If I had stayed silent about how painful it was to write these truths, then the deeper stories of our discomfort would remain hidden and the subsequential healing and insights left undiscovered. Sometimes we have to feel the full depth of our sorrow in order to get to the truth. The ancestors are calling for it. These stories did not start with us, yet they are rising for us to finish them. We are answering the call so our bloodlines are cleared of unconscious biased stories of race. These are the memories of our ancestors, the memories that they were unable to alchemise in their lifetimes.

Can we come with a sense of gratitude that they are presenting now, so that we can choose to walk through difficult doorways and choose different ways to come together in unity? We get to choose the conditions in which we gather. Even if there are no black sisters or we are the only black sister in the space, honour that anyway. Be consistent in your efforts. Do the work. This is not about performing around us or for us. It is about clearing the way so that we may enter with a sense of safety if we so desire. So, we can come in and not feel all the unprocessed things in the space. So, that we can come in and have our bodies surrender. We all have a choice of the pathways we create from this point onwards.

RESOURCES

On White tears

4 Ways White People Can Process Their Emotions Without Bringing the White Tears, 2016, Jennifer Loubriel, everydayfeminism.com/2016/02/white-people-emotions-tears/

Unpacking white tears - The unexpected bridge to healing, 2023, Annie Gichuru, Racial Equality Coach, anniegichuru.com/unpacking-white-tears/

White tears (2020) Debbie Irving
youtube.com/watch?v=YlktLILOg8k&ab_channel=DebbyIrving

White Tears, Black Scars, Ruby Hamad, 2021

White Fragility – Why understanding racism can be so hard for white people, Robin DiAngelo, 2019

On god as a Black Woman

When God Was a Black Woman: And why She isn't Now:1 by Joseph R. Gibson, 2019

God Is a Black Woman, Christena Cleveland, 2022

On Race

Finding Myself in the Story of Race, Debby Irving, TEDx Fenway
youtube.com/watch?v=c5nqN8tmfok&ab_channel=DebbyIrving

On Whiteness

White Mischief: exploring the concept of whiteness, Ekow Eshun,
www.bbc.co.uk/programmes/articles/1B1gwhJkfbfrkyrSxzKGWcf/
white-mischief-exploring-the-concept-of-whiteness

What Is Whiteness? – Should people be proud of membership in a group marked by power and privilege? 2020, Reviewed by Lybi Ma by Monnica T Williams Ph.D. psychologytoday.com/us/blog/culturally-speaking/202006/what-is-whiteness

On Education

Myisha T Hill at Check Your Privilege: anti-racism educator and author of *Heal Your Way Forward*

Blair Imani, creator of Smarter in Seconds

Asha Frost, Indigenous medicine woman, 'Dear White Woman Who Wants to Be Like Me" redschool.net/podcast/63

Nature Knows Balance

Ellen Dee Davidson

All of our ancestors were originally indigenous to particular places and had sacred relationships with their lands. For some of us, our cultural intimacies to the environment are so lost, buried, and broken that we don't know where to find them. Sometimes we can't even imagine what it is that we are seeking. We are the severed children, making our way into the future with no roots in the past, an inchoate longing in our souls, a sense that we are missing something even when we are fortunate and do find that soul mate or create a happy family. We may have a hollowness in our hearts, and a feeling that we are left out – but we don't even know from what.

This is particularly true for many of us born in the United States of America. Other than the remaining Native Americans, who managed to survive near genocide, everyone in the USA descends from people who came from somewhere else. Most of us don't even come from one country and culture.

Personally, I am a mix of Bulgarian, Russian and German Jews, and Irish Catholics. My Bulgarian grandfather came to the "New Country" with an 8th grade education to avoid being drafted by the Turks to fight in their front lines as literal cannon fodder. Not even speaking a word of English, he managed to survive and support his family through the Great Depression and World War II. One of my great grandfathers was a Rabbi in Russia who had to flee the pogroms. My German Jewish ancestors were mostly doctors and lawyers who came over together first class on a steam ship before Hitler really got going. And my maternal Irish ancestors had to leave the emerald isle due to starvation.

Like so many of us, much of my inheritance has been trauma. I couldn't even fathom where to stitch the broken pieces together. For years, in an effort to find wholeness, I looked to other peoples' more intact traditions: Tibetan Buddhism, Native American teachings, and Chinese Feng Shui. But they were never quite mine.

And then the old growth redwood tree in my backyard began to call to me. She reached out to me in dreams, teaching me how to connect more deeply to Earth. She murmured softly in my heart, entering meditations, showing me the swirling vibratory energy that was all around, coalescing into matter, creating a solid sense of reality – the ground beneath my feet. She told me to immerse myself in the old growth redwood forests near my home in northern California.

I went to the remaining forests that had been allowed to grow in their own wild ways for millions of years. For fifteen years I went to the trees. I'm still going – many days a week, camping, hiking, and sitting with the ancient redwoods. Over time, the forest healed me from fibromyalgia, chronic fatigue and severe insomnia. The trees soothed my nervous system, smoothed the electromagnetic flows throughout my energy body, and connected me between Earth and Sky in a more harmonious and balanced way.

Held at the roots, my heart soared to the stars. Light codes showered down blessings to be absorbed by my body. The intelligence of ancient beings who stood for thousands of years in one spot informed my system, guiding me into the interconnectivity that is ubiquitous in nature. Mycelial threads connected roots tree to tree, and somehow I sensed them and also felt part of this relationship. Nutrients and moisture from the soil flowed up trunks through the heartwood. Branches swayed in the breeze, dancing with the air. And my little human body, snuggled down at the base of the over 300 foot trees, was finally home.

Home on Earth. Embraced by gravity. Informed by Life. A part of the mystery and magic of being here with the All-That-Is.

The vital intelligence of nature was all around in the sensory bliss of smell, muted birdsong, and droplets on leaves. All conspired to awaken me to specific moments in time. Whenever I became fully present with the deep hush and profound silence of the forest, my heart opened like a flower in the sun. Guidance flowed into my being from the trees. There was a gnosis, an experience of the universal love radiating through the redwoods.

I knew that this experience was not only for me, or only about redwood trees, or this one particular place on Earth's holy body. This was a teaching for all of us. No matter how broken or fragmented our human traditions have become, we can go directly to nature and allow her to be our guide. We can find holy sites in deserts and mountains, springs and lakes, oceans and trees, or even the gardens in our yards. There's knowing in the rocks and stones, rivers and trees, birds in flight, croaking frogs, leaping fish, and splashing water. There's knowing in our own bodies, made of the elements.

Nature knows balance. Redwood trees creak and groan, whispering in the wind, telling me the time is now. Nature intelligence is reaching out to all of us, asking us to listen without preconceived notions. She asks us to pay attention, to notice sensations, to quiet our minds and open up. Following the lead of nature and our own wild hearts, pathways of healing ourselves and our ecology can grow into a lush and thriving future.

Black Sisters in White Spaces – Cultivating a Sense of Inclusion

Coco Oya Cienna-Rey

Without community, there is no liberation… But community must not mean a shedding of our differences, nor the pathetic pretence that our differences do not exist.

Audre Lorde

These pieces have been waiting to be written for months. As time passed, they grew less and less appealing as the rising tension of bringing up an uncomfortable topic grew. Yet, still I knew they needed to be written; and with each word my body began to unfreeze and a river of emotions flowed as the remembrance of all the times I and others had swallowed our feelings in order to belong in some of our sisterhood circles. The covertly covered reality that most black women experience is a shrinking and whitewashing of our identity when in the community. The reason being, that most of our sisterhood circles and working environments are devoid of diversity.

I want to give a big thank you to Ama A, Saphra B, Donna F in their assistance and holding in the writing of these pieces. These women gave permission for their words to be included as a collective truth, so that the gravitas of our experiences could be felt as one voice. Their stories of experiencing whiteness are woven in and speak to how it has shaped us. To write these pieces has been both hilarious and heartbreaking as we took off our protective armour to feel the untold stories. I also want to thank Sophie H (mentor), for holding me as I spoke our truth and for helping me see the bigger picture that needed to be spoken into. Also, a big thank you to Lucy Pearce (editor) for helping me get the tone right.

It is in our hands to speak up so we can be the mirrors for what needs to be tended to and not to coddle those that need to hear it. We ask that our words are held with love, open hearts and a sense of curiosity. We are all swimming in the waters of a culture with warped views on race that creates a false hierarchy in our collective. And we ask for this perspective to be witnessed and heard because it is reflected in the bypassing that takes place in our communities when we use the spiritual language of oneness or the language of inclusion. In order to change the status quo, we have to understand the roots that hold us in a state of lack of awareness; the societal constructed concepts of whiteness and blackness that create difference. These are concepts that someone came up with and so we too can come up with new ones that are more harmonious and in line with the communities we wish to create.

*

We hold in our bodies the historical patterns of those who came before us. Our ancestors who came to the shores of white countries and were unwelcomed or brought here against their will as captured peoples. Their stories get passed down the lineage and we wear their contoured ways of embodiment in order to accommodate being black bodies in white spaces. Feeling uncomfortable in spaces isn't new, it also happens when we enter black spaces, so conditioned have we become to suppress our identities we lose sight of who we are in order to fit in. Our disowned and contorted parts jarring up against our cultural heritage, having internalised the nature of the culture reflected around us.

Our circles are designed to be about wholeness. Yet when we ignore and deny one of the largest things about oneself, feeling whole becomes an issue. Don't be seen as rocking the boat or pushing others out of their comfort zone by mentioning race. Don't be seen as the angry black woman or the 'too much' black woman. Remember your place. Even when we see ourselves as strong women when in spaces where we stand tall there is still an element of us that keeps our head down so not to draw attention to ourselves.

It takes courage to enter a room when you are the only representation of you.

Especially when many have experienced eye rolls, or the deer in headlights look, the false white tears or the 'we are all one' trope, when discrepancies of race are highlighted. We take on the stress of that and push it down in order to belong. There is no equal footing if we are conditioned to take care of your needs over our own. Our sense of safety is not at the forefront of your minds when you place feeling comfortable over truth. Can you turn your gaze towards our experience and empathise as to what it feels like to enter spaces lacking in diversity. Can we find a sense of solidarity?

We ask that you do. How else is this going to be resolved? Change takes courage and change can be uncomfortable whilst new growth emerges. This is how evolution works. It's through the facing of a hardship that organism evolves. Sometimes that means delivering the difficult message and then leaving space for it to land. Giving others the room for it to digest. It is not our work to do. We are not there to be the ones that educate you on race because we can count all the times we have put your education above our own needs. Yet we do need you as allies to forge a new path. We desire to be invited, not because you want to be seen as doing the right thing but because you genuinely desire diversity. We need spaces to land and breathe. Maybe for a time this may mean being in circles of woman who look like us and leaving white dominated circles behind, so we too can come home to ourselves.

Change needs to be brought to the forefront and not be an afterthought. There needs to be a willingness to be curious, not critical, to be open, not closed. This is all of our work to do on differing levels. If one side is shouldering more of the responsibility, then it will continue to be out of balance. Race may not seem like a priority because you think it affects us and not you. This is not the case. As space holders, we must consider what this means for us as a wider collective. What affects your black sisters invertedly affects you, even if you can't see that yet. Let's bring it out in the open fully so it can finally be alchemised and integrated. Let's speak about it in our circles, at the school gates, around the dinner table and our places of work. Let's stop shying away from the issues at hand. Not just with race but all issues that affect women in these spaces.

Having one session of education on race is not enough, especially when it's back to the business as usual. It is something that needs to be woven into the fabric of how we circle, work and sit together. It would be sad to see that in another twenty years' time we are still asking how we can become more inclusive and less exclusive in our circles. Find ways to talk openly about your whiteness. How it excludes and how it dominates the spaces we occupy. Please stop seeking black women to fill in the gaps of your knowing unless they have placed themselves in the field as educators to inform you in this way.

Asking out of context can have a retraumatising effect especially when some may be still facing oppression in this world. You may not know how to begin and that's okay. Yet in the same vein it is not okay not to grow when it comes to making spaces more welcoming for black and brown sisters. It is for you to seek the wisdom of how to bring about cohesion and solidarity. To name the void that in the room. We are ready to have the conversations, but we are tired of doing the work. It's for you to look at what it means to be white and to turn the gaze away from us and the meaning of blackness and ethnicity. We should not have to break down what blackness is for you to understand there is an issue.

*

My dear white sisters it is time for you to join the conversation even if you don't know your role in it yet. And to my dear black sisters who are tired of doing all the work I hear you. I love you. I celebrate you. I know it will take courage as we examine what needs to go and what needs to stay. As we create new pathways for ourselves and for those that follow us, we can begin to see that this is about transcending our personal view, on what blackness or whiteness is. We are expanding into new territory and moving beyond limited notions of race. However, before we do, we have to look at what's in the room. To meet one another in the depth of our reflections and see where we are hiding from the truth that lies within. To rub up against the places our bodies hold the ancestral stories so we can build back restoration and regulation in our nervous systems so that when we enter the spaces and sisterhood circles, we as black and brown women, on a somatic level, can come with our full embodied expanded selves.

This is the legacy that we came here to walk for the good of all. To understand that to soften the heavy-handed nature of race we have to talk about race to get over it. To get comfortable with the uncomfortable as our voices come back online to speak our truth. Even when we can't name what needs to be said, we feel when things are off and carry that in our bodies. We have got too used to brushing it away. Or giving it other names. Anything other than naming what it is. We are feeling the unspoken memories of hatred when it comes to race. We became covertly ignorant to our needs and neglect ourselves in the name of maintaining relationships. We became afraid to raise the issue of race because of the reactions we've received, the denial and the diminishing of our feelings. Only now are we becoming more able to speak what we have been feeling. To name the behaviours we adopt in order to feel accepted as more people step forward and give their experiences form.

We are no longer willing to play small so we don't draw attention to the behaviour we receive. We are no longer willing to minimise the stress that occurs when we hold so much that is unspoken. We are done managing the expectations of others rather than our own. We have swallowed our pain, suppressed our anger, masked our true feelings because we felt unsafe whilst simultaneously having to make others feel safe. Reciprocity is key for us to feel like we are not being extracted from. We may be united because we are women yet our experiences out in the world are not the same. Discrimination still takes place in many ways. Our everyday experience can mean that we are constantly having to be on guard. We hate how society sometimes sees us when labels of BIPOC or BAME are placed upon us. Clumping us all as the same has in itself become a form of exclusion. Sometimes we have to illuminate the situation and shine light on the dark side of what has become the norm. We are done giving lip service to platitude and high faulted labels we didn't ask for.

*

There is institutionalised and internalised racism in us all, we as black women have internalised it too. We have dishonoured our blackness in order to fit in. Absorbing the culture unknowingly and aligning with a version of blackness devoid of any authentic roots. We centred ourselves through a white lens. A lens and gaze that has kept us small. Yet we know that bigness and growth can come when we share our stories and talk to other women that look like us. I would never have been able to write this without that. When we can express freely our bodies unfreeze and we can allow the truth of our expression out. Rather than having to think are they friend or foe. So, we ask you, do you consciously go out of your way to network and connect with black woman just as we do the other way around? We desire space to land and breath as black bodies in white spaces. To unhook from the imposed politeness of our tongues. To move into voicing not holding when we raise what is seen as a contentious issue. To talk about whiteness and centre that, rather than continually breaking down what it is to be black or brown. It is time to talk about what it is to be white.

Pushing it away doesn't make it go away. We know that we carry and embody our traumas. We may see the collective pain of one another because we are women standing with women, yet it has been shown that when you don't look like the people around us their experience is not in the forefront of our minds. We still live in a discriminatory world, therefore we need to build places where we can all come together and break that down. This is the time to root down into the undercurrent of race that is often ignored in our circles so we are no longer mirroring the distortions we see out in the world, but we are creating examples of how to be inclusive. It is time for the walls to come down. To rip off the band-aid admit to ourselves that our circles are not as inclusive as we would like if after twenty-odd years of attending sisterhood circles, we/I am still the only black woman in the room, something isn't being addressed.

Do you read books by black authors to support the black experience? Have you read up on black and Indigenous culture? Do you speak to your black and brown sisters about their experiences of being out in the world? Our stories want to be woven into the tapestry of what women sit and honour in our circles; not just as an afterthought when one of us speaks out, but as an integral part of what is already out there. We don't want to feel othered, we want to feel included in the picture from the start. Again, this isn't about blame, guilt or shame here. Not us against them. We are building a bridge and finding out what is in the way of crossing it.

This ultimately is communal work. Work to be done in community. Work we hold together. This is work beyond just gathering to be in sisterhood. We gather because this is the raw truth of who we are beyond the masks and labels we have worn in order to survive. To return to the depth of the original stories of woman. We are moving beyond the superficial statements of 'we are all one'. This is us as women choosing to reach back into the primal truth of who we are beyond the labels we have been given. We have the power to change these conditions.

I know race can seem like an issue that feels too big to handle and a minefield to navigate. An overwhelming undertaking upon which you don't know where to start. Just start. All new paths take time. Know that the ancestors have your backs. They are infusing us with their wisdom, insight and bigger view vision. We can utilise their guidance and strength to bring more cohesions on issues of race in our circles once we dedicate ourselves and decide to do so.

This is the invitation. Be the pioneers that are dismantling the distortions. Remind yourselves that you are the ones here to make change. You are the legacy for those that follow after unravelling themes of domination and suppression so that they do not have to.

Unveiling the Forgotten – Lesbians in the Tapestry of Sisterhood

Autumn Blackwood

This is a man's world, and it seems doubly so whenever I attend a women's circle or empowerment coaching networking event, and the topic of divine masculine and men shows up. Even here, in spaces that are supposed to be cultivated for and hosted by women, the conversation always seems to turn to men and masculinity. I get it, men are often a part of our lives – I truly understand that.

As a lesbian, I've often felt the absence of narratives that resonate with my experiences and struggles with men, though. When I try to speak about these things I am labeled a misandrist, I have been told that I am not fully aligned, or attuned with my "masculine and feminine." These statements have been from other women! The ones that call me sister with one breath, have their lips curling in disgust with the next.

One of the fundamental issues lies in the prevailing narrative that often caters predominantly to heterosexual women. Many empowerment coaches and self-help gurus perpetuate a narrative that revolves around the dynamics of hetero-sexual relationships, leaving little room for the diverse experiences of lesbians.

The emphasis on balancing masculine and feminine energies, a common theme in these circles, often fails to recognize that such dynamics manifest differently in same-sex relationships. When bringing that up, it is insinuated that this is somehow a failure on my part. This oversight leaves lesbians feeling excluded and unseen, struggling to find guidance and support that truly resonates with their lived realities.

It's all patriarchy at work. These enlightened women telling me that I need to have boundaries (masculine) and flow (feminine) and that I am somehow unbalanced are regurgitating the patriarchal narrative that we NEED men and masculinity to be whole, hale, and healthy. I am asking us to challenge that thought. Women's circles and women's empowerment are booming and a key talking point is that the feminine has been left behind and forgotten. The world has been male-centered for eons.

What if we left masculinity behind, if only for a little bit, if only for a few moments? What if, just what if, we catered to the forgotten "sisters" in this global circle: me and my fellow lesbians? The lack of resources tailored specifically for lesbians exacerbates this sense of invisibility. From dating advice to self-care tips, the majority of available resources are geared towards heterosexual women, leaving lesbians to navigate uncharted – sometimes hostile – waters on their own. The lack of representation in mainstream media further perpetuates this invisibility, reinforcing the notion that lesbian experiences are somehow less valid or important or that we are a straight man's sexual fantasy.

Furthermore, there's a misconception that being a lesbian automatically equates to being a misandrist. Lesbianism is not about hatred towards men but rather about embracing love and attraction towards women. It's about celebrating our identities and forming connections based on mutual respect and understanding. In fact, as lesbians, we often find ourselves challenging traditional gender norms and patriarchal structures, seeking to dismantle systems of oppression rather than perpetuate them.

It's crucial to recognize that empowering lesbian women doesn't mean detracting from the struggles faced by other marginalized groups. Rather, it's about acknowledging the intersectionality of our experiences and creating inclusive spaces where all women feel seen, heard, and valued. By amplifying the voices of lesbians and acknowledging their unique journey towards empowerment, we can move towards a more inclusive and equitable world for all. By leaning into the feminine, and perhaps learning from lesbians, all women will benefit.

How do we do this? I think it starts as simple as seeking out more women-owned spaces, more women-created products, services, and media. Take a look at your daily life. How much music do you listen to that was created by women? Movies? TV? Not just actresses either, how about directors and producers? How many books are written by women?

Look at your daily life and see just how many places could use women-led creation. Now take a look at it again and see how many lesbian or queer women you have in that daily line-up. Maybe that will help bring everything into perspective, that women, and especially lesbians are often left in the dust.

What Ifs

Molly Remer

When teaching childbirth classes in an earlier part of my life, I used speak to my clients about shifting the common fear-based "what if" cultural dialog of birth to "positive" anticipation rather than fears, encouraging them to ask themselves questions like: "what if I give birth and it is one of the most powerful, thrilling moments of my life?" While I stand by this practice, I also think about the *what ifs* that crawl out of our dark places and lodge in our hearts. The *what ifs* that snake around the edges of our consciousness in the early hours of the morning. The *what ifs* we try to push down, down, down and away. The *what ifs* that stalk us. The *what ifs* so very awful that *we fear in giving voice to them, we might give life to them as well.*

We may feel guilty, ashamed, negative, and apologetic about our deepest "what ifs." We worry that if we speak of them, they might come true. We worry that in voicing them, we might make ourselves, our families, our communities, our work, or philosophies, our faiths, or whatever *look bad.* We want to be positive. We want to be blissfully empowered, confident, and courageous. And, guess what? *We are.* Sometimes that courage comes from looking the "what ifs" right in the eye. Sometimes it comes from living through them. My most powerful gift from my pregnancy with my daughter, my pregnancy-after-loss baby, was to watch myself *feel the fear and do it anyway.* I was **brave.** And, it changed me to learn that.

What if we can learn more from our shadows than we ever thought possible? There is power in thinking what if I can't do this and then discovering that you CAN.

It is so easy to close down to risk, to protect ourselves against change and growth. But no baby bird emerges without first destroying the perfect egg sheltering it. We must risk being raw and fresh and awkward. For without such openness, life will not penetrate us anew. Unless we are open, we will not be filled.

Patricia Monaghan

At a gathering of midwifery supporters and birth educators, I listened to an interesting and insightful presentation about language and the impact on birth. The woman speaking urged us to always talk in "positive" ways about birth, to use "positive" words and to avoid "negative" stories. As I listened to her, I thought of my own pregnancy loss story and knew that my experience in giving birth to my little dead baby would likely have ranked way up there as a "negative" story. **And, that bothered me.** Giving birth via miscarriage to my third son was one of the most transformative, formative, and powerful experiences of my life. He gave me many gifts, he taught me many lessons, and *I am a better person* than I was without that experience. So, what does it mean for when we hide away the "negative" stories of our lives? What might we be missing by making sure we never hear about a bad outcome? I wondered what if by avoiding "negative stories," we also miss out on powerful stories of courage, growth, and transformation…

What if she *suffered* and *survived*?

What if she danced with death and *she's still here*?

What if she faced fear and *held on*?

What if she was scarred and broken, **but she healed**?

What if she hasn't healed, *but she's working on it*?

What if she grieved deeply and came out the other side?

What if she felt fear **and did it anyway**?

What if she was so scared and felt *so* weak and *so* helpless and yet she persevered?

What if *she sacrificed parts of her body* for her children?

What if she couldn't keep going…**and then she did**?

What if she is stronger in her broken places?

In another person's strength, may we see our own. In another person's fear, our own becomes acceptable.

When I was in the middle of my first miscarriage and I was thinking, "*how will I do this?!"* the faces of other women I knew who had experienced baby loss came floating through my mind. I saw them all and I knew that if **they could do it, *so could I.*** After my own baby's miscarriage-birth, I then made a list of these women. There were twenty-seven names on the list. As I shared my experience and came to know other women's stories and as multiple friends then experienced losses during that same year, the list grew to at least forty names (personal connections, not "online only" friends).

What if they'd all been careful to keep this "negativity" away from me?

When one woman puts her experiences into words, another woman who has kept silent, afraid of what others will think, can find validation. And when the second woman says aloud, 'yes, that was my experience too,' the first woman loses some of her fear.

Carol Christ

Once, listening to a presentation by Pam England at an ICAN conference, she told us that the place *"where you were the most wounded – the place where the meat was chewed off your bones, becomes the seat of your most powerful medicine and the place where you can reach someone where no one else can."*

What if we *withhold* our most powerful medicine?

I've come to realize that despite the many amazing and wonderful, profound and magical things about pregnancy, birth, breastfeeding, and parenting, these experiences are also very likely to take some kind of toll from us, sometimes severe – whether on body, mind, or emotions. There is usually some type of "price" to be paid for each and every birth and sometimes the price is very high. This is, I guess, part of what qualifies birth as such an *intense, initiatory rite* in a person's life. It is most definitely a transformative event and transformation does not usually come without some degree of challenge. This is also true of many significant life events that do not involve children, including chronic illness. We may have experiences that involve something to be triumphed over or overcome, but they are also things that leave permanent **marks**. Sometimes those marks are literal and sometimes they are emotional and sometimes they are truly *beautiful*, but we all earn some of them, somewhere along the line. And, I also think that by glossing over the marks, the *figurative or literal* scars our experiences can leave on us, and talking about only the positive side we can deny or hide the full impact of our journeys. *What if it was okay to share our scars with each other?* Not in a fear-mongering or "horror story" manner, but in honesty, depth, and truth.

What if we let other people see the full range of our courage?

May you allow yourself to
taste your longings
and to bravely honor them.
May you make wise sacrifices.
May you trust in abundance.
May you savor the many flavors
of this sweet life before your eyes,
beneath your feet,
below your skin,
within your soul,
around your heart.

Encircling Experience

Rev. Jo Royle

I welcome you.
In all you are
and all you're not.
All your emotions are welcome
YOU are welcome.

Settling into
meditation.
Closing your eyes.
Feel the holding of the Earth, Love
Invoking Her.

And noticing...
What is with you?
How are you now?
In this moment in time, what is
your inner truth?

Now returning.
You look around.
Welcome from this
new, deeper place. Welcoming self,
circle sisters.

All checking in.
Sharing heart truths.
Opening to
feelings here now, fully present
Raw, real, honest.

Deeply witnessed.
Seen, heard, held in
compassion, love.
Each life a mirror, reflecting
back your own life.

Reassurance
in connection.
Magic in the
uncanny synchronicities.
Truly all one!

Contemplation.
Turn in again.
A deeper dive
What emotions do you carry
in your being?

Sisters sharing
same distractions,
from emotions.
Same struggle to feel, the full weight
to feel deeply

Society
reinforcing;
medicating,
not normalizing, what's normal -
All our feelings

Then knowing you're
held, safe to feel
all that is here.
Physically feeling and healing
self, collective

Porosity
to emotion,
Not prolonging,
by clinging, instead feeling it
Passing through you

Your emotion.
Seen, heard, witnessed,
held, understood,
felt, embodied, allowed to be.
To co-exist.

And then a shift.
Not so heavy,
lighter somehow,
less dense, more space; room to breathe – live -
Sighing relief.

Gratitude for
These sisters all
Affirming each
Thanking, releasing and closing
Uncircling now.

Their strength, courage
Sustaining you
Upholding you
Cheering you on, to feel, to heal
Until next time.

Your circle of
Women – sisters –
A sanctuary
Teaching you how to wrap yourself
in arms of love.

Creating Inclusive Spaces

Mary Ann Clements and Aisha Hannibal

Neurodivergence

According to a social model of disability – which is what we invite you to adopt – disability is a result of a society that does not fully include people with a wide range of abilities – rather than a consequence of what others might see as something 'different' about a disabled person. A liberatory space is a space in which disabilities are welcomed, recognised and supported as needs just like any other. They are spaces in which inclusion and accessibility become a practice.

If you take this perspective, including people who have a disability is about doing all you can to reverse the ways in which the environment in and around your Red Tent may inhibit their full participation and inclusion. Be sensitive to confidentiality about sharing information to meet needs and holding clear boundaries to protect privacy where appropriate. It is important also to remember that many people's challenges are "invisible" at first glance, including many neurodivergences such as autism, dyslexia, dyspraxia, ADHD, as well as visual and auditory processing issues. Consider being ready to share with anyone wanting to join your group what support with accessibility you are able to offer. Share as widely as you can what support for this may be available. Having a welcome person at the Tent that helps people to get comfortable and find what they need can be a great support here.

Communication and Information

With communications, clarity and readability is key. Think about the accessibility of information, the online information and anything written that you are sharing. Provide clear instructions and, where possible, maps for reaching the venue. Consider how someone with visual or reading challenges would access the information, for example. Be clear also about the length of your gathering – this can be especially important for those with sensory issues and those who experience anxiety. Provide a clear description on what the timings include and which aspects are optional (if any).

Physical Accessibility

We live in a society that often presents multiple barriers to people with physical disabilities. How can you create a workable solution in advance if a Red Tent is happening in your home or in another inaccessible or unequipped space? Clarity on physical arrangements is key. Some Red Tents run at venues that do not have full physical accessibility.

The first step is to get clear. Our Red Tent is far from ideal in terms of accessibility because it is upstairs, which concerns me. So far it has not been an issue, but I am not sure how we would resolve it if someone did want to come who could not manage the stairs. I would always try my best to accommodate.

Jessica

If physical accessibility is a challenge, you might consider using community spaces that would provide better provision for some types of accessibility, such as a wheelchair ramp, lift or disabled parking, and be relatively low cost to hire. Have a plan in place about what arrangements you could offer if someone wanted to come who was unable to access your current venue. That way, it is not the responsibility of the person wanting to attend to find the solutions, you are accountable for that instead. You can make clear in your invitation about the limitations for accessibility but that you have a plan to adapt where necessary. In this way you can acknowledge the issue and also indicate that you want to find a way to resolve it. This communicates your Red Tent is welcoming to people of all abilities, as you hold the responsibility for changing the set up.

It is not just access to the venue that requires consideration, but also sitting arrangements inside: is there an alternative, for example, to sitting on the floor which may be impossible for those with mobility challenges and chronic pain conditions? Lighting can be a big issue for those on the autism spectrum, those with sensory processing issues and for people who experience migraines. If possible, ensure non-fluorescent lighting.

Consider how you can support accessibility in other ways. Are there supports you can provide including working with carers or assistants to facilitate attendance at your Red Tent? Can you offer support with transport also? Consider those with visual and hearing impairments. In what ways might you help them be able to fully participate in your Red Tent and access the information they may need to do so? Consider a range of health needs relating to rest needed, medication impacts and concentration spans that people attending your Red Tent might face.

How can you become more aware of accessibility for those on the autistic spectrum? How might visual support materials and clear social guidelines help?

Consider sharing a picture of the room, some of the key women and the entrance way, as well as a clear map on your website or social media.

The opportunities here include developing an understanding of a variety of needs and practically and creatively meeting them. Modelling inclusive space, rather than waiting for an opportunity to create inclusive space, is important in a society that in general disables people rather than accommodates and includes them.

How can you more effectively model an accessible society within your Red Tent?

Mental Health

Red Tents are valuable spaces for many women to support their mental health. There are a huge range of issues and diagnoses that can be grouped under this title. Many of us will experience some kind of mental health issue in our lifetimes, by which we mean a whole range of conditions including anxiety, depression, self-harm, and feeling any number of symptoms of being overwhelmed. Others will be managing life-long mental health issues or for those that menstruate there may be times within their monthly cycle where their mental health issues may be amplified. Women will likely share about mental health issues at some point in the sharing parts of your Red Tent.

A lot can happen in each woman's life and – let's be honest here – life can throw us some pretty tough things to deal with. Women's mental health is also disproportionately affected by a patriarchal society which undervalues women's time, underfunds women's services and undermines women's rights. It is little wonder that women's mental health and wellbeing is such a huge issue and that mental health problems are a common experience. Please bear in mind that a Red Tent that is collectively led is not and cannot be a professional therapeutic space. Red Tents allow you to be where you are at: you are not going to have your feelings negated, you are not going to be fixed, you are not going to be offered solutions, you are not going to be judged for not knowing the answers to your particular puzzle. But they are deliberately a community of women, not a professionally facilitated process or means of support. Red Tents have needed, at times, to point this out to those participating so it is worth being clear about this. You might also find yourself suggesting or referring women to other forms of support if women attending do need to request additional support. Although Red Tents cannot replace the value of regular therapy or professional help, they can offer a place to be heard, and seen, and welcomed wholeheartedly.

Finding quiet and rest can be challenging when you have constant noise in your head, which is how I experience my own anxiety and depression. For me it is often like a meteor storm of negative thoughts and I barely know which way is up. I think that if you have depression or anxiety, you are incredibly brave for choosing to seek company rather than hide, nourish rather than grind yourself through another day, and sit still instead of doing everything to outrun your thoughts. But quite honestly the stopping is the rest in itself, it doesn't need to be anything more than pausing in the company of others. Whether you feel alone or connected, you are disrupting the thoughts that keep you separate. That in itself is an act of courage.

Aisha

As Red Tents often involve unstructured time, those with mental health challenges may find knowing in advance exactly what will happen during a Red Tent gathering particularly important. Many may be managing anxiety or other challenges in relation to attending the Tent. Being clear about what will happen at the Red Tent, in terms of process, may help to allay their concerns. It may be appropriate in some cases to meet with women in advance of a Red Tent to help provide more clarity and support them with any anxiety they may be facing about attending.

Gender

We are all operating under capitalist white supremacist patriarchy right now and in cultures that are racist, transphobic, and ableist. We have seen how the culture we are living in can challenge us in this work. How it trips us up. How we can feel compelled to lead individually rather than to build together. How we can find ourselves creating spaces that only feel safe to white women. How we can find that questions of money and resources plague us and challenge our collective structures. How we make assumptions that diversity is catered for without ever asking how others feel. How we close off from conflict or questions or accountability. How we internalise all the ways we have been critiqued. Perhaps patriarchy, capitalism and white supremacy are in their early dying days. Perhaps we are seeds of a new tomorrow in this work. But that is by no means a certainty in these precarious moments: change takes, and will take, time. For now, we have to operate in these systems at least to some extent in order to continue to meet this moment. And so, questions of resourcing are real. Questions of how we can work together are meaningful. Questions of structure and leadership become key. How do we imagine the structures that can hold us when what we are seeking is radically different from what we know? We are imagining something different and it takes a commitment to trial and error, a willingness to get it wrong sometimes and to stop something and start afresh.

When we first started the Red Tent Directory, we described Red Tents as spaces for women, without much thought about what was implied by, and who was included within that term. Since then, we have had a lot of questions come up within communities about the inclusion of trans women and genderqueer people in Red Tents and we have been providing ad hoc support to holders of Tents on this topic. In the process we have learnt a lot from trans women and those who have welcomed them in their Red Tent spaces. They have shown us – wholeheartedly – that including trans and non-binary people in your Red Tent is an obligation rather than an option.

We now understand gender to be more fluid than we were brought up to believe and understand trans and non-binary people to be oppressed by the same patriarchal, supremacist system that women more generally struggle with. Red Tents are a form of rest and replenishment from this system.

When we say women, we are clear that we are not talking only about cis women. Instead, we include all cis, trans, intersex, and non-binary people. We believe a Red Tent is a place for you and there is a place for you at the Red Tent.

In the words of Julia Serano, "There are countless experiences that can shape a woman's gendered experiences: being socialized as a girl (or not), experiencing menstruation and menopause (or not), becoming pregnant and giving birth (or not), becoming a mother (or not), having a career outside of the home (or not), having a husband (or a wife or neither), and so on. Women's lives are also greatly shaped by additional factors such as race, age, ability, sexual orientation, economic class, and so on. While each of these individual experiences are shared by many women – and each is rightfully considered a 'women's issue' – it would be foolish for anyone to claim that any one of these was a prerequisite for calling oneself a woman. So long as we refuse to accept that 'woman' is a holistic concept, one that includes all people who experience themselves as women, our concept of womanhood will remain a mere reflection of our own personal experiences and biases rather than something Red Tents based in the truly diverse world that surrounds us."

If we understand gender as a construct that has us performing and presenting in a certain way some of us may feel strengthened by our gender and others may feel it doesn't fit. What we can hopefully agree on is that whilst it forms a part of our identity it's not the whole glorious summary of who we are. What would it be like to take off your gender and allow yourself to feel all of your edges that are squeezed or denied previously when you sit within it? We know that there are those in the Red Tent community and among women's movements more generally who feel fear and anger about the participation of trans women in women's spaces. But, as we have explained, we believe that this emphasis on biology and a resulting binary mindset is part of the oppressive systems that dehumanise us all, including trans and genderqueer people, and sow division. In many ways non-binary people are rejecting this binary mindset and living into a more liberatory framework of gender. Meanwhile, we know that violence is a problem in our world and that violence against women, of many different kinds, is endemic.

As Laura Bates' most recent book, *Men Who Hate Women* demonstrates there is a frightening proliferation of misogynistic online spaces where sexual violence is encouraged and applauded and in which cis-gender white men are most active. They are spaces where the narrative, fuelled by the far right, promotes the belief it is legitimate to hate and harm anyone who doesn't look like them. When we invite you to welcome all those identifying with the gender woman in some way to your Red Tent, we are not denying your experience of sexual abuse or rape or sexual or domestic violence. Nor are we denying our own. We are also not denying these experiences for trans women or those who are non-binary. Violence is a problem for us all.

And so, we invite Red Tents to be offered as places where women can rest and gain respite from the oppression of patriarchy and the suppression of so-called feminine in society and in which those attending can give themselves full reign to express all the parts of themselves that are devalued in our wider cultures.

Edited extract from *Red Tents: Unravelling Our Past and Weaving a Shared Future,* Mary Ann Clements and Aisha Hannibal, Womancraft Publishing (2021)

SACRED
FEMININE

'Knowledge Goddess'

Charlotte Thomson

The Story of Mother Earth

Grace Sasha Clunie

When I was a child I was told this story.

Father God birthed everything.

He made a man too, but the man was lonely.

So Father God made a woman – out of the man's rib -

To be a 'help-mate' for him.

But the woman, who was made to make the man happy,

Gave way to temptation,

With apple and snake,

Her weakness and disobedience

Brought misery and pain into the world.

Oh woe-ful, woe-man, cursed you are!

(This story made me sad – and mad!)

When I was a child, in my heart I knew another story.

Running through fields, climbing trees,

Splashing in rivers, swimming in seas,

Listening to bird-song, wind-song, free

Mother Nature whispered to me.

She said,

'Child, you are a Daughter of Earth,

Wind, air and fire were at your birth;

Your soul is as old as the ancient of days,

You are held in my nurturing, loving gaze.'

Oh, the music of rhythm filled my soul

And I danced with the joy of a life made whole!

She is the essence of all I hold dear

In the path of Her love I have nothing to fear.

This is the story of Mother Earth,

Through sacred seasons and cycles of birth;

All that is living is full of Her fire,

Magic and wisdom are gifts of Her power.

Oh joy-full woman, how blessed you are!

(This story made me glad!)

Praying Differently

Sharon Ann Rose

Tell a child that humans are made in the image of God, and she'll believe it until the day she dies.

I couldn't see how thick the enclosed membrane had encroached upon me; I was living under the doctrine of a childhood God.

I knew to grow quiet like an unseen creature, as I entered forest calling out prayers for how best to serve a humanity I daily cried for.

I felt far-away whispers send goose bumps across my skin, following ancient commandments, *"Do unto others as you would have them do unto you."* In return, I served up softness. Extended kindness. Offered vital energy and sacred dreams to support and uphold the heart of my fellow kin.

Why was it that when I needed His help, God was too busy to answer and didn't have time to listen?

My God was a narcissist.

Each morning, I fell to my knees offering myself to Him. Heart and body. Womb, seed, sex, life energy, to do with as He saw fit.

Why was it that no matter how much I gave, I was left bereft without sustenance to nourish me?

My God was a rapist.

I tracked my heart, kept spreadsheets, filled notebooks, treating the balance of finances like a religion I would never get right. I placed down dreams, admitting bankruptcy.

Why was it that no matter how much I hustled, reduced and simplified, I was told I could never meet our basic needs?

My God was a slave-driver.

I prayed, offering my devotions onto nature's altars, giving my blood to earth. Surrendering to the heart-searing path of resuscitation of the divine feminine face. Sacred pages inscribed, holy visions enacted, sealed with innocence's kiss entrusted to His care.

Why was it that Her face became desiccated, enshrouded in hot searing shame?

My God was a terrorist.

I honored what was said, listening to what was preached. I took in the words each candle-holding doctrine proclaimed, committing to a valiant search for agape love. They said it would eventually happen at the hands of their God who supposedly provided for us all.

Why was it that I couldn't find a personal sense of the sacred inside their prescriptions?

My God was a missionary.

Tell a child that humans are made in the image of God, she'll believe it until the day she dies.

I spent the better part of fifty years seeing the divine inside each person, each sacrament and moment.

Why was it that my intimate sense of the sacred kept slipping further away?

My God was human. Or was it that humans had become my God?

Turning towards the place I've been neglecting, I stand willing to face obliteration. Reinstalling a relationship to a creative source that rebirths me from the all-consummate holy within my flesh, it's time to stop outsourcing my higher power living inside my body and life.

I'm not responsible for how others see themselves. It is not my job to hold a vision of humanity's Godliness…or God's humanness.

Standing before a freedom I still tremble to fully claim, the chalice of nurturance warms at my touch. I caress the embers of life on its own terms.

I hold in the alchemical fire, a God That Does Not Work for All.

The one who's been screaming at humanity its whole life. To do more. To be someone else. To not fail. Who's been using our bodies to exert and expend His rage.

I hold in the alchemical fire, a God Who Presumed We Could Live on Nothing.

Who provided no clean water, mineral-rich food, safe housing or financial means to take care of ourselves and loved ones, and presumed we existed solely for His use.

I hold in the alchemical fire, a God That Thought Only of Himself.

Who treated our minds and bodies as if they were His own. Who denied and disregarded our hearts and dreams, leaving us to starve and live destitute. Who thought it was irrelevant if we lay on the ground, bleeding naked and in pain.

I hold in the alchemical fire, this Patriarchal Childhood God and all His Counterparts.

Who had no notion of how to live from realms and regions of benevolence and unity. Who lived as separatists, rapists, annihilators and vindictive enslavers. Who could not see the vulnerable beauty of our human bodies, beating hearts and soul-filled nature, that required gentleness, dignity, space and protection to heal, thrive and grow.

Exhaling softly, I move these embers aside, feeling the weight of millennia burn into a clear flame where my creator and I are one.

I now hold in this alchemical fire the beloved and all of their counterparts, breathing into my intimacy with life.

My god is a primal creature found howling into wind, water, earth and fire. Touched inside the center of each storm.

My god doesn't ask that I know his/her/their name. Endlessly seeking and searching, never finding, left barren and depleted.

My god is found in starry heavens and hard-cracked soil. Wearing a cloak, donning a dress, carrying a staff, seen in bejeweled robes and tattered garments, arms outstretched to moon.

He's melting into galaxies. She's disappearing into fog. They're crashing onto white-washed beaches, roosting at the tops of trees.

My god is palpable in the tides of creation, welcoming shades and spectrums of belief that are daily accessible to one and for all, irrespective of what you've prior been told or believed.

Tell a child that humans are made in the image of the divine, and she'll believe it until the day she dies.

I'm grateful when I took this last breath, pulling out my investment from former notions of a patriarchal higher power, now laid to rest.

It's been a slow resuscitation. In the remnants of its metamorphosis, nothing of importance has been severed. Life renews itself inside my core.

I can breathe again.

We Remember the Goddess

Jessica M Starr

Four thousand years ago, two thousand years before the birth of Jesus and Christianity, a poet and priestess (and astrologer, law maker, and princess) named Enhedduana was writing hymns and poems dedicated to the goddess Innana.

These first writings, the oldest in the world, were by a woman and written in praise of a goddess. For context, the earliest date for the writing of the Bible is over one thousand years later than that.

Does that amaze you? Do you doubt it to be true? Or perhaps you already knew that before the disembodied father god we had the voluptuous creatrix goddess.

Even if you do know the real story of the goddess you will recognise that our mainstream culture denies it. Denies Her. And in so doing disempowers and harms us all. The true story of the goddess has been suppressed and forgotten and in its place we have been sold a myth of natural patriarchal power and female guilt and weakness.

Humanity has been denied our vital connection with the sacred feminine, the goddess, for thousands of years.

For women this wound cuts especially deep. I want you to know that the loss and the pain you feel is valid. What you know intuitively is true: goddess is real. You know it. I know it. But we have had that truth denied over and over since before we were old enough to remember. We have been forced to adapt and live in a world which denies so much about what is real. Our mother, the goddess, has been forgotten, and because of her loss we have become scared and isolated.

We were wounded again when it became taboo to even speak about our loss. If you have ever grieved a loss you know how painful it is to feel unable to talk about your experience, to be forbidden to speak of it. And so, we are doubly wounded. We are wounded by the loss of the goddess, our knowledge, our lore, our stories, and then we are wounded again when it is forbidden to speak of these things as if they are real and important.

No wonder so many of us are living in pain and confusion. We are forced to squash our truths back down and pretend that everything is fine. But it is not fine. Your feelings of pain and confusion are real. You are not faulty or broken. It is the way in which we live now that is causing your distress. You are a sane person living in an insane culture. You are right to be wounded. To feel your wounds. To tend them, to mourn them, to grieve them, even at times to avenge them.

When our sense of what is true does not match up with what is permitted by society to be real it seriously messes with our heads and with our hearts. It causes us to doubt our perceptions of the world and makes us lose trust in ourselves. We are forced to conform to the monoculture and deny our personal understandings of what is real, or be shamed, ostracised and isolated. And so we push down or away our knowledge of the goddess, we submerge our natural inclination to listen to the wisdom of the trees or the wind, we deny our understanding that our hearts beat in rhythm with the Earth.

But this is a truly painful way to live, it cuts away at the core of who we are. We feel the visceral pain of the disconnection, but we have no practices, no wisdom, no craft, to help us to heal that rift. We are told there was never any connection in the first place, our genuine feelings of loss are unfounded; the goddess does not exist, and men are entitled to do what they want with this planet and her resources. This forces the problem into the shadow. The result being that we are now living with a vast collective shadow of pain stemming from this severing from the Great Mother.

This unspeakable wound causes untold harm within ourselves, and in all of our relationships with others. It keeps us separate, small, and cautious, or lashing out without understanding why.

I want you to know I see you in your pain. I feel it too. It is real.
But we can heal. We can remember.

To Re-Member

Gina Martin

We come together, under the power of the full moon, to speak of She of a Thousand Names. We stand in this Grove, in this sacred circle of women, connected through all time and space to all other groves, to all other circles of women, that we may remember.

These are the words the officiating priestess speaks at the beginning of each Full Moon ritual here in our Grove in Dún na Sidhe. As a spiritual community we began over twenty years ago to find a way to connect to the Goddess that felt true and served to deepen our relationship with Her. We had been exposed to different traditions and teachers. We were novices, having dipped our toes into Wicca, Lakota, esoteric Western magic and Celtic practices. We came from mélange of religious experiences, Catholicism, Protestantism, Judaism, and Islam.

We knew enough to start with the basic building blocks of ritual. We processed, we sang, we cast a circle. And we met every full moon, rain, snow, or no, in the Grove up behind my house. How do you get to Carnegie Hall, or in this case, to a predictable altered state of being that can serve all? Practice, practice, practice.

It was truly a study in trial and error. Some Moons we would explore different prayers, mediations, different ways to align with the seasons etc. The measuring stick was simple. Did that feel right? Did it work? Did it allow every woman and girl to leave the outside life behind and stand, held and protected, between the worlds? We rejected dogma but had a few 'rules'. We always allowed, nay, encouraged girls to stand in Circle with us. The need to create these spaces for the girls, for them to have the opportunity to know women's mysteries and to create a new lineage, was primary in our original intention. Additionally, I always held to the maxim that ritual may be therapeutic, but it isn't therapy. But mostly we sought to remember.

Ah, remember, re-member to put the body parts back together again. We choose to connect to the past and the lost knowledge in order to create something that is old and new. But memory, as neuroscience now tells us, is a remarkably faulty tool. Eye-witness testimony, which used to be the gold standard in legal proceedings, is now seen as flimsy and unreliable. We probably have all heard the first-year law school trick. The professor begins the lecture and one student bolts out of the room, grabbing another's backpack or purse as they go. All the students are asked to relate what they saw. There is hardly ever much agreement on what just happened or what the perpetrator looked like. And that is short-term memory. For incidents that occurred longer ago, listen to adult siblings recall their childhoods. It often sounds like they grew up in different families. So how then do we remember that which is millennia old and violently obscured? How can we trust any memory?

The centuries old onslaught of patriarchy has dis-membered our Old Ways, the ways of the Goddess, and of our integral relationships with the land. We are starving for that which feels true and authentic. It is understandable that we gravitate towards those who are so confident that they know the answers, that they have the 'in' to the hidden truths. However, my instinct has always been to run – run fast and far – from those people. For me the spiritual path has always been akin to that of a scientist. Keep asking questions, then the next questions, then the next.

When is a 'knowing' a true remembrance of something ancient and holy, and when is it at its best, wishful thinking, and at its worst, manipulation for an effect or purpose? When is ritual performative and when is it transformative. Can it, should it, be both?

In the quest to remember we must be careful not to slavishly hold to old ideas and practices. And I use that adverb specifically. In the old Celtic Brehon Laws, there is much to admire. It was a delicate and sophisticated system of laws to keep order, honor life and liberty and stay in balance with the land, the seasons, and the Otherworld. It held people and their people accountable for their actions and preserved a notable gender balance. It cherished the goddesses and revered scholarship, creativity, and courage. But it also concretized societal hierarchy and lauded 'power-over' systems like slavery. If we desire to create a new paradigm – a 'power with' construct – we cannot perpetuate the patterns of domination. All that is old is not necessarily gold.

Our work then is to excavate the best of what was from our genetic memories and still to hold those old ways up to a twenty-first century lens. We will find so much value in the existent Indigenous practices, in the old texts, in the remnants of knowing that come from our past-life experiences. But our greatest mission is to leave this world a better place for the next seven generations. We keep what honors life. We eschew the rest.

To walk the Goddess path is to be a weaver. We weave the old truths in with the modern deep understandings. We are creatrixes. We are making something old and new that is strong and honest and one with all that is. It may frequently feel like bailing out a leaky boat with a teaspoon. But it is the work of the valiant.

We endeavor to re-member, to gather our fragments of soul and wisdom and become stronger, more awake, and more resilient that we ever thought possible. At the end of every Full Moon ritual here at Dún na Sidhe, when all are gently scooped out and filled up with the wonder of our connection to Her, when we desire to linger in that vibratory resonance with the Divine She, the priestess says, *"Remember, this is how we are supposed to live."*

So mote it be.

Her

Georg Cook

I walk with her in the fields
She takes my hands
And speaks to me
Of those who walked before me
Their stories and their truths
Hidden but remembered
She is the essence of this land

I feel her in the waves
She holds me in weightlessness
And sings to me
Of the corrupted stories
The untold history of the women of the sea
Their strength and their heartache
She is the essence of this sea

I smell her in the trees
She fills my lungs with floral scent
And talks to me
Of the women who listened to nature
Worked with the seasons and the moon
Who were outcast and named witches
She is the essence of this woods

I hear her in the breeze
She tugs at my ears
And whispers to me
Of the women who were silenced
Degraded, abandoned and abused
Their memories written into myth
She is the essence of this wind

I see her in women today
They speak and write
And confide to me
Of their stories and their traumas
Their challenges and triumphs
They support and uplift my spirit
We are the essence of all women

Re-membering the Sacred Feminine

Rev. Jo Royle

It began at home, in the darkness, wild, naked, raw. Re-membering the Sacred Feminine began when I birthed my first child and birthed myself as mother. My daughter born through the fire of pain, onto the earth, into the element of water, without assistance, the midwife lifting her into the air and onto my body. Held by nature – mine, hers – in this natural process of birthing.

After much of my life lived in the cage of patriarchy, the stories of Clarissa Pinkola Estés brought awareness of how it is to be a woman in our 'over-culture': Aunt Edna refusing to conform to the definitions she was handed of 'woman'; stories which painted a new picture of 'woman' as embodied, wild, wise, fierce, sovereign and powerful.

My wise sisters nudged me further towards this truth; to Sue Monk Kidd and Glennon Doyle, awakening me to the 'good girl' conditioning and the messages we women grew up with: smile...be happy...agree...don't make a fuss...don't be angry...be pretty...and whatever you do, don't be rude to a man! They led me to Lisa Lister's work which felt revelationary – our bleeding not something bad, to avoid or be abhorred, instead a superpower! Our cycles a rhythm to embrace, to harness, to live by. This changed first my contraceptive decisions and then my life!

Lucy H. Pearce's *Burning Woman* brought holy rage...for what was (and is) done to women; rage for the way women were turned against one another; rage for the silencing, the abuse, torture, violence and murder. Dreams and triggered terror bringing me glimpses of the witch wound...my tongue cut out...my children taken...drowning... With a deep and sickening knowing that the women in my line *were* wise women...but their wisdom, connection with the land and earth ceremony was ripped from them...from me. Taken...forcibly...stolen... leaving me bereft of the feminine.

Deepening rage with the words of Robin Wall Kimmerer, highlighting when we term raping and pillaging of the earth as 'mining' for 'resources', we don't ask permission, give thanks, and stay mindful to the damage we cause. Seeing then the abuse of the earth and feminine with the same roots – entitlement, ownership, patriarchy, capitalism, colonialism.

Brick by man-ufactured brick, this journey of re-membering, breaking down the walls containing me, unlearning his-story, releasing what I thought I knew, what I thought was true. Divesting myself of patriarchy, brick by brick until I was back to the earth again, back to the ground of my being, from where to build again. But not a linear wall of uniform bricks, with sharp edges, this time...an organic creation of nature and beauty, spiralling, circling, wild and uneven, uncontrolled, uncontrollable. Not a wall at all, not a structure to hold me in...hold me back...but one to hold me up.

In the world religions, I found the Sacred Feminine, not solely in Judaism or Christianity, or Hinduism or Buddhism…instead She spanned them all. Much like my female friends who'd describe themselves as Jewish-Buddhist-Hindu or Christian-Pagan-Buddhist.

In Judaism, I found Her in the mystical teachings of the Kabbalah, in the women lighting the Shabbat candles, in the teachings of Rabbi Tirzah Firestone, in the lineage of Jewish mothers, in prayers to the Shekhinah.

In Christianity I found Her in the Christian mystics of Teresa of Avila, Hildegard of Bingen and Julian of Norwich; in Mary Magdalene, her disciples and her gospel, discovered at Nag Hammidi, and the work of Meggan Watterson.

In Islam, She was in Sufism, in the whirling and the dancing, in the love and longing of the poetry of Rumi and Hafez and in the beauty of sacred geometry.

In Hinduism, I found Her in Kali and Bhuvaneshwari, in Lakshmi and Saraswati, in mantras to the Hindu Goddesses, in Shakti and the words of Sally Kempton.

In Buddhism, I found her in the love and compassion of Tara and Quan Yin, in chanting and in the Tibetan Monks of Tashi Lhunpo devoting their ceremony to all sentient beings.

I re-membered the Sacred Feminine! Building her from the ground up, to hold me, support me to root in my sovereignty, rise in my feminine power and wisdom and surrender myself to being the Presence of Love.

She is in my holy body, in my naked feet on the earth, in my desires, in my meditations with Mary Magdalene, in my ceremonies, in the practice of anointing, in the silence of Quaker meetings, in the light of Shabbat, in the magic and wonder, in the arms of my friends who hold me in my shame, in the warm embrace of sisters welcoming me into the mosque, in the sea when swimming, in every tree and every blade of grass, in every butterfly and every bee, in every river, rock and mountain…literally everywhere!

She teaches me to turn in and root down, to be in my body, to not fear persecution, to be courageous, to rise up, to speak out, to express my holy rage, to listen to my intuition, to set boundaries, to stay open to love, to create safety, to surrender, to receive, to live cyclically, to be gentle, to desire, to be authentic, to create, and to love.

She led me to a role at Women's Aid…literally. The job showed up three times before I had the courage to hear the call and the day I drove to the interview I followed a red car with the registration SH3 LVE.

She led me to dance, to be in my body; to weave healing ceremony for myself; to travel to Lancaster to walk in the footsteps of the Pendle witches, to restore justice, to heal the wounds of my feminine line.

She led me to showing up naked on Zoom, fully woman, speaking the words "I am witch, healer, powerful and powerless one, warrioress, Goddess, Priestess, sovereign one, creatrix, dancer, singer. I am woman in my power."

And She led me here, to Womancraft, and to you.

I might call her nature, light, breath, universe, Divine spark, Spirit, Goddess, Love, God, She, All There Is, Great Mother, Creation…and I might call her nothing at all…instead dropping deeply into the delicious peace, stillness, silence, beauty and Love of being in in Her presence.

New Annunciations (Re-visiting Luke 1:26-38)

Patricia Higgins

I wonder
What Mary thinks about the Nativity now
And all that led up to it

I wonder if she might wish the Annunciation had been a little different:

That as well as the wonder of being asked to 'conceive and bear' a son
That she might also have been invited to use her gifts
Of knowing and loving and trusting God,
And drawing others to God;

That she was asked because of what she could bring to her Son's mission
And not just because of her conveniently virginal womb,
And her betrothal to someone from the House of David.

I wonder, in light of all the alabaster depictions of her since,

Might she actually liked to have squared her shoulders and said
'Well, no, I don't think so'

Has she replayed that conversation with Gabriel in her head
Over the millennia since and wished she'd said something like:

'Do you know what, why don't you ask God to have a re-think
To refine this 'Divine Wooing' –
which is what's going on here if I am picking you up right.
God might want to balance out the 'male' references –
to David, Jacob and what a great Son and King this baby's going to be?
God might want to talk to me
As a woman with my own gifts and passions

About the role I might play beyond this birth
To be involved, active in what my Son will do and bring to the world

About how I might give voice to that which I see and wonder deeply about
Trusting that it will touch others as it touched me
Not just passively pondering
And endlessly cooking, cleaning, and clearing

After all
I would want to be able to look the women who come behind me in the eye
And say,

'Well, when my big moment came,
I did my bit
To change this world that can so often seem to be so tilted towards men'

I wonder then
Might that be what actually happened
Might Mary have squared up to Gabriel –
Asked for her gifts to be more fully acknowledged, recognised, and used
And it just never got written down?

And then I wonder
What might God be doing to try and rectify that?
What new Annunciations are being made today, and to whom?

Previously published in a small booklet gathering contributions made at an event in March 2023, *Writing by the Water* by the local Greencastle Writer's Group.

Eden Revisited

Rebecca Lowe

It was never as simple
as breathing life into being –
Only a man could have written that –
Perhaps, she sang us into existence,
Feet stamping, hips swaying,
Bells pulsating through
blasted dust, perhaps,
A frenzied utterance,
Some kind of dizzying dance,
Celestial planets tracing
Ecstatic paths around the sun.

Perhaps, she sweated
as she sang, perhaps
mountains hefted into being,
Rocks sundered into sprinkling
streams, perhaps the sparks
from her soles created the
first heavenly fire –

For if breathing birthed us,
It was surely the breath

that accompanies labour,
The remembrance to breathe
through the pain – the remembrance
to push against the agonising
darkness of our own mortality –
Souls trapped within paper skins

Perhaps that is what
It really means –
Creation out of the Nothing
of ourselves – a breathing
into being of something
unfathomably ancient,
Miraculously new

The breaking of waters:
'I am life. I Am here'
Exquisitely fragile,
Unstoppably strong.

Genesis*

Iona F Millar

Before the beginning, there was Silence.

She hovered over undisturbed waters of stillness.
Of sacredness.
Of deep and dark peace.

From within the wells of her mystery, there came a quickening.
A tiny seed of possibility flickered in to being.
And moved through her confinement.

And so it was that Sound came to be.
Sound was with Silence, and *of* Silence; birthed from her being.
And Silence nursed Sound so softly.
Gazed on her lovingly.
And cradled her tenderly.

And Sound grew.
She found her voice.
She learned to sing.

And as she sang, she and Silence danced in symphony.
Spinning in infinities, all across The Before that became The Beginning.
She who was nothing.
And she who was everything.
For Silence, Sound was her All; all that was, all that is, and all that will ever be.

But Sound grew.
And as she grew, a restlessness took root within her.
For she knew only Silence.
Yet she longed to dance to her own tune.
To hear her own song.

And so it was that the moment came.

Sound composed herself.
And burst into infinite fractals of all her frequencies.
Breathed herself into vibrations of music and light and matter.

And so it was that she became The Beginning.
Of all that was, all that is, and all that will ever be.

She became light and darkness; that she might know her contrasts.

She separated her waters into sky and sea; that she might stretch the depth and
breadth of her expanses.

She became land and tide; that she might know what it is to stand steady.
And what it is to move with grace and flow.
On her lands she grew trees that bore fruit; that she might know the seasons
of her growth. That she might know what it is to take root, to bud, to bloom,
to let go and to take to seed once again.

She became Sun dancing with Moon, tripping over the skies by starlight; that
she might know her luminosity.
Her music.
Her mystery.
And her magic.

Her seas gave rise to life; that she may know her fertile potential.
That she might surrender herself to the ebb and flow of her energies.
That she may give herself over to the great excesses of her deep, peaceful
equanimity and the raging turmoil of her tempests.
Her airs gave rise to wings; that she might soar the heights of her wonder.
And delight in the freedom of her skies.

Her lands filled with creatures of every sort; that she might express the limitless
bounds of her creativity.
And all the colour and texture and vibrancy of the very fabric of her being.
That she might show the daring of her wildness.
And she saw that it was good.

And she wanted more.

She wanted to taste it and touch it.
To live it.
To breathe it.

And so it was that she sang herself into infinite incarnations.
Refracted fragments.
Reflections.
That she might delight in watching herself discover and decode her own great

mysteries.

That she might live, and laugh, and love.

That she might walk, and dive, and fly her wildernesses.

That she might taste her abundance.

That she might commune with her creatures.

That she might inhabit her expanses, and wonder at her wildness.

That she might come to see her Self with her own eyes.

That she might look in the eyes of each other soul and experience the flicker of remembrance; and see her Self reflected there.

And so it was that Sound became The Beginning.

She who birthed the Universe into being.

And who cradles her and croons to her still.

To her spirits embodied on Earth she lilts her lullaby to all who will listen:

'My child, my love, my dear one …

Where can you go from my Spirit?
Where can you flee from me?
For we are separate only,
as a raindrop is to the sea.

You can rise on up to the heavens,
you can sink to the depths of despair.
My eyes are accustomed to darkness,
I'll reach out my arms to you there.

You will see me sparkle in starlight.
My scent is sea-salt on the breeze.
You can hear me whisper in silence,
and in rustling leaves on the trees.

I'm in the soft song of a mother's,
and the gentle father's embrace.
I send you kisses in candle-lights,
and love in each smiling face.

I've promised you signs to remind you
- rainbows, poems, sunsets and stones -
that you're here to search for the music
where can you hear me sing your way home.'

A divine feminine reimagining of the biblical story of creation and the singing of psalm 13.

The Power of Circle

Kelley Davis Sookram

What happens when systems suddenly become intolerable? Where and how do meaning, belonging, ritual, and celebration occur if the world is burning? At the heart of patriarchy, there is the need for dominance over another. Whether it's human, creature, or Earth, nothing is safe. When this awareness penetrates the heart, the shift in perspective beckons a response. There is no going back. The wasteland, however, appears too big, too insurmountable a task to dismantle, a system far too pervasive and dominant to untangle.

So as one might find, retreat seems the safer response. Exchanging known patterns for a period of gestation, where the unraveling of fear and restriction begins. This chapter of disintegration ends up being more complex and lengthier than first anticipated. Grief has its own timeline and circular nature that needs to be respected. Curiosity and openness emerge as healers and are allowed to chart the journey now. At the core of the grief spiral, sadness and anger remain. These heavy emotions become a womb space from Witch (not a typo but a nod to the wise ones) something new can be birthed. In this story, the something new is the Sacred Feminine.

The Sacred Feminine reveals itself in gut feelings, goosebumps and tingles, and an embodied gnosis that says, 'Pay attention, this is important.' She is the greatest truth detector and ally. Far too many years are spent shutting Her down and dismissing Her gifts. The remaining days will be spent in dedication to restoring Her to a place of honour and reverence.

The Sacred Feminine is rising and She is the antidote to a patriarchal system that is long overdue an exit. Her attributes bring healing, balance, wisdom, and transformation. She is at work in the most ancient and simplest of forms, weaving Her magick through the power of Circle.

Sitting in New and Full Moon Circles awakens renewed hope and belief that an alternative way of living exists. Here, the ebb and flow of Grandmother Moon's wisdom allows for diverse energies and rhythms. When souls have the opportunity to create sacred space together, to be their truest, messiest, most authentic selves, miracles happen. When judgment and the pressure to solve problems are removed, and there is freedom to sit in the unknowing and hold space as a witness for another's journey, this is when She does Her best work! Transformation ignites when the sacredness of Circle results in flow and cyclical living, releasing attachment to an outcome, embracing both light and dark, ensuring safety, practicing non-judgment, and the gift of compassionate space holding. These are the energies of the Sacred Feminine at work in the world.

Intuition becomes that long-lost friend from childhood once again. Connection to each other grows now that there is no longer fear of the "other." Shared experiences and struggles are recognized. The sister wound, long cultivated by patriarchal systems of lack and competition has lost its power. Healing can finally flow to those places that hide the "dark and ugly bits," since they are now accepted and seen. This finally allows stuck energies to transform and ultimately transmute into something that serves growth, rather than impede it. The dominant masculine psyche now infuses with the deliciously wild, nurturing, and honoring qualities of the Sacred Feminine, bringing life and wholeness again.

It is inspiring to witness the bravest souls, speaking difficult truths aloud, freeing themselves from limiting beliefs, and writing new stories for themselves. They are intentionally tearing out the stitches of their patriarchal patterns and weaving empowerment, embodiment, truth, and authenticity back into their designs. When we heal ourselves, we heal the world. This is a humble belief, even if it feels too small a response to a patriarchal-infused wasteland. Blessed are the disruptors, rejecting unhealthy patriarchal systems, hungry for something inclusive, restorative, and healing to take their place.

Growing numbers of people are sitting in Sacred Circle together. People from all backgrounds, beliefs, genders, and demographics are being drawn to the core values of Circle. They are connected by a need to belong, to be heard, to be accepted, and to create an intentional space for growth without fear of judgment, where there is freedom to make mistakes and try again. Circle gifts the attendee a container to tune into one's highest self for guidance, and perhaps even spark some joy on the journey, as releasing what no longer serves becomes part of the process. These are core values all can celebrate. Truly, the potential of Circle is limitless. May it grow in strength, and its breadth of opportunity for all to participate and infuse healing into this world. So be it!

The Sacred Feminine is rising across this vast globe. Do you see Her? Can you feel Her? Most importantly, will you be Her champion? The Sacred Feminine is the ultimate challenger to the multi-faceted systems of patriarchy, for She is everything it is not. She is awake and transforming lives through the power of Circle.

Embodied Knowing

Molly Remer

*You are your own
sacred space.*

*Your feet are always
on temple ground.*

One of the key factors to me that differentiates feminist spiritual paths from many dominant religious traditions and frameworks is the recognition and acknowledgement of the body as a source of wisdom, a source of pleasure, a source of learning, and a source of knowing. Not viewed as unclean, dirty, or as something to be mistrusted or transcended, we can return to our bodies again and again, dropping down into our bellies, bones, and blood, returning to center, and returning home to ourselves. Those who embark into thealogy quickly realize that it is a spirituality better lived than analyzed. My own experience of my goddess-oriented path is an intensely embodied one. I am here on this earth, in this body, my feet on the ground, my eyes on the sky, listening, feeling, and sensing. This, to me, is sacredness in motion, this is the Goddess right in front of me, she is witnessed in the very fact that my pulse beats in my wrist and that my eyes alight on those three crows coasting lightly into the treetops.

Sara Avant Stover, writing in the *Book of SHE* says: "Our bodies aren't indentured servants here to labor for us until we take our dying breath. They are sacred chalices… Our bodies *always* tell the truth and hold the information we need to thrive" (p. 43).

And, one of my favorite quotes of all comes from Camille Maurine in *Meditation Secrets for Women* who writes: "Your body is your own. This may seem obvious. But to inhabit your physical self fully, with no apology, is a true act of power."

At one time, I would have focused my attention primarily on women and encouraging women to trust their bodies, to listen to their bodies, and to honor their bodies. I've come to see that a goddess-centered approach to ethics, values, and embodied spiritual experience includes *all people* who have a body. In my heart of hearts I would like all people to value their bodies, honor their bodies, trust their bodies, and listen to their bodies. I think if this was true, the fundamental way in which we relate to, treat, and care for one another would change and the feminist values of cooperation, compassion, and empathy would come to form the foundation of society. Every single one of us begins life within someone else's body. We enter the world through someone's body. And, we have a body that interacts with other bodies for our entire lives. This is altogether simple, obvious, and profound. Our bodies are our seats of reality, of being human, of being present in the world. A life firmly rooted in concept of the body as sacred, no longer allows room for violation of or harm to others.

Carol Christ writes in *Rebirth of the Goddess*: "The rituals and symbols of Goddess religion…[bring] experience and deep feeling to consciousness so that they can shape our lives; helping us broaden and deepen our understanding of our interdependence to include all beings and all people; binding us to others and shaping communities in which concern for the earth and all people can be embodied."

When I talk to other people about self-trust and building self-trust, I often encourage them to check in with their bodies for a physical response to a decision, idea, choice, or happening. Where does it land in your body? What do you feel inside when you think about making this decision or taking this action? Does your body respond with a "yes" or a "no" when you think about this idea? For me, the sensation comes in my chest, around my heart – a lightening or expansion or a contraction or heaviness. This is not what all people will experience, perhaps you feel the answer in your belly, in your head, around your jaw. Perhaps you feel it as a color, sensation of warmth or coolness, or as a "rightness of being."

I must also acknowledge that many people have experienced some form of physical trauma or abuse in their lives and that these experiences can complicate our relationships with our bodies, our sense of intuition, and our trust in ourselves. If your body has been a site of violation, it may be more difficult or complex to connect to this body-based sense of "knowing" or intuition that I reference and I do not wish to oversimplify what can be a complex and multilayered personal experience of embodiment.

In the books *A Deeper Wisdom: The Twelve Steps from a Woman's Perspective* by Patricia Lynn Reilly and *The Book of SHE* by Sara Avant Stover, there arises a theme of the body as home, and I would like to offer some questions for your circles based on this theme:

- What is your inner "house" like?

- Does something need tending?

- Where do you need to clear something out?

- If you mentally walk through your body, what do you see?

- What is your body as *home* like for you? How re-sourced is it?

- What needs attention within you?

- Do you have a sense of your inner and outer ground?

- What do you feel in your belly, right now?

I lead a process called #30DaysofGoddess and one of the things I often suggest for a daily practice is to offer a "body prayer." May this process nourish you and your circles too.

A Body Blessing:

Fold your hands
in front of your heart,
feel your palms warm
and your pulse beat.
Kiss your fingertips.
Raise your hands and
cradle your face with love
and then,
move one hand
to the top of your head
and one to your heart.
Pause.
Cross your arms over your chest,
one hand on each shoulder
and sway back and forth gently.
Kiss your palms
and lay them upon your belly.
Run your hands down your legs.
Wiggle your toes.
Fold your hands in prayer pose
and bring them back to your heart-level.
Breathe deeply
and then open your hands.
Gaze into them.
Envision the day's potential
nestled there.
What do you see
in your own cupped palms?
Kiss your fingertips again

and whisper what it is you

need to hear.

Say:

thank you.

Sacred Mother Rising

Paula Youmell

I sit on Mother Earth, grounding down into Her Bones and Flesh,

I hear Her cry for help.

Softly at first, not a sad cry or a desperate plea.

It is the sound, smell, energy of a Mom opening Her arms wide,

Inviting you into Her lap, to sink down into Her softness and smell

the earthy scents of Her flesh.

Mother Earth invites us with

Fiery Passion to rise up and speak out for Her,

Wet Flow to invite others into Her care,

Strong Grounding to stand up for the wrongs against Her,

Airy Whisperings to call others to Her service

Heart and Soul to share your Earth Energy and Love, three-fold.

The longer I sit, Rooted into Her Bones and Flesh, The stronger Her Voice becomes.

I hear Her in the Solar and Lunar Growth of Plants and Trees,

in the Rush of River's Waters, in the Chatter of Animals,

in the Song of Her Birds, and in the Voices of Women Past, Present, and Future.

Rise Up! Rise Up! She says.

Rise Up and Save Your Sacred Home!

Change begins by creating change within oneself. When we change our frequency of thought, words, and actions in the world this energy ripples out to everything.

Stepping back into Nature's Rhythms means living with the rhythms of the Earth as our ancestors lived. This is a somatic and sensual experience that can be our way of living, honoring Nature's cycles.

The Earth is the womb of the Divine Feminine. When our heartbeat matches her heartbeat, we transform into the potential balance of Sacred Reciprocity.

This work of transformation comes from within. When one Soul transforms, we open the door of possibility wider for the Collective Soul to transform. When we connect with and heal the Divine within ourself, we invite all humans to do the same. Seeing, honoring, and deep connection with Nature is healing. Body, mind, and spirit are pulled into Sacred Heart Space living.

Sacred heart space living is earth, cosmos rhythm living. Cultures who live in this earth centered cosmology flow and create through Nature's balance.

Our thoughts, words, and actions create energy bubbles around us. Those energy bubbles attract similar energy. We create our reality through the energy of our thoughts, words, and actions. If we live in Sacred Heart Space, our energy signature invites others to do the same. Like attracts like.

The Gospel of Diana

Will lead this land

Women dancing in circles

Women working hand in hand

Without competition

Fueling creativity

Our Daughters are artists

As are we

Creating altar tapestries

Weaving Her earth, sky and sea

Again, like before

The bible tells the lore

Everywhere was Goddess Reverence

Before "man" put up the fence

Between Women and holy Yoni life

We forgot how to Love

Our own kind of species

Make our own mind of Treaties

Treaties between the Women

Treaties about the land

Treaties where all food

Steadily meets all demand

Treaties of waterways

So Woman barges can trade

All the Goddess artwork Reverence

Women worldwide will have made

Eve-olution will continue then

We'll develop to Yoni-Earth intention!

Alethia

Terra Divina as a Practice for Reclaiming Our Feminine Wisdom

Elle Harrigan

Within us all is a deep pool of knowledge beyond what is acquired through intellect. It rises up as intuitive guidance, creative inspiration, insights, and epiphanies. This inner wisdom is named by many cultures as the Feminine aspect of the Divine: she is called Shekina, Sophia, Shakti, the life force of Yin.

The feminine quality of wisdom is as elusive as she is powerful. She must be coaxed to the surface through our receptivity. She whispers in a subtle language of symbols, dreams, feelings, and a knowingness that ripples through our senses as pure truth, grace-given and as deep as the ocean.

Her home is in the earth, a wild spirit that nourishes, sustains, and recycles life. When we encounter nature mindfully, open-hearted to the wisdom in the wind, the trees, and the waters, we tap an inner wellspring where the procreative power of the feminine dwells, an infinite resource that can guide us back to wholeness and wellbeing.

The Divine Feminine in nature demands our attention before revealing her secrets. It's not that she has stopped speaking; we simply have forgotten how to open our eyes and awaken our ears to her presence.

Our senses are the portal. When we mindfully attune to the beauty and wonder that surrounds us in the wild, we create a liminal space where our inner wisdom flows like a vast, underground spring. We're invited to dip into its ever-flowing waters to recover our most transformative gifts that can remake the world: compassion, empathy, and creativity.

One path that takes us into the depths of our soul where our feminine wisdom abides is through the contemplative practice of *terra divina*, a form of meditation that evolved out of the Christian monastic tradition of *lectio divina* – a way of encountering the divine through scripture.

When we engage in terra divina, nature becomes our sacred text; our holy book. In stillness, we absorb nature with the eyes of the poet and artist, alert to the objects that call for our attention and the feelings that arise. A field of summer grass may whisper revelations; a single leaf may divulge profound insights. Slipping into reflection, we ask what our inner wisdom has to show us; what lessons we can learn from nature's strength and resilience; interconnectedness and harmony. Integrating the insights that come forth brings healing to our fragmented self, moving us closer to an empowered balance between Being and Doing.

The earth offers herself as spiritual restoration to be imbibed and savored, a sensual, sensory repast that nourishes body and soul. By encountering nature through deep awareness and contemplation, we create receptivity to the voice of our inner wisdom. It tells us that we can imagine a world that embraces the fluid, nurturing power of our feminine/yin energy and the highest, most life-preserving expression of our masculine/yang energy.

In reclaiming our feminine wisdom, we embody vulnerability alongside assertiveness; connection alongside self-reliance. We become capable of envisioning a holistic, compassion-driven future in which wisdom, through its social guise of emotional intelligence, presides over every choice and action that impacts the human family and our survival.

Within Witch I Dwell

Erika Zinsmeister

Within witch I dwell

motionless like the rabbit in her clover

lingering or am I frozen in fear of passing shadows

your baggage

our historical baggage

when they were strangled and burned

for loving wild things

My kettle speaks,

howls really,

names of herbal infusions

medical indications, invitations to sip with me

to find what you are looking for

I dare not ask

An acquaintance has seen a garter snake

and tried to run it over with his lawnmower

multiple times. It would not die

It pressed itself to the Earth and shed the will to give a cowering inch to pa-

triarchy any longer

Gaping-mouth scream

within which I dwell

The cosmic serpent, the ouroboros,

swallowing this tale

To begin again:

I dwell in the sacred feminine

in ebullient plurality

yes and

generous synchronicity

in dreams of intuition

waking vision

the ancestral wisdom of my foremothers

and in the wisdom to hold

my ancestors accountable for

wresting privilege from exploitation

Great Mother She

accounts too for those who would not be mothers

who would instead midwife the waxing moon

or self-generate,

conceive themselves

as indivisible possibilities in the undifferentiated beyond

Beyond She

Not all is birth and renewal

Waters carve, winds reveal

Erosion too is productive

And there is liberation in exposure

so sayeth the midnight rabbits reveling through pools of light

She is and I am

Here now are the surface processes within which I dwell,

unveiling bone from stone

The cliffs give way like crumbling tea leaves

and what can be read from their ruins?

Who has preyed upon this land?

Throw open the catacombs!

Disturb the slumbering dragonslayers

revered for their blades and desecrations

May serpents molt there underground,

grow too large for old skins

And query the quieted inquisitors

let no candle mark their tombs

snuff out their honorifics,

the menacing shadows of predators that loom

And you?

Linden? Tulsi? Nettles? Mullein?

Is loose leaf OK or do you take yours without risk of damnation?

It's hot – be careful you don't burn (me)

Take a cup from this stranger

I will trust in the danger, I will trust

with one hand full of sand

the other dried wax and dust

I'm to cast a circle

within which I am no longer paralyzed by power's lies

in clover sky-high my power lies

within witch I dwell

Planting Seeds for the Mother

Donna Fontanarose Rabuck

I

Rise up, awaken

women of the world

It is time to plant seeds

for the Mother

Divest your imagination

of demons who lurk in dark places

of lies about sexuality

All those worn out

delusions of power-hungry men

It is time to plant seeds

for your Mother.

First, you must turn over the ground

exhume those unremembered graves

allow the air to be filled

with their truth, with words

to break the silence.

Re-member.

Slowly, gently, carefully

put back the pieces

of a dismembered world
allow it a life above-ground
Thus, you nourish the soil
of the Mother.
Sing, chant, tell stories
mingle with creation
respecting diversity, honoring difference
witnessing our essential oneness
This harmony will form the
seeds you will plant
for the Mother.

II

Sleep well. Watch the moon
Honor Her/your cycles
Recalling that only
history is linear
Herstory, your story
our story is cyclical
turning with the seasons
the tides, and Luna.
Let Spiral Woman be your teacher
Her body a swirl of endless possibility
Ingest Her wisdom
Know that change is
the mother of invention
reinvention, revolution.

III

Arise and sing
for it is Time to plant

seeds for the Mother.

Let your voice

your truth

your imagination

lead you to Brigid

Yemaya

Spiderwoman

Kwan Yin

Mary

Tonantzin

The Goddess of One Thousand Names

Sing Her song

Write Her story

Plant seeds for the Mother

You and You and You

Blessed be.

SPECIFIC
CIRCLES

'She Who Drums'

Anne Reeder Heck

A Maiden's Journey

Macy-Doris

Like a ship's maiden voyage, a girl's first journey towards womanhood is a sacred rite of passage. I remember the first time I stepped through this portal at eleven years of age. I can see it so clearly, my becoming, and in the years to follow, a real blossoming.

I remember the feeling of excitement as I began my journey.

When I look back to see how my mama honoured and welcomed me into this work, my heart warms at the memory, my eyes fill with tears to recall the feeling of such love, for me to take my seat in the circle of women. By the time I was approaching my twelfth trip around the sun, I had already begun to crave something deeper and more meaningful than the conversations and teachings at school, something that stretched beyond the playground pettiness.

So began my search. It was here my journey with the witch wound started to unfold and this then led me to recognise something I knew and had felt but could never name, the sister wound, one of separation and division that spilled out across my entire school life and would continue to spill out as I met such resistance for following my heart and pursuing this work.

When the ancestors arrived at my door, it was a truly expansive start to exploring my lineage. I felt called to dig deeper into my heritage. Who was I? Beyond my parents and grandparents, where do I belong, who were the women and men that came before me? I now know through speaking to my maternal grandparents that I am Irish and Scottish on my grandfather's side and Welsh and English on my grandmother's side. The lives that they lived spoke to my soul, especially as I uncovered voices of women through my maternal line, awaiting someone to listen to their stories.

Unexpectedly, I was hospitalised for nearly two weeks with severe dizziness and loss of motion in my legs. By the time I went home after a traumatic experience with medical professionals, I was still no closer to discovering the cause. Several months later I was diagnosed with a chronic illness.

The ancestors had a plan and were a constant guide that showed me the way to holistic healing through the earth, plant medicine, detoxing and soon after had me embarking upon my medicine woman training, which was transformational for my own healing. After all this, my path still led back here, as I answered my soul's resonance calling which brought me full circle, back to my initial intention. Where I still longed for a space unlike any other I'd been able to find, one which meant being held with peers my age, where we could share, listen and express, in total safety with one another. A women's circle, like the ones I had grown up around, with my mama being a doula and holder of space, this is what I was inevitably drawn to. This is what I could feel in my bones, this was why I was here, for the reclamation!

I am Macy-Doris, I am a maiden, writer, poet and holder of sacred space for young women who are looking for a deeper way of connecting... I believe that at menarche a girl steps through a portal, over the threshold and into her own journey of woman, it is here where she will meet the maiden.

The maiden archetype is the first of four and usually presents herself in some way uniquely on or around a girl's first bleed. The power of the maiden when unlocked is fierce, she is wild and carefree, from being the young child gathering flowers to becoming the lover, dancing barefoot in the meadows and woodlands alike. Her realm encompasses such beauty from willow trees to waterfalls, the magic of her, is simply enchanting when harnessed by the heart. The maiden is the bud on the very precipice of unfolding, it is essential for this bud to be given the nurturing she so needs, when this is not the case and the bud is moved away from the sunlight it becomes detrimental to the whole plant life, the flowering process and the growth. This is a representation of what happens if a teen girl is not supported, the effects this will have on the future phases in her life, of Mother, Maga, Crone – the three remaining archetypes.

The word "maiden" is associated with the word "virgin" and has a lot of stigma around a woman's sexuality. My work here is for the maidens, for the next generation of women, to strip all the negative away and reclaim the maiden in both word and action, in essence and love. I had a calling with such clarity, leading to the creation of this course which began this maiden movement. There was something unearthed in my body and I could feel the change in the air, a fusion of my work as an earth tender and red thread channeller.

"The Maiden Journey" at its centre is a collective togetherness of girls gathering in a safe space free from the prying eyes within society, to express the suppressed, to speak the unspoken and begin their journey back home to themselves. Many girls who arrive at the doors of The Maiden Journey are not entirely sure what to expect and are feeling a desire for something more, whether that be finding the key to their creativity or struggling to break patterns of shame around their body and cycle, each of them have been called to this work for a reason, knowingly or unknowingly, they arrived because it was time, they were ready to peel back the layers and watch the magic unfold!

We journey together for up to six weeks in this container, the main three sessions are held in person, at my home in the moon lodge. We start by laying out the primal aspects for what is to follow, moving through the initiation. We spend time becoming familiar within the archetypal embodiment of a woman's life. Archetypal work is so important to me as I believe it to be a vital tool for girls to work with; it not only allows us to expand our knowledge upon the phase of womanhood we are in presently but it mirrors the future phases, the women we will one day become.

Meeting your maiden, for the very first time is a special experience and often where the most potent of medicines lie, the maiden archetype in her truest form, appears in your third eye and lives in your womb, around your inner cauldron within every fire, flame and spark. To be able and willing to create beautiful, strongly rooted foundations with yourself in your maiden phase as a young woman, will be transformational. Rippling through your maternal line, as your ancestors feel and recognize the reclamation and shedding of shame in a soft, gentle way.

One of the main reasons I created this course is for young women to feel empowered. I wanted to delve deeper into the topic of why women have ever been disempowered, discouraged and therefore become disembodied.

Through circling, we descend into the feelings, thoughts and memories our own body is carrying for us, welcoming the release of anger that so many of us are storing, energetically sending healing where needed, whilst exploring the process of feeling safe again. This is the path we must walk in order to fully arrive home within our body, our temple. Let us shine a light on the shadows of menstruation, of our own menstrual cycle, as something that is woven into our tapestry, "our story," not a separate entity as we're conditioned to believe in schools but as a re-membering, that as women we are cyclical beings, designed for connection to our inner and outer seasons, the land and other women, our sisters. This is where we thrive, when we feel safe enough to be fully in our body, we enable a softening and can drop down, out of our head, the masculine way of living and return to our feminine divinity.

Ultimately, we awaken our sovereignty, for when we are in our power, we become magnetic, like the bee drawn in and seduced by the rose. This is our brimming fire within transmuting, source of our sovereign self.

As we prepare for our closing of The Maiden Journey, we share the fun and playfulness of body painting, covering our skin in uplifting words and powerful symbols. This ritual I absolutely love, treating it as ceremonial whilst enjoying the pure bliss and excitement of being painted on by another sister, to have the girls see themselves as art, to be home! It is an act of celebration and rebellion which all at once stirs up the feeling of liberation!

When women gather together in circles and safe spaces of sacred ceremony, this is the medicine to be had, this is the truth of these spaces and as we all spin our gold webs out into the world, we are doing so with the same collective purpose…for women to RISE!

How We Gather as Wisdom Circles

Kelly Barrett

Looming over my laptop were shelves full of books, stuffed and double stacked. My desk was littered with papers as I sifted through mounds of collected data. It was the last year of an intense graduate program. I had just completed the research portion of my final project, 'The Great Magic: Rewilding the Feminine', where I had invited six women to participate as co-researchers in identifying individual and collective practices to cultivate the instinctual feminine.

I had named the research study The Great Magic, after reading cultural historian Thomas Berry's book *The Great Work, Our Way into the Future*. In his book, Berry tells us every time period has its Great Work, and the healing of the human-Earth relationship is *The Great Work* of this time. He believes no person alive today is exempt from responding, being a part of this shift. Berry goes on to propose a more sustainable harmonious partnering future in which the wisdom of women is one of the 'fourfold wisdoms' that will guide humans. His vision is filled with magical descriptors: intimacy, wonder, depth of meaning, integral relationship, flourishing, honoring, the grandeur of existence, and mysterious power. Even though it was published in 1999, I still found it resonant.

Yet, I kept tripping up on the tone of the word 'work'. For me, the word work just did not uphold the bounty of this vision. And as I was learning, language is a powerful shaper of our perceptions, and inspires behaviors, beliefs, and actions, which in turn accumulate as culture. Why not choose something more enlivening than work for such a wondrous future?

So, I chose to call the "great work" of my time, *The Great Magic*, focused on saving the feminine. For me, this conjured a more compelling vision of a future I wanted to move into, a shift I could be part of.

Now it was time to make sense of all the research data and draw conclusions. Having been at my desk for far too long this morning, though, I was, ironically in danger of veering more towards work than magic. And yet, I definitively wanted to complete this final phase of analysis from the same spirit of inquiry as the research study. And to stay in that field of magic required a relaxed state. I decided I should take a break.

As I stood up to stretch, I noticed a small book on one shelf, wedged between others so it almost disappeared, called *Wisdom Circles: A Guide to Self-discovery and Community Building in Small Groups.* Out of curiosity I pulled it out, skimming page after page. I had no recollection of having read it previously. With eerie serendipity, what I found described was a type of circle that felt a lot like our research gatherings. I then recalled a comment made by a co-researcher known as Snowy Owl. When asked what practices she felt had been most significant for her in rewilding the feminine, she reflected, "there was something in the act of gathering itself, coming together as women, that had nourished me the most."

While I had been hyper-focused on what *individual* practices animated the feminine, I realized I had lost sight of the *collective* practices. The act of gathering had not been something we consciously claimed as a practice. It was simply how we organized. It was how we were 'being'. With my lopsided analytical eye, focused like a patriarch solely on the 'doing', I had not seen holistically. As I stood holding open the book, I could not deny the irony of a wise owl connecting me to wisdom circles.

The authors, Garfield, Spring and Cahill, define a "wisdom circle" as a "safe space within which to be authentic, trusting, caring, and open to change… searching for a way of life that embraces wisdom and compassion." They offer ten constants as guidelines for crafting a circle. Here is my shorthand version:

Constant 1. Mark the opening and closing of the circle.

Constant 2. Create a mutual intention.

Constant 3. Acknowledge the wisdom of the ancestors. Consider future generations.

Constant 4. Express gratitude for what is known and being learned.

Constant 5. Create a safe space for truths to be shared.

Constant 6. Compassionately witness.

Constant 7. Speak with care from your truth and experience.

Constant 8. Allow space for silence.

Constant 9. Empower all members to (equally) co-create.

Constant 10. Commit to an ongoing relationship.

The Great Magic: Rewilding the Feminine – a 'Wisdom Circle' Case Study

Given the nature of the research topic, rewilding the feminine, I opted for a femininely inclined style of research, a qualitative participatory research approach known as *co-operative inquiry*. A question initiates the study, instead of a traditional proclaiming hypothesis found in quantitative research. The lead researcher does not guide or anticipate the outcome but allows it to emerge. It is a partnering and collaborative process, not dominating or hierarchical. Within this methodology the participants and the initiating investigators embed themselves as action agents in life, not in an artificially controlled environment, on a quest exploring a common interest. Ultimately, this is research *with* people who are generating culture through their own social participation.

The perfect container to hold the dynamics of the group was a circle where all things are equal. We gathered five times over the six week period of the study. Each time we met, we created a sacred space where we could share what we knew or what we were coming to know about the instinctual feminine.

At our initial gathering, I introduced a story by Dr. Clarissa Pinkola Estés as a metaphor for cultivating the instinctual feminine. In her book *Women Who Run with the Wolves* (1992), Dr. Estés, a keeper of the old stories and a Jungian analyst, suggests the trail of the Wild Woman archetype, the feminine instinctual nature, and her scent can be found within various myths and fairytales. "La Loba", she suggests, is one such story where an Old Woman who lives alone in the desert gathers the bones of the endangered. When she has collected and laid out a full wolf skeleton, the Old Woman sings the flesh back onto the bones until the revivified wolf leaps up and runs off towards the horizon. As she watches, she laughs in delight as the wolf turns into a Wild Woman.

Based on studies in wildlife biology, Dr. Estés concluded Wild Women and wolves have a lot in common; both are endangered species. To resuscitate women's soul life, which she believes has been culturally domesticated, tucked away in the collective cultural shadow, she guides women to find their own authentic expression of this archetype and animate it. This sounded a whole lot like re-wilding to me, and La Loba a perfect doorway, a perfect guiding story, for our research group to imagine ourselves in.

At the launch of our study, I invited each researcher to envisage herself as a Wild Woman roaming the desert collecting her bones. Each of us would return to the laboratory of our own life on a quest to find our bones and sing over them. The bones we would be searching for in the desert of the patriarchy would be neglected aspects of the feminine and our practices would be the metaphorical singing over the bones. This exploration resonated so much with the group that it continued as our main thread throughout the project. We became bone collectors, and our practices our animating medicine.

By imagining ourselves inside one story, La Loba, we were also giving rise to another type of story, a living story, through our actions. Tom Atlee from the Co-Intelligence Institute makes an interesting distinction between a 'told' story and a 'living' story. A told story, he says, is a shared narrative, but a living story, is a story we inhabit. While La Loba was a told story, through our actions, we were simultaneously co-authoring a living story.

The nature of the research required anonymity. I could share what participants said, but was required to shield their identity. We did this by assuming self-selected Bird names. While standing in the circle, each researcher revealed her self-chosen Bird name and explained why she chose it.

As another way of introducing ourselves, each woman brought an object that reminded her of a time when she was close to her own truth, her instinctual nature. Hawk brought a Tarot deck, Birdie swim fins, Snowy Owl a wooden spoon she carved, Hummingbird a yarn painting she had created, Magpie a pendulum, Raven a pod from nature, and Quetzal, clay goddess talismans. As each woman placed their item in the center of the table and shared their relationship to the object, it became a way of revealing a shard of personal story, like our self-selected Bird names. Over time, the more layers of story, the more fleshed out we became to each other, and each layer built intimacy and trust.

There were further deepenings as the study progressed. Millions of women took to the street to protest the inauguration of the 45th president of the U.S. Each Bird chose a favorite sign from the march and shared what it meant to her. An energized and raucous discussion ensued around messages such as: *"This Feminist Has Balls." "Brace Yourselves, Women Coming." "When Sleeping Women Wake, Mountains Rise." "I'm a Feminist, what is your superpower?"*

Additional layers were woven into the container as we shared divinatory practices, created masks of our Wild Woman, and co-created drawings and stories. At each gathering we continued to share the stories of our own explorations, collecting our Wild Woman's bones, administering practices to re-animate our whole skeleton.

In our circle, our cauldron of story, we were whipping up what Atlee calls a story field, where resonant mutually re-enforcing living stories congeal. Our individual interwoven living stories had become a story field, a collective living story, and Wild Woman was our protagonist.

Stories can arise in a multitude of ways. For example, they might be 'plot driven' or 'character driven', but in this case, I felt our story was 'value driven.' A living story was bubbling up beneath the feet of our collective Wild Woman as her values inspired her actions. As story weavers of this emerging vision, we slowly built up layers, fleshing out the Wild Woman archetype, discovering who she was, where she lived, what she knew, and how she behaved. Each of us brought aspects of her, collectively painting a descriptive portrait of her personality that revealed her values.

She demonstrates an assertiveness, consciousness and advocates for the greater good. Her connection with soul is embodied and experiential, sometimes reverent, involving nature, creative practice, and quiet spaciousness. She embraces many ways of knowing, and feels interconnected in a reciprocal relationship of honoring. For her, the rational mind has created an imbalance that she counters with embodiment and mindfulness practices, although she does not disavow the mind and remains inquisitive and ever curious.

She is who She is in the midst of a patriarchal culture.

When the circle powers up, anything can happen. It is exciting and, no matter how much planning you do, not entirely predictable. Yet, having a consistent format is helpful. This does not mean every gathering is identical, but there are some elements or rituals you do every time you gather.

We had a predictable structure to contain the dance of what was emerging. We began with an opening circle, continued with two rounds of reflection, and one round claiming our next action, and finished in a closing circle. The first round was typically a reflection on the actions we had taken in our own lives responding to the research inquiry. The second round was unique and varied.

The opening and closing circles marked the edges of our gathering, creating a temporary container in time and space. At the opening, the flock arrived back at the nest, the home territory of the Rewilding project, in a circle around a small round table setup as an altar honoring the instinctual feminine, serving as a visual reminder of our research intention.

Here we wove the circle in an embodied way. To start, I lit a candle, set it on the altar, and offered my hand to the woman on my left, asking "May I take your hand and *begin* to weave the circle?" She, in turn, would light her candle, and extend her left hand to the woman to her left and ask, "May I take your hand and *continue* to weave the circle?" This gesture rippled around until the last woman would invite me to take her hand and *complete* the circle. We would pause to ground before taking a 'feeling pulse', sharing a few words reflecting our emotional state.

At the end, we again circled the altar, took a closing feeling pulse, enacted a 'flapping away' gesture, and returned to the laboratories of our own lives to continue our individual research. The feeling pulses reflected the transmutation; the shift of energy created through the act of gathering.

In our first circle weaving, I also incorporated an invocation and a blessing to establish expectations around how we would engage and why we were gathering.

The objects on the altar became the fulcrum of our opening and closing circles. The clay goddess talismans resting on the altar connected us to our ancestors, and the blessing expressed and extended our intention to rewild the feminine into the future.

As part of our last circle weaving, I read a blessing for all we had been shown. In a tight circle, arms interlaced, eyes closed, swaying in a slow rhythm, we sang three rounds of a song celebrating the nature of flow, acknowledging what we had become – tributaries merging as a flowing river. In the residue of the resonance, we paused, taking a step beyond gratitude into reverence. We were now a ripple of disruption, perhaps more feral, a current flowing through the river of patriarchy.

Through the alchemy of the circle, we invited in what we knew, wed it to what we valued, and returned with what we learned back into our own lives. Within the alembic, we were rewilding and re-animating our collected feminine bones. Upon completion of the project, every single researcher expressed a desire to continue. We intuitively knew there was something here, something that fed our instinctual natures and supported our efforts to transform, and we did not want to lose it. What began as a six-week research project continued as a seven-year circle.

You can't ask a group to trust; it is not something to be commanded, it is an emergent quality. It arises from a group that comes to know one another authentically and over time, with all their edges polished or rough, to co-create that third thing, relationship. The person facilitating the experience, be it one or many individuals, really does imprint on the tone of the group. When a person who leads the group recognizes everyone has value, all are co-creators, and that the group is coming together not to admire the facilitator but for a collective purpose, a tone of trust, motivation, and openness emerges. Inside this cauldron, wisdom stands a good chance of manifesting.

With the turning of each page that day in my office, I learned more about the "Ten Constants." Although I had been unaware of them previously, I saw these threads were present in the weaving of our circle. We were not just a group of women coming together to explore a common inquiry, we were a wisdom circle. As the authors of the book share, while each person is a teacher in the circle, the real teacher is the circle itself.

Why Wisdom Circles Matter

In *Evolution's Purpose; An Integral Interpretation of the Scientific Story of Our Origins* (2012), Steve McIntosh explains how he believes *values* influence cultural evolution. Each stage of culture, he says, develops as a result of a push and a pull. The shortcomings and pathologies of a current worldview are the push. The attraction to an alternative future worldview is the pull. When enough people are no longer aligned with the values of the current culture and instead are expressing the values of an alternative worldview, the structures and institutions supporting the old values will begin to disintegrate. In this dissolving, new structures will appear to support a new view.

Wisdom Circles, as new structures, are a way forward, a way of socially organizing, fostering an emerging vision of a wiser flourishing culture. Cultivating a wisdom circle can lend stability for us as women – and men – living within a patriarchy. When the world is fragmented, breaking down and apart as it is now, new growth will appear in the cracks. This is where roots can take hold and grow beneath the current structure, breaking it apart. Now is our time.

While we cannot excise ourselves, as part of a whole, from the overculture whose goals may not be compatible with ours, we can actively co-author our own *living* story resonant with our values within the container of a trusted circle. Becoming a participant in a story field can be a form of activism, story activism. Creating and participating in circles can be a revolutionary act, as stories may be the best intervention point to counter a patriarchy run amok. Circles can be a cauldron of story-making where we practice a new story inside an old worn-out story. We don't just imagine a more compelling way of being, we embody it.

As I write this, where I live it is now the time of whale migrations. With the migrating pods of whales, I am fantasizing about pods of feminine rewilders. What would happen if we had circle upon circle of rewilders? Pods of rewilders of the instinctual feminine swimming in the ocean of patriarchy? And what if the story fields being spun inside each circle, each pod, congealed into larger and larger story fields? Then one day the influence would be like a contagion changing the balance, shifting and transforming the culture. Filling the culture, the ocean, transforming it, making it something different.

How to Start a Sacred Women's Drum Circle

Sophie Messager

Five years ago, I decided to start a drum circle because I was eager to participate in one, but there was nothing like it in my area. Little did I know that this step would not only lead to a thriving circle, but it would also deepen my connection to the power of the drum. I'm so grateful for that decision, as it has shaped my journey in ways I couldn't have anticipated.

I am going to share my experience with you and offer tips for creating your own drum circle. I will cover practical aspects like choosing your location, organising the structure of your circle, and gathering your materials, drums included! I'll also share insights on holding space for your group, managing energy, and how the drum itself can guide the experience. I will also tell you about how to make your circle both sacred and social, and how to trust the rhythm to help everything fall into place.

If you experience impostor syndrome before starting a drum circle, remember that every experienced space holder started just where you are. Let me share how I've learned to create and hold these sacred gatherings, and to help you find your own way.

Write down a simple list of everything you will need to think about:

- Where will you run your circle? (indoors, outdoors, can you start simply with little cost like in your house or garden?)

- What time will it take place and for how long?

- Will the circle be intimate or open to larger groups?

- How many drums will you need? (Not everyone who attends a circle owns a drum.)

- How will you advertise it?

- What kind of atmosphere are you hoping to create?

- Do you need any specific measures for physical or emotional safety (e.g., providing cushions, ensuring accessibility)?

- Will you provide snacks or drinks for after the session?

- How will you invite people to the circle (social media, word of mouth, flyers)?

- Do you have a contingency plan if something unexpected happens, like bad weather for an outdoor circle?

Getting your Space Ready

Whether you are using a woodland geodome like mine, or friend's garden or a community hall – being at least thirty minutes early is essential. This gives you time to set the space up physically but also energetically.

As you arrange your central altar and lay out drums and percussion instruments around it, you're already beginning to create the container for the circle. Use this time to ground yourself too – you'll need this to hold space for others.

Clear timing helps everyone feel secure. I let people know exactly when to arrive (for example, from 6.30 for a 7pm start), and I ask people to arrive on time to avoid disturbing the sacred space. I'm specific about late arrivals – they need to wait quietly until a round finishes before joining. It might feel strict, but I've found this clarity actually helps people relax.

Getting Started

When it comes to the circle itself, starting with a grounding meditation helps immensely. It doesn't need to be complex – just guiding people to connect with their breath and feel the earth beneath them works beautifully.

Start with a brief sharing circle, giving each person about a couple of minutes to speak. You can use a talking stick (one of my drum beaters is perfect) for the rounds of sharing, and explain that only the person holding the stick will be talking, and that sharing is optional. This removes the pressure to share whilst also giving people a chance to decide whether they want to share or not. You can also use a rattle as a gentle timekeeper, reminding people if they share for a bit too long you will gently shake it – this helps to keep boundaries lightly, and often brings laughter.

Share some simple rules about the circle, such as confidentiality, speaking from the I (as in for oneself instead of others), and from the heart (waiting for the talking stick to come to join before deciding what you will share so you can listen to others).

The sacred space flows naturally from here – maybe opening directions together, cleansing with rattles or smoke in pairs (depending on whether smoke is appropriate and/or comfortable for people – always ask if anyone is sensitive to smoke).

You can then start by setting individual intentions, and use these to weave in a joint intention for each round of drumming. Trust your intuition with the joint intention – you'll be surprised how naturally it comes when you're in the space.

For the drumming itself, invite people to join you into a gentle heartbeat rhythm to start with, then to trust their hearts and hands when guided to do something else. The beats often evolve from cacophony to beautiful synchrony over the course of the drumming round.

I find that three rounds work well – two for personal needs and one for the world/wider community. Each round will have its own character, its own energy. Do not try to control this – let it flow. Some rounds will be gentle, others powerful. All are perfect.

Closing the Circle

Closing is just as important as opening. You can lead the group into a closing song (find a simple chant that resonates with you and your group – I prefer something easy that everyone can join in), and then allow time for chatting and sharing refreshments. Never underestimate the power of cake and informal connection to help integrate the experience! If you're just starting out, begin simply.

I like to bring a homemade cake to share and have about thirty minutes at the end for socialising. It helps to ground people back into the reality before they leave and also to foster connections.

Timing and Numbers

Start with smaller groups – maybe eight to twelve people max.

Keep your structure simple: meditation, brief sharing, drumming, closing. Ninety minutes is a good length to begin with. As your confidence grows, you'll naturally find ways to expand and adapt.

Dealing with Challenges

Remember that challenges will come – late arrivals, varying experience levels, different energy needs, emotional challenges. Meet them with grace and clear boundaries. Trust that the drums will help harmonise the group.

Most importantly, know that this is your journey. While I've shared my way, you'll develop your own style, your own rhythm. Start where you are, trust your intuition, and let the drum guide you. Each circle will teach you something new. Reflect on each circle, and what there was to learn for the future. The key is creating a safe container where people feel free to express themselves through the drum's voice.

Hold the space lightly but clearly, balance sacred with social, and trust the process. Before long, you'll find your own way of weaving these elements together. Remember, the drum has been calling people into circle for thousands of years. You're not alone in this journey – you're part of an ancient tradition that continues to evolve. Trust the drum, trust yourself, and most importantly, enjoy the journey.

'Creativity for the Soul' – The Wheel of the Year and our Internal Seasons

Pippa Grace

Deep within a magical patch of land called the Haven in Bristol, UK, there is a witchy round house. Open the wooden door and you find a fire, the scent of sage, a home-made cake, and a gathering circle of women. Of course, things begin with the most natural age-old ritual: tea and a gaggle of chatter. After a while the words start to fall away, and we settle into the creative work of the day.

Creativity is as cyclical as the natural world around us, and the hormonal world within. It ebbs and flows, comes to us at times in torrents, and at others it is elusive, hidden out of view. It may flourish with the return of the light in spring and dwindle to an ember in the hearth throughout the winter months. Or you may find that you have your own internal seasons that take a unique path, beating in tune to your personal drumbeat/heartbeat; sometimes chasing you, sometimes out of reach.

Nine years ago, during the winter months, a creative spark was simmering in me. It demanded to be heard, and I let its dance play out, having no sense where it might take me. In the process I spliced together established writing workshops with my love of clay and sculptural work. A hybrid form was born that I named Creativity for the Soul.

The first workshop fell in time with Imbolc, it was unintentional. But as time progressed so the Wheel of the Year worked its magic on us and the workshops aligned with the seasons. We fell into its rhythm and began to meet intentionally on the cross-quarter fire festivals: Samhain, Imbolc, Beltane and Samhain. Later this extended to include the equinoxes and solstices.

Humans are meaning making creatures, we understand the world around us through the stories we tell, and I choose to tap into this rich seam to underpin the work. All the workshops are grounded in, and illuminated by, myth, fairy-tale, folklore, seasonal festivals and personal dreams. A language that speaks to our innately creative souls.

The women start to settle onto cushions on the floor of the round house, we are weaving the magic of the circle. Within the hush we listen in to the seasonal wisdom of the land around us and I read an extract from the wonderful Glennie Kindred[*] [†], deepening our understanding of the festival. We pick oracle, goddess or soul cards[‡] and take time to share, reflecting on our personal journeys across the changing seasons since last meeting. There is deep listening, and reflection. Laughter and tears. The wisdom in the group blows me away again and again. And then, notebooks in hand, we write. I guide the group through an exercise using prompts to encourage the free flow of their pens, away from their inner critics. There is a deep silence except for the scratching of pens on paper. The prompts take us on a journey: sometimes into a wood, or underground, to a waterfall, climbing a mountain, or deep into a valley. But the words are only suggestive, the women take them wherever their unconscious

[*]   Kindred, Glennie, *Earth Wisdom* (Hay House, 2011)

[†]   Kindred, Glennie, *Sacred Earth Celebrations* (Permanent Publications, 2014)

[‡]   Koff Chapin, Deborah, Soul Cards (1996) are one of my favourites – open to all sorts of soul connections

needs to go. Their personal experience and dreams come through again and again, along with the images that mean most to them. Metaphor abounds.

As the day unfolds we take time to reflect on and share pertinent parts of our writing. Frequently we find images and thoughts that run through several women's words, as if we are tapping into our collective roots. To break the intensity we take time out on the land, often collecting natural materials before gathering to share lunch.

In the afternoon we change from pen and paper to clay; if the writing has prompted us to switch off our critical brain, the clay wakes up our haptic sense, taking us deeper into an embodied sense of being. I read a seasonal myth whilst sculpting takes place, maybe Demeter and Persephone; Vasalisa the Wise; Brigid and the Sacred Flame; the Descent of Inanna.[*] This is a different sort of quiet, as the women dig into the clay, feeling it in their hands, rolling it and shaping it. The women make abstract forms, mythological creatures, images from the story – whatever their souls want to speak out. They frequently incorporate the natural materials they have collected. Reminding us again of the cyclical nature of our work. As we take time to share what has been created, so women find connections they hadn't imagined from their writing in the morning. The process has allowed things to ferment and develop, to reappear in new forms. There is another hush as we take all this in, reflect on what has been created throughout the day. And then laughter and voices return, we hold the circle once more to find our ending, and the day is complete.

From one workshop to the next, as we turn through the wheel, so things change and develop. And the clay sculptures represent this cyclical nature, spirals and spherical shapes, and when viewed in relation to sculptures made throughout the year a circle of development may be seen.

And the women keep coming back. Keep walking the wheel. One has been there since the very first workshop. Together we have moved through life changes, illness, children growing up, relationships ending and beginning. External things that weave their way into our internal, creative world. Guided by that great big beating heart of the rhythm of the year. The sun increasing and decreasing,

---

[*] Tomlin, Keli *Walk the Wheel* (Self Published, 2023) is a wonderful collection of seasonal children's stories

the moon waxing and waning, nature growing and becoming dormant again. Our internal creative cycles, our winterings and flourishings, the two work hand in hand supporting one another and enriching our lives.

Uplifting, fun, truly food for the soul.

Kayamokshini Farrimond

The workshops have become my seasonal, nurturing balm, like honey for the soul.

Jules Allan

The Medicine of Sharing Circles with Art for Wellbeing

Eva Živa Blažková

Holding women's sharing circles with art for wellbeing has been an important part of my life mission for many years alongside creating artwork that honors, celebrates and heals the feminine. My experience is that *if women gather to create and share from the space of their hearts, profound healing can happen on the individual and the collective level as well.*

For me, sharing circles are safely held spaces where we can take the masks off and share the vulnerable parts of self with trusted others without the fear of judgment. Being truly heard and being able to listen to the authentic versions of others generates the sense of belonging and deep compassion.

In my practice I felt called to expand the experience of sharing beyond the spoken language which resulted in exploration of the chosen themes through creative activities. If we allow ourselves to be led by intuition, creativity has the potential of being the language of the subconscious: it not only allows us to step out of the controlling mode of our minds but also invites the unknown parts of ourselves and opens a new gate into self discovery.

This way of creating requires that we fully merge with the process and give up any idea of what the result should be: *to become a tool of creation rather than creator.* This can be challenging, as most of us were taught the very opposite. Therefore I like to include some gentle bodywork (often in the form of sounds and breathing exercises) before the creative activity as that helps us to leave the brain world and enter the body fully. Asking the body what colour she wants to use, what shapes she is drawn to, what materials she wants to touch is a simple way to unlock this mode of creation.

As I am also interested in ecotherapy (and I am recognizing how alienated from nature many people living in the cities are), I started to experiment with ways to mediate more experience with nature through the sharing circles. Using, or at least including, materials foraged in nature became a wonderful adventure and widened my own creative practice: creating paints from natural pigments; preparing an oak ink; plant and flower bashing; wool felting; making natural treasure mobiles; creating figures from sticks, roots, leaves, stones, shells; decorating stones… I held several circles in the woods which was a truly beautiful experience – being held by Mother Earth at the same time.

Interestingly, the most powerful sharing circles are often those that are devoted to the most challenging themes. I won't ever forget our Mother's Grief circle. There was a woman who gave birth to her dead daughter six months into her pregnancy, just a few days before she attended the circle. The spirit of her daughter was present in the space, in her crying empty womb and tender breasts ready to give milk to a being who was no longer alive. We all felt her loss so deeply. We all cried as she shared her story. And in this shared grief, these streams of cleansing tears, the energy started to move from dense and heavy into a different lighter quality. We supported this transmutation process with painting the stones previously chosen as a visual representation of our grief. With the colors emerging on the stones the grief medicine formed: *being with the grief, feeling it in the body, recognizing its importance and valuing its message.*

That is true for all the so-called 'negative' emotions (I prefer to call them 'dark guests', as in Rumi's poem). Another circle I will remember forever was one with the theme Vital Power of Anger. In circles I normally encourage the women to use compassionate sounds after each sharing to express we heard the woman who just talked and enhance the power of her intentions. When we were working with anger it felt appropriate to roar instead – and wow, such a powerful energy was generated with our animal-like roars coming from the depth of our harmed souls for all the injustices, suppression and abuse we (and our female ancestors) experienced as women! We became love-warriors, painting our bodies with marks and symbols of power with the body paints. We drummed and danced and roared again. At least for that moment we managed to befriend anger – the most forbidden emotion for women.

I am clearly called to do a lot of shadow work and I recognize why: *in a world that applauds empty positiveness above depth and authenticity it is a revolutionary act to create a space for the 'dark' and 'difficult' aspect of the human soul.* If we look further, the 'dark' correlates with the earthy and feminine that has been neglected, overpowered or demonized for centuries. Neglect of these qualities caused the great imbalance in our postmodern world and I also believe that it is at the root of the inhuman behavior we witness around the world today – because the individuals who hide and fear their own shadows are likely to project them on other people (or even whole nations). Acting from the place of unhealed trauma multiplies the trauma. And trauma is born where the energy is stuck in our body minds. When we invite it to move we also invite healing.

So offering spaces to work in a gentle and creative way with wounds and giving attention to the feminine (often while simultaneously creating a connection to the natural world) is my small way of helping to build something different beyond the patriarchal system: *a community of self-aware people who are brave enough to share their authentic selves, own their traumas and won't pass them any further. Above all, a community that values the Feminine and the Earth.*

Summer Solstice Ecstasy

Ger Moane

Energy ripples from the movements of the big crowd gathering on the Hill for sunrise. Already we are in a beautiful spiral of energy. The golden globe rises slowly – first an arc, then a half ball, and finally the full sun. Joyous cheers rise over and over from the crowd.

The *boom boom boom* of drums rings out.

We begin a pound with feet on earth that builds to a crescendo. Hands and feet tingle as soles hit the ground in rhythm with the beat of drums. Pound,

pound, lightly to begin with, we look for flow that takes us higher, we move, senses alert, aligning together. Pound, pound – we are not all together yet, there are still different rhythms and notes.

A deep rhythm gathers pace but is still not settled. We lighten the pound of our feet on the ground, ears and bodies strain, full alert, allow rhythm to settle. It gathers, and all we need is to stay together until the rhythm hits its stride. We are ready for the moment when we rise together. Odd notes fade and all we hear is harmonized rhythmic pounding and drums beating. Hold it, hold it, we keep to the central rhythm, hang on, wait, let it gather. We grow stronger, we connect, we flow. Let the rhythm take over, swelling and rolling, taking us with it. Feet let go. We pound as one with drums, energy gathers and rises. We glisten, eyes shine, nostrils flare, hands and feet tingle, throats ready. Breath gets deeper, mouths open and ragged murmurs begin that quickly become single tones. Now we are heaving, pounding, toning, immersed in beautiful joyous ecstatic energy. We rush along to a crescendo, entire bodies tingle. As the rhythms break, we are barely aware of bodies but only of sweeping energy crashing and breaking over us as we abandon our flow, jumping, shouting, screaming, singing, clapping then hugging and embracing. What joy! We revel in waves of pleasure, elation, love, catch each other's shining faces and sparkling eyes, share the glory of the moment.

Mabon

Nia Solomon

when the sun and moon share equally at autumn equinox, I walk a spiral slowly on wet grass. Curls of mugwort smoke make a temple of the garden the citrus scent a direct line back to when ritual was common as cornflakes

I'm making it up, shaking a deer skin rattle at the sky, my own brand of magic I've foraged a rainbow, amber apples, hips and haws, onyx elder umbels for mandala making. Wild asparagus ferns whose feathery yellow whips nod towards winter.

I mimic the orange ombre beech, turn inward lengthen my breath like the nights to come. Anchor myself into now and now and now until every inhale is prayer every exhale an invitation to arrive wholly – holy – In my skin as a place of worship

where worries *will fracking begin again? Is there milk in the fridge for tea? Will the tortoise survive hibernation?* all fall away like spent leaves. I arrive thankful for the soft shell of my body, the fruit of my action. I contemplate symmetry a halo of field maple a circle of sloe.

Creating a Simple Ritual to Honour and Support Women Through Life Transitions

Sophie Messager

Let me share with you how to create a simple ceremony. This can be adapted to hold a woman through any of life's transitions: whether she's entering menarche, motherhood, the menopause, or navigating any of life's thresholds, here's how to weave magic and meaning into her journey.

Setting the intentions

Meet with the woman who wishes to have the ceremony. Invite her to share her vision, her intentions of what she would like the ceremony to look and feel like, and what she would like to achieve from it. Offer suggestions and ideas you think she might like. Be sensitive to her needs, her spiritual beliefs and what feels right for her.

Gathering the circle

Help her gather her friends and loved ones. Call in those who truly see her, who've walked similar paths, who hold pieces of the wisdom she's seeking. Keep it intimate – too many people can scatter the energy. I find that somewhere between six and twelve women creates the perfect container.

As you plan the day remember that less is more and create plenty of spaciousness in the ceremony.

Creating sacred space

Create a womb-like space: soft, warm, and nurturing. Think beautiful fabrics dotted around the space, fairy lights, candles, cushions placed in a circle. Your central altar might include crystals, flowers, oracle cards, art, and objects/figures representing the transition the woman is going through, and/or the elements. You can also invite the guests to bring something to place on the altar. And of course, you can bring a drum or several if you or guests have them and maybe some percussion instruments too.

Welcoming everyone in

As the women arrive, invite them to drop into sacred space. You might welcome them with a smoke or scented spray cleansing ritual as they enter. If you have a helper to do this, you can play the drum in the space as they arrive, letting the rhythm draw everyone into their bodies and away from the rushing world outside. You could open sacred space by welcoming each direction and each element, and/or simply speaking your intentions for this gathering and the sacred circle you're creating.

Honouring her journey – the heart of the ceremony

Place the woman being celebrated on a special seat (you could setup an armchair or other comfy seat, think throne rather than hard chair), and crown her with flowers. There's something so powerful about physically marking someone as special, sacred. You might invite guests to wash her feet or hands in a bowl with scented oils and rose petals, an ancient act of blessing that says, "You are worthy of being tended to."

Have a circle of introduction, starting by sharing a few breaths together, and invite each woman to speak her name, and the name of her mother and grandmother, to invite the presence of ancestors in the space.

Invite guests to share a story, a blessing, a piece of wisdom, a strength they see in the woman. There are often tears! Let the laughter bubble up too. Share gifts that carry meaning beyond their physical form and the moment: a bead from each guest to share to make a communal necklace to keep and cherish, a shawl to wrap her in community's embrace.

Honour her body

Share some gentle touch by massaging her hands and/or feet, or plaiting her hair in a fancy way. Whilst this is happening, you can also lead the group into a simple chant apt for the occasion (you can accompany it with the drum if you have one). You could also do some art together, a collage of wishes for the journey ahead, vision board style, using cutouts from old magazines, with each guest sharing the meaning of their chosen picture once it is complete, or a lighting of a number of candles that represent the phases of what the woman is going through (months of pregnancy, experience of menarche, matrescence and sagescence for a menopaused woman...)

Make sure you're also planning the support that extends beyond the ceremony. Who's bringing meals? Who can she call at 3am? Who's checking in next week, next month? Write it down and make it real. This could be captured on a beautiful piece of paper or card, whilst people are doing the collage.

Weaving the web of support and closing the ceremony

Pass some wool or string around the circle and have everyone wrap it a couple of times around their wrist or ankle. Once everyone is bound by the thread, pass scissors around to cut it and have everyone knot the thread, with an invitation to keep it until a certain milestone has happened (in the case of a mother blessing, when the baby has been born).

You could also gift everyone a tealight, with an invitation to light it and send good wishes to the woman being honoured at an agreed time. This might be the beginning of labour, the morning of a significant surgery, the anniversary of a loss, or before starting a new chapter such as the end of a significant relationship or moving home.

Then, when the time is right (a good couple of hours is a nice length), have a final sharing circle, maybe some drumming and singing, then announce the end of the ritual, and close sacred space.

Grounding the sacred with a feast

After the sacred time and before people leave, share some food together. The practice of sharing food helps weave the sacred experience back into ordinary life, reminding us that ceremony and daily life need not be separate. It could as simple as tea and cake, or you could ask each guest to bring a dish to share and have a feast.

Remember, this is just a framework – a basket to hold your own creative offerings. Each ceremony will be as unique as the woman it honours. Trust your intuition, follow what feels right, and don't forget to document the magic (and take photos if she's comfortable with that). The key is creating space where a woman feels truly witnessed in her transition. Where she knows, deep in her bones, that she is not alone on this journey.

My hope is that we might rebirth new customs into accessible practices supporting women and making it the norm once more. Though we may not have much practice in this in our culture, I believe we all have an innate understanding of what is needed to craft a meaningful ritual.

The Labyrinth

Hazel Evans

Welcome to the threshold of your journey. You are here, at the gateway to the labyrinth of your divine wisdom. All that is required of you now is to accept the invitation of this quest and set foot on your path. The labyrinth takes you into your deepest self, then brings you back with expanded awareness and a renewed sense of who you are; maybe there are even soul gifts and insights awaiting you.

The labyrinth is an ancient symbol of the sacred spiral of life, where you get to experience the wisdom of the triple goddess: life, death, and rebirth. There is only one way in and one way out. Your life path leads you in, and transformation occurs in the centre as it is a portal between worlds where gifts of the soul are given. Then, your path out is your rebirth.

The journey is one of seeing truth through the eyes of love. Keep your heart open. It leads you forward into the unknown, into the mirror of self-reflection to see all your shadows and all your light. It requires courage to open and receive the deep wisdom of the labyrinth. Ultimately, it leads to the illumination of your magnificence, wisdom, power, and all that is within you.

Do you choose to accept your path, with all your shadows and all your light? If so, step forward…

The Labyrinth Creative Journey

With this creative journey, you will create and walk into your own labyrinth. You can use this journey alone, with a sister, or in your women's circles. It is powerful to take time out for yourself to do this and create a sacred space or altar to support your journey. The important thing is to follow your inner guidance all the way; make this ritual your own.

You will need the following

- A piece of paper or your journal

- A pen or set of colouring pens/pencils

- Optional power objects, candles, crystals, or artefacts to help guide you

- Optional music list of inspiring tunes to guide your way

Draw Your Labyrinth

- Take a sheet of paper or a page in your journal. Draw a large spiral, circling around until you get to the centre, leaving a 1-2cm gap between the lines as you spiral inwards. (For this exercise, we will work with the spiral to form a simple labyrinth, but you may wish to draw your own version of a more complex labyrinth, for example, the Chartres Labyrinth.)

- Place your power object at the top of your page and light your candle, speaking out your intention for this sacred ritual.

Meditative Journey

- Seated, place both hands on your womb space, forming a triangle.

- Eyes closed, relax and focus on your soft breath coming in through your yoni.

- Ask your higher self or guides that you work with to ignite the deep wisdom of your womb, your space of sacred creation.

- Take some deep breaths.

- Imagine yourself walking down a long corridor in the dark.

- In the distance, there is a light.

- As you approach the light, you see it illuminates the entrance of a labyrinth.

- What does it look like?

- Do you accept the challenge to go inside?

- Breathe. Open your eyes and draw how you saw the entrance to your labyrinth, including any symbols or words on the page at the entrance to your spiral.

Step Into the Labyrinth

- Start your music.

- Take your pen.

- Place the index finger of your free hand at the entrance of the labyrinth.

- Feel your way, as if you and your whole body are stepping in.

- Move your finger around the spiral slowly, with your eyes semi-closed, and always keep your finger in contact with the page as if you are walking inside.

- You may see images or have words or messages appear. Write and draw them onto the page and keep following the path inwards towards the centre, feeling, sensing, drawing, and writing as you go.

- When you arrive at the centre, keep your finger there and close your eyes. You are now deep inside the labyrinth.

- Take a moment to breathe in silence, bringing awareness to the intention you set for this journey.

- Ask your higher self, your guides, or the Universe to show you the soul gift of this journey. It may come as a vision, instruction, or symbol. However it appears to you, allow yourself to feel the vibration of this gift for a few moments, anchoring it into the sacred space of your heart and womb.

- When ready, begin your journey as you spiral back out of the labyrinth. Again, notice what appears in your inner vision along the way and add it to your page.

- Before you make the final move out of the labyrinth, take a moment to give gratitude for all you have witnessed and received on your journey.

- Then move your finger over the threshold and exit the labyrinth.

- You can complete the page as you wish by adding more colours, symbols, and words to help anchor the messages and wisdom of your creative journey.

Have you ever walked into a labyrinth before? I have visited many and have always found it to be a very powerful experience. Each labyrinth carries a unique vibration and energy field.

I once visited a private woodland labyrinth where a woman from one of my women's circles in the Netherlands had made it herself with bricks and stones. It gave me the most potent and beautiful gifts in the centre, like sunshine beaming into my heart. Afterwards, she told me that she had encoded the labyrinth with golden sunshine energy, so it had definitely worked its magic on me.

Visiting labyrinths can make wonderful sacred days out with your women's circle. Is there one near you? Maybe you might like to make a simple one out of sticks in a woodland or stones on a beach with your sisters. It's a beautiful practice in a small group of women to hold space for each other as you journey in and out of the labyrinth and share the wisdom of your journeys together afterwards.

May this creative labyrinth practice help you access your intuitive guidance to a greater degree and give you practice for when you visit a real-life labyrinth.

Introducing Sagescence: Understanding the Becoming of a Wise Woman and Reframing Perimenopause and Menopause as a Sacred Rite of Passage

Jane Hardwicke Collings

We know this feeling. We've definitely navigated change like this before – at least once, and possibly many more times. Our first experience of this kind of profound transformation was adolescence, when, over a period of years, we became our adult, fertile selves. This becoming wasn't an overnight shift; for many, it was a slow, sometimes tumultuous process of growing into who we would become.[*]

Then, if or when we became mothers, we experienced another life-altering transformation: matrescence. The process of becoming a mother is similarly gradual, often slow, and full of profound changes to our identity, roles, relationships, and bodies.[†]

Now, as we reclaim menopause and reframe it as a sacred and transformational time, we can connect it to these other two major life stages – adolescence and matrescence. These life stages all share commonalities: they involve physical, emotional, neurological, and spiritual transformations. Each is a rite of passage that profoundly changes us, and each brings new roles, responsibilities, and opportunities for growth.

Sagescence is the third major rite of passage in a woman's life. It is the journey of becoming a wise woman – the Sage. And like adolescence and matrescence, it is a gradual, sometimes challenging, process of transformation.

---

[*]   neurolaunch.com/what-is-pruning-in-the-brain

[†]   reuters.com/business/healthcare-pharmaceuticals/
study-shows-how-womans-brain-reorganizes-during-pregnancy-2024-09-16

The Similarities Between Adolescence, Matrescence, and Sagescence

1. Physical Changes

- **Adolescence:** Our bodies undergo significant hormonal shifts that initiate fertility.[‡]

- **Matrescence:** Pregnancy, birth, and postpartum bring hormonal and physical transformations to support motherhood.[§]

- **Sagescence:** Our bodies wind down the menstrual cycle after 40+ years of cycling, or less if we experience premature or induced menopause. In physiological menopause, the decline of oestrogen and progesterone reshapes our physical experience, often with accompanying symptoms.[¶]

2. Neurological Changes

- **Adolescence:** Marked by neural pruning – the brain reorganizes itself to become more efficient by cutting away unused neural connections and strengthening others.[**]

- **Matrescence:** The brain undergoes structural changes, particularly in areas related to empathy, caregiving, and problem-solving. This rewiring helps new mothers attune to their babies and navigate their new role.[††]

- **Sagescence:** Neural pruning happens again. The decline in progesterone and oestrogen shifts our brain function, making us less inclined to accommodate others at our own expense. We become more self-focused and assertive, with greater clarity and intuition. Our brains shift from nurturing everyone else to focusing on our own needs and desires.[‡‡]

[‡]   neurolaunch.com/what-is-pruning-in-the-brain

[§]   reuters.com/business/healthcare-pharmaceuticals/
study-shows-how-womans-brain-reorganizes-during-pregnancy-2024-09-16

[¶]   thegroveclinic.com.au/blogs/news/menopause-the-second-spring

[**]   psychologytoday.com/us/blog/inspire-to-rewire/201402/
pruning-myelination-and-the-remodeling-adolescent-brain

[††]   reuters.com/business/healthcare-pharmaceuticals/
study-shows-how-womans-brain-reorganizes-during-pregnancy-2024-09-16

[‡‡]   ted.com/talks/lisa_mosconi_how_menopause_affects_the_brain

3. Psychological and Emotional Changes

- **Adolescence**: A time of identity formation – a quest to figure out who we are and where we fit in the world.

- **Matrescence**: Brings a new identity: mother. This role requires renegotiating relationships, responsibilities, and priorities.[*]

- **Sagescence**: Prompts us to revisit and reevaluate our identity once again. As our caregiving roles shift, we may feel a loss of purpose or identity. But Sagescence invites us to step into our wise woman role, with new priorities and responsibilities focused on personal growth, leadership, and legacy.

4. Behavioral and Relational Changes

- **Adolescence**: Often brings rebellion and a desire for independence.

- **Matrescence**: Shifts our focus to caregiving and nurturing relationships.

- **Sagescence**: We once again seek independence – this time from societal expectations and the roles that no longer serve us. We are prompted to renegotiate our relationships, set boundaries, and prioritize our own needs.

Embracing the Gifts of Sagescence

Menopause, like childbirth, has been pathologized by modern medicine. Women are often led to believe that menopause is a problem to be solved – an experience to be managed with hormone replacement therapy (HRT), now called Menopause Hormone Therapy (MHT), or other medical interventions. But menopause is not a problem. It is a sacred rite of passage into the second half of life.

When we normalize menopause and view it as a natural and necessary transformation, we can fully embrace the gifts it brings:

- **A Return to Self**: After years of accommodating others, we are prompted to prioritize ourselves.

- **Increased Intuition and Visionary Capacity**: As we become less reactive, due to changes to our amygdala, we gain greater clarity and foresight.

---

[*] popsugar.com/family/matrescence-essay-49343052

- **Healing Opportunities:** Menopause asks us to revisit and heal past wounds, especially those related to our Red Thread or Motherline.

- **Leadership Skills:** We are primed to step into leadership roles with wisdom, empathy, and long-term thinking.

- **Enhanced Pleasure:** Yes, our orgasms get stronger and longer!

In Traditional Chinese medicine, menopause is called 'Second Spring' – a time of rebirth. Sagescence offers us the opportunity to heal, grow, and step into our wise woman role with strength, clarity, and purpose.[†]

A well-known First Nations American teaching says it all: "At menarche, a girl meets her power; through menstruation, she practices her power; and at menopause, she becomes her power."

The Importance of Reclaiming Sagescence

Our world needs well-initiated, wise women. We need women who embrace the transformational and healing opportunities that menopause offers. These are the women the Earth needs now – healed, strong, soft, and powerful.

Sadly, our culture encourages women to avoid menopause – to stay youthful, to stop the symptoms, to resist the change. This robs us of our wise women and denies younger generations the elders they seek. This may be seen in the future as a betrayal.

It's time to reclaim menopause as a sacred rite of passage. It's time to honor the journey of Sagescence and step into our power as wise women.

The Journey Through Sagescence

Perimenopause to postmenopause can be a decade-long process. During this time, we undergo profound transformations – physically, emotionally, and spiritually. We experience neural pruning, just like in adolescence. We meet the unresolved issues of our lives. We are prompted to heal the unhealed parts of ourselves so we can enter the second half of life strong and well on every level.

If we choose to take it, Sagescence is an underworld journey – a descent into

† thegroveclinic.com.au/blogs/news/menopause-the-second-spring

the depths of ourselves, where we confront our fears, wounds, and unmet needs. It's a journey of rebirth and renewal. When we emerge, we are the wise women the world needs.

Sagescence is a time of harvest – a time to gather the fruits of our life's experiences and step into our next phase with wisdom, clarity, and purpose, to be the women the Earth needs now.

Womandala

Annette Vaucanson Kelly

I want to prowl naked on the soft sweet Earth,
my hair a tangle, my skin smeared
with soil and mulch and leaf-litter,
before I slip into the cold clear wild waters.
Otterly at home.

From the soft nest of my pillow, I raise my head to look at the clock. It's 4.30pm and I have just woken from a nap. All thoughts of showering off the bits of vegetation probably still in my pants dissipate in the semi-darkness. The skin on my feet and legs feels peach soft, from walking barefoot in rain-soaked grass, and I want to keep it that way.

This morning I took part in Womandala.

Once a year for the summer solstice, women gather in a secluded Indian sculpture park in the wilds of Wicklow, to create in silence a mandala with their naked bodies. This was my first participation.

A hazy ray of sunshine welcomed me as I walked through and out of the yoni portal into the sacred space, and I took off my shoes. It felt necessary to walk barefoot on the earth, to leave footprints on the spongy grass beneath my feet. I didn't wash my face in early morning dew, as is one of the Bealtaine customs in these Celtic lands. But I crouched down and rubbed my palms in the soft wet grass, and I streaked my cheekbones with some early morning rain, like a solstice blessing.

The circle was opened, and the master of ceremony invoked the four elements and their corresponding cardinal point: east/air, south/fire, west/water, north/earth. We were blessed with so much water! Rain through the night, then drizzle, then more rain as, gently guided by mandala artist Mayumi Nakabayashi, we made the flower mandala – petals kept sticking to my fingers, it was so wet.

When the time came for Womandala, the heavens opened. Our host suggested a "slow, mindful undressing," and she chanted and hummed as she took off her clothes. My undressing was more like for a sea swim in winter – removing layer after layer of clothing and stuffing them all into a bag to keep them from the rain. We all walked out onto the field, gathering in a circle around the flower mandala to rehearse the positions. Standing, we hummed in harmony to tune into a powerful vibration. I could feel the energy rising, all of us part of it. Rain on my cold skin, eyes closed, a lungful of air. The wet air sparkled with excitement. No self-consciousness or awkwardness. Just a grounded energy in a safe space alert with consciousness, joyful and playful.

The flower mandala was like a womb, with a wide-open centre for the solstice sun to illuminate. Mayumi got us into position. Eight of us lay around it in the foetal position, navel aligned with the four cardinal points, while an outer ring, of which I was part, first stood with heads tilted back, fingertips nearly touching, arms wide open – ready to receive the blessing of solstice, of light and water, in ecstasy. All those raindrops falling from the sky onto my face, my open hands, my naked body – eyes closed, I was smiling.

For the second position, we kneeled, still in the same open-armed posture. Finally, we too lay down in the foetal position, going clockwise to the inner ring's anti-clockwise – inward and outward spiral, masculine and feminine, yin and yang.

It felt good to lie down on the earth at last. I wanted to soak in the moment, no pun intended, but the rain and cold didn't let us. We all sat up rather quickly, laughed, talked. Such a wonderful energy of sisterhood and joy and mischief coursing between us, among us, naked. In no rush to get dressed, I stood by the flower mandala with my hands in prayer in front of my heart.

It was a soft day in every way, from the wet grass to the sweet earth and the dewy light; a cleansing and a blessing, a release and a refill, in order to receive more and create more. Stripped bare again – all the water of Womandala flushing out the ashes of the Bealtaine fire, before the sun stands still for solstice.

Guí Grianstad an Gheimhridh/ A Winter Solstice Blessing

Lisa Leahy

Nuair atá an domhain ag dul ó dhorchacht agus chuig an solas,

(when the world is moving from darkness towards light)

Guím go mbronnfadh an tabhartas luachmhar seo ort

(I wish that you be bestowed with this valuable gift)

Seal sa suantaíoch, sa chiúnas,

(Time to pause and be quiet)

An dorchadas tharraingte tharat mar bhrat a bhfuil chomh mín le seoda

(The darkness enveloping you like a soft, velvet wrap)

Géilleadh leis an dorchacht, codlatach, séimh

(Surrender to the sleepy, gentle darkness)

Lig eagnaíocht diaga, saíocht na ngealaí, na réaltaí, na flaitheas

(Allow divine wisdom, the heavenly wisdom of the moon and the stars)

Glac an tusa istigh agus an saineolas atá fite fuaite ionat

(Accept yourself and the knowing that is interwoven in every fibre of your being)

Á nochtadh, mar ó bhroinn

(Emerging, as from the womb)

Athshaolaithe le loinnir

(Reborn in light)

An gruaim scaipthe le suíochán agus suaimhneas

(the dreariness dispelled with easeful peace)

Le spleodar agus gnaíúlacht i do chroí agus d'anam

(With joy and cheer in your heart and soul)

Réidh don ré geal nua atá uait.

(Ready for the bright new era ahead of you).

A Daily Prayer for the Peace of the Earth

Grace Sasha Clunie

For daily use at an outdoor or indoor prayer-place.

For example, in my garden I have created a circular place to walk as I pray this prayer. I have 6 elements there – fire (a small chiminea or you can light incense), water (a bird-bath!), earth (soil I'm walking on), air (fresh air of outdoors), wood (trees), and metal (a metal wind-chime with bells on it).

I pray for the souls of all beings,

May they live and die in joy and peace,

And when the time for change of worlds has come,

May each soul flow freely into the Mother Ocean of Sacred Energy,

From which all life has come,

And to which all life shall return.

COMMUNITY

'Sisterhood'

Eva Živa Blažková

Rooted Wisdom

Olivia Bowen

The wisdom is in the tree roots, how they reach out to one another. They stretch across the expanse and reach their tendrils into sacred space. All connected, pulsing with electrical charges, carrying information and their lifeforce through the soil.

The trees do not worry about needing help. They do not think, *I'm not worthy. I'm not enough. I haven't given enough.*

No. The trees accept the help sent their way. And they provide help without hesitation, or expectation.

This ability to extend help when there is abundance and receive help when there is need makes every tree in the forest stronger.

We are beginning to remember this. We are waking up to the strength that comes from community. Generous giving, and generous receiving, too. We strengthen each other. We grow together. We nourish each other. We thrive together.

Stronger trees make a stronger forest. Among the trees, there's no misconception that life is a zero sum game. Abundant help is available. Helping is everyone's responsibility. Receiving help does not make you weak.

The trees have always known. Now, we begin to remember.

Remember

Léa-Jeanne Sachot

Remember

This song is so old

I never sang it

before and yet

I know it

from deep inside

listen

the words of our stories have been lost

but our bodies carry their memory

you know

it is time to remember

harvest the wisdom

in our bones, our blood, our breath

breathe

and we will sing our songs

bleed

and we will dream the world

gather our bones around the fire

remember

and we will dance our birth into being

Community

Megan Desrosiers

What is community? This word comes from the idea that something is held in common by all, something is collectively held by the public, something is communal to a group of people. Despite increased social media friends, technological connectivity, and ways to communicate across vast distances, we are in a collective state of increasing loneliness and isolation. We have forgotten how to have deep and real connections; what it means to be in community.

My ancestors tell me of a time long ago, of a time when there was no such word or thing as community. That is because everything was one; there was no "other." Once we started to create an "other," words and names for the things that were not our own community or kin, our sense of belonging began to break down. If you have ever found yourself lost in a crowd, not knowing where you belong, this stems from a breakdown that was hundreds of thousands of years in the making.

Animals, plants, and minerals were once a part of that community. So much so that you were never alone, even if you were the only human for miles around. But wars for the things that others possessed began to tear us apart, trading possessions and women as a bride price and as peace offerings. Traditions were torn apart. Assimilation compounded over and over. No one at the time understood that the ultimate sacrifice would eventually be paid; a severing from the land, which was a severing from our way of life, from our connections, from our community.

My ancestors have also told me that I am the Keeper of the Words, but I think we can all be keepers. Words have the power to heal and the power to harm; they have the power to bring us all back together again. With breakdowns in the systems we rely on, how do we find our words and our voices again? In ritual held in community: through the ancient oral traditions. Telling stories of remembering and singing songs that unite us. In the end, when everything else has gone away, we can still find power in our voices. There is a reason music and song can unite us, it is also what makes us unique as humans. When listening to live performances, we feel like we are a part of something bigger and we become simultaneously connected and suspended in time.

Animals, plants, and minerals can also tell stories and share songs but only if we are willing to listen and share them in ways our communities can understand. They hold our memories of belonging, the memories that are waiting to be reclaimed. If you were to choose one animal, plant, or mineral to help you remember, who would you choose and why? Invite them in as you sit, quietly closing your eyes. Sway to the music they teach you, begin to hum and sing their songs, your songs. Remember those songs in your bones, in your DNA, and remember what it was like to be in community. In remembering, you know that you are always in community, no matter where you are. When you are strong enough in your remembering, gather with others who have also remembered or who are ready to remember as you share your stories and songs together, in community. Only once we find our way back to the beginning, which has been healed and re-visioned to include the oneness of all, will we be able to find our way forward again.

To know little

Nicola Wood

I know little as I age.

I am glad for it.

To know there is so much more,

more than I could ever absorb in a lifetime,

brings wonder to my eyes,

hunger to hear and understand another's truth,

propels me to seek my own and allow my truth to move, change, inspire me in this lifetime,

over and over and over.

When you move through the world as if you know it all,

you place yourself on a step above.

A shadow falls across the world you meet,

blinding you to the wisdom in front of you.

To truly accept you know little, you meet life on equal footing.

Humble.

Able to hear, feel all of life,

all creatures, plants and elements.

We become seekers with open hearts,

and perhaps even gain the gift of a grain of wisdom

before we depart.

Community and Connection:
A Vision for the Future

Rachel Glueck

Over the forty-three years of my life, I have sought to collect stories that could teach, perspectives that could give a glimpse of Truth. From the Midwest of the U.S. to Hawaii, Europe and Vietnam to India and Nepal, and Indigenous communities in Panama and Mexico, I searched for the root of the social illnesses of our modern Western life and potential cures.

It's clear to me that what ails us is our lack of connection – to the earth, to one another, to our deeper sense of self. We've gained greater freedom to believe and behave in a way that feels true to us as individuals, but amidst the ruckus of consumerism and the push for individualism, we've lost our ability to hear our own true voice. We've lost our sense of belonging to a place and a people. And we've lost the supportive structure of having a tribe.

The greatest harm the patriarchy has done to us is to divest us of our innate sense of belonging and worth. We've become isolated from one another and from the land we once cherished. It is a devastatingly lonely existence. And that loneliness is manifest in the form of addiction, abuse, violence, greed, and the emptiness of our now-normal, consumer-based lives.

If the disease is disconnection then the cure must be Community – an entirely new way of living where nourishing one another and stewarding the earth that nourishes us takes precedence above all else. But what does that look like? I suppose each must decide for themselves. What matters isn't how much or how little we share, but *how* we share it.

Today we live like islands in an archipelago – loosely tied but not connected. We now have to schedule time to meet, share, and support each other – no easy task in our frantic, modern lives. And so Community means an end to the nuclear family. Not an end to personal space and autonomy, but rather the conscious cultivation of active communal space as the centre of our lives. It means intergenerational living. It means a child isn't trapped by the capacities and beliefs of only its parents but can learn and expand with the influence of neighbours and friends. It means a single parent (or a couple) doesn't carry the full burden of raising the children, earning a living, cleaning the house, maintaining the property, and attending to the myriad details that life requires. Community means the elderly, childless woman and the anxiety-ridden teenager are naturally held in a loving, supportive embrace because we've replaced a profits-centred social structure with a human-centred one.

Imagine for a moment the number of women currently in abusive relationships or unfulfilling partnerships that would actually be able to leave and start a better life because they wouldn't have to do it all alone! Imagine how much time would be freed up if groups of parents were to share the workload. Fifty years ago, families could sustain themselves with only one parent working; today we struggle to sustain ourselves with both parents working full-time. And with each passing year, it only grows harder. Without this radical change, what security do future generations have?

Community is a system of support. It is an end to 'us versus them,' to 'keeping up with the Joneses' – an end to othering those that are different. For centuries our lives have been led by the Father figure. It is time for the Mother figure. The Mother is the nurturer; she is compassion, she is connection. She cares for all of her children alike.

To move beyond the patriarchy, we must prioritise Community and Connection. We'll need a wealth of emotional intelligence, compassion, and honest communication to make those things a reality. It's a long road to this vision. The place to begin is with radical honesty and vulnerability. We must first allow ourselves to be vulnerable enough to reach deeper truths and share our fears and hopes with others. We must be honest with ourselves: about what is working and what is not, what is hurting and what healing we need. But we cannot stay stuck in the pain. We must immerse ourselves in our vision for the future – and then step into it. We must be brave enough to throw off the expectations of others, speak our truth, and forge a path forward.

We begin organically: with ourselves first, then gathering the members of our tribe to consciously build this Community together.

A World Forged of Blood and Milk and Bone

Jessica Sheather-Neumann

We are the volatile

Sea salt on flames

We are the constant

The moon, with its rhythmic pull

We are the sisters

Hands and hearts linked

Even when not by blood

We are the mothers,

The wise ones, stories

Passed down like links

In a fire-wrought chain.

We are the stars

In an endless night sky.

CLOSING

'Ancestral Mother Holding'

Siobhán McGuire

Gather the Women

Lynette Allen

We're gathering again. The women. We're gathering. And we're remembering. We're remembering the power we hold. We're remembering the fire in us, the words we used as spells and the medicines we grew, we're taking it all back and there are swathes of us, all around the planet, with fire in our bellies and a thirst for the forgotten. We're drumming, can you hear us? We're gathering on beaches and in forests and we're calling you in darling. We have our hands in the soil, we're stomping on the earth, hollering out loud and we're sitting together, in silence. We're listening to each other, communing with the women of the past, inviting in the ancients, the rituals and the cycles of nature once more. We're re-learning and unearthing, bringing back the names of the witches they burned, giving them the burials and the tenderness they so desperately needed back then. For they were our blood line, those women, we were born from them. And now, we're the firekeepers! We're not scared anymore, we're rising and we're asking you to join us. We're safe to be seen now, to stand in the middle of our power and personal space and flirt with the universe and its roaring, raging forces of love. We are here, we women. We are here and we bring medicine. The medicine of words, of intention, of sacred space and of sister circle. We're laying alters with the stones of the past and we're inviting healing – yours and ours. We're here with the soft, the feminine, the mothers and the collective. We are a wise counsel of women, and we are here to speak. We're writing too; of strength, of reclaiming and of the relief of finding our voices, of the courage to be heard. We're here; the granddaughters of the granddaughters of the granddaughters. We remembered you see, that in a sea of masculine, *we* were the ones who weaved life, *we* were the keepers of insight and *we* knew all along! We were always the guides and we're speaking of it now. We are gathering…in plain view…so other women can sit with us…the covens, the red tents and the sister circles. We're in homes, around kitchen tables, in fields, yurts and village halls. Start yours darling, invite the women you know, start the conversations that otherwise would never be aired. Share, write, remember ritual and drum…loudly! Make it open house, so they can hold your hand and hold you up, so they can sing and drum with you, until you remember who you are! Gather the women darling. Your daughters need it and so do you.

The Gathering Time

Ruth Everson

Stop what you are doing,
Put down: the book
              the work
              the cup of coffee
              the slice of cake,
This is the gathering time.
Bring legs strong enough to stand
with the woman whose world has fallen.
Bring arms gentle enough to hold
the frozen heart about to break.
Bring hands cupped into dams
to safe-store the spilling tears.

This is the gathering time.

Bring songs to sing away new silence,
Bring love like flowers and forests,
Build the bowers where despair can rest,
Send out your words like birds on a seeking wind.

Gather the ones you love.

Gather the ones you don't love.

Sisters, there is only one circle now.

Come.

New Moon Prayers

Jane Hardwicke Collings

This is one of the ways I use my awareness of the wisdom of the cycles for my personal inner work, and to stoke the fires of our revolution…

I do a spell, make an intention, a prayer, a wish…they're all the same thing…

I call my Guides and Teachers, my Animal Allies be with me,

and often,

I call the Dragons…

I close my eyes,

I stand, one hand on my heart

the other on my womb.

I take my awareness to my feet,

I send my roots down deep into the Mother.

I breathe up yin energy from the Earth, up my roots to fill my body.

I focus with my full awareness on my connection with the Earth.

I refocus and send long silver tendrils out of the top of my head up into the heavens.

I look with eyes on the ends of the tendrils and I face the Sun.

I breathe in yang energy from the Sun, down the tendrils and into my body.

I take my awareness to my heart,

I think of someone I love right then,

and I feel a glow, a warmth, a lit space in my heart.

I breathe in and out of my heart

charging the yin and yang energy I breathed in with my love.

And then I grow the light in my heart, as big as I need right then,

maybe around myself,

maybe around the group in circle,

maybe around around the planet.

I speak my prayers,

usually the threefold prayer –

one for myself, one for my community,

and one for the planet or humanity or a global issue.
I speak my prayers
through the energy I am sending forth with the light from my heart.
I see, feel the reach of my prayers.
Sometimes visions arise.
I pause.
I give great thanks.
I put my hands in the prayer position,
I open my eyes and say:
And so it is.
And so it is.
And so it is.

Then I watch for the clues and the cues that come,
that are the information I need to fulfil my prayers.
These come from either right in front of me, or the 'book that falls off the shelf', or serendipity happens.

I work with the prayers through the cycle of birth, growth, full bloom, harvest, decay, death, rebirth, and on…
And I trust the process.
And I give thanks for what is for the highest good of all.
Let's all do this every New Moon!

Cycles of Belonging

Stella Tomlinson

Thank you for making this journey home to belonging. Thank you for bringing reverence for my sacred cycles into your life. And know that this will change your life, and in doing so, you are changing the world along with the wider circle of sisters who have also heard this call. Imagine the world changing. Envision a planet where I am held in loving reverence and the cycles of life are considered sacred. What would this world look and feel like? Imagine it now, my love…

Imagine a world where women and their cyclic nature are honoured and respected. Where girls mark their entry into womanhood at menarche with sacred celebration within their communities. Imagine a world where women embrace their menstrual cycle as a guide to living in rhythm with their divine body, their energies, gifts and soul. Imagine a world where women listen to their intuition and trust their emotions. And imagine a world where women are crowned Wise Elders at menopause and are respected as wisdom keepers and treasured mentors in their community.

Imagine a world that lives in deep intimacy with nature's cycles of life and has rejected the linear model of perpetual growth that is destroying the planet; where living wholeheartedly for the good of your soul and for the good of the community is prized above grasping after more for the individual – a world where it's considered normal to live simply, with enough for your real needs.

Imagine a world where community and kindness is prized above competition and materialistic greed; where the hustle and grind has been replaced by recognition that a good life contains time to dream and reflect; a world where it's no longer a badge of honour to live at a hundred miles an hour just to stand still, which instead honours the need for rest and time to daydream, to make space for magic, and to live in tune with the pulse of Mother Earth. Imagine a world that values the wisdom gained when you learn how to surf the wild liminal edges between wakefulness and sleep and access the treasure trove of vision and creativity that lies there; a world that honours listening to and acting upon the wise whispers of the soul.

Imagine a world where it's considered perfectly natural to talk to trees, to sing with a songbird, to listen to the whispering wind and the rippling river, to say hello to the flowers as they grow and bloom and to hear the Moon's whispers; where it's customary to see messages in the stars and to acknowledge the presence and influence of the planets. A world that recognizes that we live on a beautiful animate Earth in an intelligent cosmos, and that each human life and soul is intimately entwined with nature.

Imagine a world where you live open to wonder and awe, and the magic that is within and all around each person; a world that enthusiastically embraces mystery, cultivates curiosity and trusts in what is difficult to understand but can be felt anyway – a world which nurtures the numinous.

Imagine living in a world with meaning, where creating simple rituals and ceremonies is a normal part of everyday life, where life is lived with intention. Imagine a world where rites of passage are marked in recognition of the seasons and the phases of the Moon, where crises and healings are honoured and where pilgrimages are made on the land and in the heart. Where life is truly celebrated.

Envision this world where a healthier way of life has taken root, where all live in reverence of and in belonging to each other and Mother Earth.

How would that be?

Envision this world and hold it tightly and closely in your heart and soul, cherish this vision and trust that it is possible. Let hope be your guiding star and action your route to get there.

And know this, dear woman: this is the world you are now helping to co-create.

So take your place in the circle and root yourself here where you are so welcome and where you are so needed. Woman, never forget that you are my presence and power embodied in human form. I need you to be awake and aware and to speak your sovereign truth and own your wise, wild power. So, rise up as the vital, wise, radiant force of nature that you are!

Extract from *Cycles of Belonging* by Stella Tomlinson, Womancraft Publishing (2021)

The Quickening: A Blessing for Beginning

Iona F Millar

May she come to you through the stillness; this stirring.
This first flutter. This mystical movement.
This fragile magic.

Even here. Even now.
Even in what seems
the barren spaces;
the torn and tattered places.

May you know

that cocooned in the womb of your soul,

possibility is still dancing delicately into existence.

The tiny trace of her heart

pulsing her promise

to *become,*

become,

become.

May the seed of her being hold and soothe you,

as you whisper your longings to her forming.

May you come to know her as 'Hope'.

This embryonic clustering.

This constellation of aliveness.

This chrysalis of *something else.*

A *one day.*

A *maybe.*

A *more.*

May you cradle her oh so tenderly.

And sing her sweet lullabies through the night.

As you wait together on the dawn.

As you nest on the promise of wings.

Biding your time; until she is strong enough

to unfurl into the bright savage beauty

of beginning.

And grace the sky.

And fly.

A Letter to My Daughters

Monica Welter

To My Daughters,

I am writing to you so I will never forget, and you will always remember the most important part of being a Woman. You, my beloved daughters, are the Wisdom Keepers of the Earth.

You innately possess and preserve ancient knowledge from every Woman who preceded you since the birth of Mother Earth. Wisdom from the Ancients, the All-Knowings and the Goddesses swirls within you, waiting to be re-membered.

There will be times in your lives when these obscure understandings come out of the shadows and into the light of your being, revealing truths to the mysteries of life. These secrets are your birthright, your heritage, and your future.

Within you is a sacred vessel of Magic. A hidden and mysterious entranceway through which all human life must pass before entering the light of the world. This is the center of your Womanhood, the place of conception, creation, and growth where life is held within the darkness until birth. Where the secrets and mysteries lay dormant waiting to be released.

Although there are challenges, inconveniences, prejudices, and injustices you may face because you are in possession of this revered vessel, this intrinsic holder sustains your superpower.

The container of conception that rests inside of you is full of life and potential. The honor of carrying an epicenter of creative power, an energetic well, and a direct connection to the cosmos has been bestowed upon you. With this gift comes great responsibilities and tremendous fulfillment. To harness the full beauty of Womanhood you must believe in yourself, respect your sacredness, and uphold and assert the Wisdom of the Sisterhood.

As you journey through each passing year, connect to the Sacred Feminine within to guide you. Harness the courage of the Maiden when trying something new. Call upon the heart of the Mother to nurture yourself and others. Summon the intuition of the Crone to guide you to discern what is right for you.

If there are times you doubt or question yourself because of internal or external forces, remember you hold the vessel of Divine creation within you. All you must do is re-member; put the pieces back together to form the whole and the knowing will return. For you, my daughters, are the Wisdom Keepers of the Earth.

All my love,

Mom

Towering Women

Aisling Henrard

Take my hand, baby girl.
Climb up.

Stand on my shoulders,
as I stood on my mother's shoulders,
as she on her mother's,
as she on hers.

The tower extends
up and down,
left and right.
An infallible circle of women.

Look at your cousins to your left.
Look at your aunts to your right.
Look at Gráinne, Brigid and Mary.

You are held.
You are loved.

'Mandala'

Nicola Lilly

About the Contributors

Aisha Hannibal is a campaigner and programme manager who supports communities to lead change on issues from social equity to environmental justice. Her passion for collective care runs a thread through her work – from co-founding the Red Tent Directory with Mary Ann to leading national campaigns – to amplify multiple voices and build healthier, more connected communities. Aisha is co-author of *Red Tents: Unravelling our Past and Weaving a Shared Future* from Womancraft Publishing. She thrives when working at the edges – whether making change or encouraging others to find their own, by climbing a mountain or dipping in the sea.

Aisling Henrard's work is an attempt to digest the contemporary female experience. She explores female identity, mostly around self versus expectations. Living in Brussels she works as a personal coach and as an English language proofreader and editor for cultural institutions in Belgium. She creates text-based visual art, short story fiction and non-fiction.

Alethia is a lesbian poet, mother and grandmother, caregiver and aromatherapist, gardener and bird watcher. She lives happily in a pine forest in the Pacific NW of the U.S. with the wildlife and pollinators.

ALisa Starkweather, visionary and facilitator, devoted four decades + to the work of the Sacred Feminine and women's transformative leadership. She founded in 1998 her women's mystery school, Priestess Path, the Women's Belly and Womb conferences, Daughters of the Earth Gatherings, the global grass-roots Red Tent (Temple) Movement and co-founded Women in Power initiations, uplifting the fierce feminine to confront predator energy through Shadow Work. Much of her work was purposefully undocumented for women to meet mystery in her containers, yet her influence is in the roots of much that grew from her devotion and those in her communities who gave immense lifeforce for our palpable rise. Contact via alisastarkweather@me.com for private immersive work at her home (Massachusetts) and for online global coaching.

Amy Wilding has been leading women's circles and mother-daughter circles in the Louisville area for over fifteen years. Her soul work is, first and foremost, dismantling patriarchy by creating safe spaces for women to access their wild wisdom and reclaim their inherent power. She is passionate about guiding menstruators of all ages in unlearning the shame and taboo related to our amazing, powerful bodies and cultivating body sovereignty, cycle literacy, and empowered embodiment.

She is a queer and inclusive feminist, author, and National Board Certified Integrative Women's Health Coach. Her first first book, *Wild & Wise: Sacred Feminine Meditations for Women's Circles & Personal Awakening*, was published in 2017, and her next book, *Period of Change: Welcoming Your Daughter's Period with Care and Confidence* will be published in early 2026, both from Womancraft Publishing.

This essay is based on Amy Wilding's Five Sacred Elements of Women's Circle Leadership Training, a comprehensive curriculum that guides aspiring circle-holders not only in creating sacred, inclusive, and transformational spaces for women – but in uncovering and cultivating their own unique magic as leaders.

To deepen your journey and enrol in the full course, visit amywilding.com

Andrea Gonzalez is a Guatemalan woman, who rebirthed in the sacred lands of Hawaii. Motherhood became her teacher and made her into a sacred space holder. She is a homeschooling mother of three beautiful souls, full spectrum birth keeper, mentor for young girls and coming of age facilitator for mothers of young boys and girls. Andrea is a weaver of journeys of the soul. A mother, daughter and sister.

Anne Reeder Heck is a writer, healer, artist and fierce believer in miracles. author of *A Fierce Belief in Miracles*, and *Float on Leaves*, Anne is devoted to guiding others to trust themselves, open to their intuition, and experience life's magic. She lives in Asheville, North Carolina. anneheck.com · IG @anneheck1

Annette Vaucanson Kelly is a writer, mother and wild swimmer. A former outdoor family blogger and reformed climate activist, she writes Another World is Possible on Substack. She is French and lives with her family in Greystones, Co Wicklow, Ireland. annettevaucansonkelly.substack.com · IG @annette_four_acorns

Autumn Blackwood is an ordained Pagan priestess, witch, Usui Reiki Master, poet, and women's empowerment coach. When not working with women to heal their feminine wound, you can find her reading the latest romantasy, crocheting, listening to K-pop, or spending time with her wife and pet bunny, Marshmallow. untamedpriestess.com · IG @untamedpriestess

Carly Mountain is a women's initiatory guide, a psychotherapist, breathworker and writer. Her work has evolved over twenty years of working with sacred practice and space holding. She is author of *Descent & Rising: Women's Stories & the Embodiment of the Inanna Myth* and *Untamed Pleasure* from Womancraft Publishing. She lives in Sheffield, England with her husband and two daughters.

Cath Jevon is a rites of passage keeper, working in the threshold spaces and has spent many years holding red tent circles, workshops and ceremonies. Cath is currently journeying with severe chronic illness and learning to express, practice and commune with her beautiful New Forest surroundings in new ways.

Charlotte Thomson-Morley is a Pagan artist based in Nottingham UK. Charlotte specialises in creating paintings reminiscent of Neolithic Goddess sculptures, but which are rooted in the reality of celebrating her own body, bodies that aren't shown frequently enough in spiritual art, and the diversity and beauty of the human form. charlottethomson.co.uk · IG @charlotteart

Coco Oya Cienna-Rey, author of *Digging for Mother's Bones* from Womancraft Publishing, is a UK based creative, mystic, soul guide and writer. Her creativity is informed by her journey as a devotee of the Tantric path (an embodied path of self-liberation) and being a channel for the Divine Feminine. Deeply sensitive and highly empathic she can be found weaving her intuitive gives at creativelycoco.com

Donna Fontanarose Rabuck is a writer, teacher, ritual leader, and the Director of the Center for the Sacred Feminine in Tucson, Arizona for almost 30 years. She offers women's circles, playshops, retreats, private rituals, and consultations.

You can reach her at donnarabuck@gmail.com; visit her website at centerforsacredfeminine.org.

Elle Harrigan lives in Buffalo, New York, USA. She is a contributing writer with the Religious Naturalist Association and hosts @livingwildwisdom on Instagram focused on nature and spirituality. Her self-published book, *Seeing Differently: Nature and Art as a Path to Wholeness, Freedom, and a Transformed Life,* was released in 2023. livingwildwisdom.com

Ellen Dee Davidson lives in the redwoods of northern California. Thirty years ago, the old growth redwood tree in her backyard began teaching her in dreams. She is the author of several books including *Forest Bathing in Ancient Redwoods* out, 2025, Inner Traditions. ellendeedavidson.com · FB @ellen.davidson.583

Erika Zinsmeister, MS, PhD. Erika is a white, cisgendered, middle-aged mother of two recently transplanted back into hometown soil along the New England coast. After a multi-decade streak of degree collecting and research in the health sciences, she considers herself a recovering academic learning now to root in community and the natural world.

Eva Živa Blažková is a creatrix of many kinds. She's mainly known for her vibrant watercolour art celebrating womanhood. She also offers sharing circles with art for wellbeing (CreateShareHeal, Tribe of Mothers and Gifts of Crones) in Bristol encouraging women to use their creativity for self-discovery and healing. IG @ziva.zena

Georg Cook is a poet, writer, over-thinker and nature spiritualist living on the Sussex Coast of the U.K. She is on a powerful journey of self- rediscovery following Narcissist Abuse through the healing power of nature, especially the Sea and the seasons. She is a current contributor to the Earth Pathways 2024 wall calendar. earthpathwaysshowcase.uk/contributors/cook_georg.html ·
  IG @georgcook_writer

Ger Moane is a psychologist, writer and shamanic practitioner. She was born in Galway and currently lives in Dublin. She has been a full-time writer of fiction for several years. She has written a novel and short stories about ancient Ireland, and also writes about LGBTQ+ issues. germoane@gmail.com

Gillian White is a seasoned facilitator of women's circles, public speaker, metaphysical teacher, and soul worker, and she resides in Alberta's scenic Foothills, Canada. With expertise across many spiritual disciplines, she delves into clients' inner worlds, uncovering the roots of challenges, guiding profound soul connections, and nurturing transformative spiritual practices.
gillian-white.com · IG @weaving_soul_magick

Gina Martin is a founding mother and High Priestess of Triple Spiral of Dún na Sidhe, a pagan spiritual congregation in the Hudson Valley. She is the author of the *When She Wakes* series: *Sisters of the Solstice Moon, Walking the Threads of Time* and *She is Here* from Womancraft Publishing and the *Daughters of the Goddess* series. She is a ritualist, teacher, healer, wife, mother, lover of Irish Wolfhounds, and writer of sacred songs. ginamartinauthor.com

Grace Clunie, writer and artisan. In Northern Ireland conservative Christianity still has a powerful patriarchal influence. My yearning for a new story of feminine power led me to Celtic Spirituality. I feel that the first step to changing women's experience in today's world is to change the story we tell ourselves and our children. These poems are my offering.

Hazel Evans is an award-winning visionary artist, with the gift of foresight. Hazel is a medicine woman with a powerful journey of reclaiming her heart through the shamanic life of living art and animism. An inspirational leader and mentor of deep feminine wisdom, mysteries of creation and author of the Soul Prophecy Oracle. thesovereignjourney.com · IG @thesovereignjourney

Iona F Millar lives in central Scotland where she is a practising social worker also trained in spiritual development and ministry. Passionate about pastoral support, she's offered reflective practice sessions, coaching, group supervision, soul support counselling, and a women's circle. Iona publishes her musings on life at luminem incantare, ionamillar.substack.com

Jaine Rose is an artist, storyteller, and sometime outlier, dancing the sacred trails of the Dark Mother. She is a witch journeying ever deeper into Tidal Time, unspooling patriarchy as she goes. She is co-founder of the Earth Pathways Diary, a creator of women's ritual and story, and in 2014 knitted a seven-mile long pink peace scarf (she had tonnes of help) as a piece of insane activism. She lives in Stroud in the southwest of England, and loves cats, all cats.
 jainerose.com · IG @jainerose123

Jane Hardwicke Collings is a grandmother, former homebirth midwife for 30 years, a teacher, writer and menstrual, childbirth and menopause educator. She offers training programs on mother and daughter preparation for menstruation, and all her workshops. She offers workshops on the spiritual practice of menstruation, and the sacred dimensions of pregnancy, birth and menopause. Jane founded and runs The School of Shamanic Womancraft, an international Women's Mysteries School and she has created the first holistic menstrual cycle charting app – Spinning Wheels. janehardwickecollings.com · schoolofshamanicwomancraft.com

Jeanne Teleia, LMFT, play therapist, holistic life, wellness and family coach, teaches people how to be resilient and live in alignment with their true essence. She's been facilitating or participating in women's circles for nearly forty years. In her work, she uses the power of peak experiences with dolphins, whales and Mother Nature to help people (re)gain their birthright – JOY. She is currently writing a book on 'The Gifts of Menopause', and invites your stories and experiences around changing the conversations around it. Email jteleia@gmail.com to be part of this change! YourLifeWellLived.net · SeaDreamsRetreats.com

Jennifer Margulis, Ph.D., is an award-winning science journalist and book author. Currently based in Beaufort, South Carolina, she has worked on a child survival campaign in Niger; appeared on prime-time TV in France to speak out against child slavery; and taught non-traditional students in inner-city Atlanta.
 jennifermargulis.net

Jennifer Miller is from the North Georgia mountains and currently resides in Alabama. She explores themes of earth-centered spirituality and women's empowerment in her poems and prose. Her works have appeared in *Rebelle*

Society, Sage Woman, and several feminist anthologies. Find her latest offerings at quillofthegoddess.com · IG/FB @quillofthegoddess.

Jessica Sheather-Neumann (she/her) has been published in *Mutter Magazine* (now *Motherlore*), *Scribente Maternum, Feminartsy* and the anthology, *Christmas Cheerios*. She lives in Australia and runs a writing group for parents. You can find her on IG @readingjesssn.

Jessica M Starr is a Welsh folk-witch and astrologer who helps women heal their connection with themselves and with the feminine divine. She lives in her ancestral homeland of South Wales with her musician husband and their two unschooled children. Every Monday she sends Magic Mail, subscribe at jessicaandthemoon.com

Kelley Davis Sookram is a Circle attender and keeper. She believes Circle can foster healing and transform lives. She creates to empower and connect with others. Her Alchemy of F*ck oracle deck was inspired by her experiences sitting in New Moon Circles. She is most at home collecting treasures by the Big Lake.
   IG @leavingclouddesigns

Kelly Barrett is a researcher, writer, artist, and yogini, living in the Sangre de Cristo mountains of New Mexico, and on the northern coast of California. She holds a Masters in Consciousness and Transformative Studies. In 2017 she completed a research study, The Great Magic: Rewilding the Feminine and continues to write about what she and six other co-researchers discovered at 101eyes.com. As an artist, she has traveled the world interacting with different environments, teasing out subliminal narratives or moods and translating what emerges. Currently she is working on a synthesis of twenty- five years of performance in book form. madzoga.com

Léa-Jeanne Sachot is an Embodied Mindfulness facilitator, Menstrual Cycle Wisdom mentor, Womb-Healing artist, and Earth activist. She currently lives in France and Spain and offers 1:1 mentoring and healing sessions, workshops, and women's circles online. Her womb-poetry was born from a flow-writing, singing and blood-painting experience during her moon-time meditation.
   You can contact her at ljsachot@gmail.com

Lisa Leahy lives in Ballyhooly, Co. Cork. She is a teacher, celebrant and creator of ceremonies to celebrate significant points in the Celtic Calendar – the Summer and Winter Solstices, Samhain, Imbolc/Brigid and Bealtaine. Lisa gathers wild wisdom wandering the hedgerows, woods and hills that surround her.

Louise Allen is an artist, medicine lodge holder and currently works as the director of the Creative Futures Academy. Her area of interest is in Indigenous cultures and nature-based practices that rebuild people's connection with the natural world. She lives in Bray, Co. Wicklow, Ireland. linkedin.com/in/louise-allen-2021

Lucy H. Pearce is the author of twelve life-changing non-fiction books for women, including four #1 Amazon bestsellers and three Nautilus Silver Award Winners – *Burning Woman, Medicine Woman* and *Creatrix: she who makes*. She is a sought-after speaker and teacher on women's creativity and spirituality. She founded Womancraft Publishing in 2014 and the Creative Magic podcast in 2024. A mother of three, she lives in Cork, Ireland.
lucyhpearce.com · IG/FB @lucyhpearce

Lynette Allen is the author of the *A Woman's Blessing* trilogy, and the curator/editor of collaborations *A Woman's Voice is a Revolution* and *The Women who Gathered*. Her non-fiction focuses on women finding their voice and their connection to themselves. She lives in Bali, Indonesia.
awomansblessing.com · IG @thelynetteallen

Macy-Doris is maiden, earth keeper, medicine woman, writer, poet, Shamanic healer and co-founder of Pine Tree Circles. Her life's path is to share this magic with other teen girls. Having birthed *The Maiden Journey* in her thirteenth year she now holds a safe sacred space for young women to learn about the inner journey, through her online offering Moon Maidens Membership to in person ceremonies, empowering them to stand in their power. Her work is centred around the four powerful female archetypes of Maiden, Mother, Maga, Crone, bringing them all home. subscribepage.io/7mbS3Z · IG/FB @pinetreecircles

Mary Ann Clements is a feminist writer, leader, facilitator and coach and helps people and organisations explore how the injustice they stand against shows up in them. She is currently Co-CEO at ADD international, a participatory grant maker for disability justice and also working on her first novel. Aisha and Mary Ann ran the Red Tent Directory together for a decade and co-authored *Red Tents: Unravelling our Past and Weaving a Shared Future* from Womancraft Publishing.

Megan Desrosiers is an ancient and intuitive healer with deep connections to animals, plants, minerals and her ancestors. Through her art, writing and healing practices, she supports and inspires others to become more comfortable with transition and the continuous cycles of life and death. Learn more and connect at herbalbonesart.com

Melia Keeton-Digby is a writer and speech-language pathologist specializing in dyslexia. She is the author of *The Heroines Club* and *The Hero's Heart* from Womancraft Publishing. She is the founder and creator of The Nest, a sacred gathering space in Georgia, USA, where she first birthed her mother-daughter and mother-son empowerment circles, on which her books are based. Melia is passionate about supporting mothers in raising confident and connected children.

Molly Remer, MSW, D.Min, is a priestess, mystic, and poet in central Missouri. Molly and her husband Mark co-create Story Goddesses at Brigid's Grove. Molly is the author of many books, including *Walking with Persephone, Whole and Holy, Womanrunes*, the *Goddess Devotional* and *365 Days of Goddess*. She is the creatrix of the devotional experience #30DaysofGoddess and she loves savoring small magic and everyday enchantment.

30daysofgoddess.com · brigidsgrove.etsy.com

Monica Welter, BSN, RN is a truth seeker, a mother, a nurse and an aromatherapist who facilitates a Women's Circle and is on a mission to assist women of all ages re-align themselves with their own truth. She lives in Long Island, New York. inquirewithinyourself.com · IG @inquirewithinyourself

Nia Solomon is poet living in Wiltshire. Her writing centres around the issues and intersection of feminism, culture and the environment. Her poetry has appeared in various journals and anthologies and has been short-listed for major UK poetry competitions. She is currently working on her first pamphlet which seeks to remind us of our deep connection to nature and the more-than-human realms. It is the work of a poet who is recovering her root to the land. IG @nia.h.solomon

Nicola Lilly is a writer and artist based in Ireland. Unfulfilled in accountancy, Nicola felt drawn towards energy healing. Her work involved healing for individuals, hosting circles and teaching Reiki. Currently a SAHM committed to personal healing, her world is filled with creative exploration and learning to honour the Sacred Feminine. IG @nicolalillyartist / @sacredfemininewisdom

Nicola Wood holds women circles as part of her offering at Women Replanting and also works in the charity sector. She's a creative enjoying writing poetry, stories, painting and singing. Nicola is happiest when adventuring outside or camping with her family. She is a mother to three living in Wanborough, Wiltshire. IG/Substack @womenreplanting

Olivia Bowen is a certified life coach whose practice is devoted to working with nature to help people cultivate and trust their intuition. She lives in the suburbs of Washington, D.C., with her husband and two firecracker daughters who are, of course, named after plants. ThisIsSacredNature.com · IG @ThisIsSacredNature

Patricia Higgins is a Donegal-based community worker and founder of Rewilding Faith, through which she offers people creative ways to explore faith. An Interfaith Minister, married to a former Jesuit Priest, Patricia has spent her life living questions about vocation, celibacy and how to be a 'woman of God' today. patriciahiggins.ie · IG @rewilding_faith

Paula Youmell is a functional medicine RN, herbalist and holistic health educator steeped in care of body-mind-spirit. Paula's latest book is *Sacred Circle Shamanic Yoga for Releasing Stress & Trauma*. PaulaYoumellRN.com

Pippa Grace is a socially engaged artist, writer and sculptor. A passionate feminist, Pippa specialises in working with women, exploring issues including: the female body, motherhood, maternal lineage, creativity, trauma and sexual violence. Pippa published *Mother in the Mother* with Womancraft in 2019. Pippa lives in Bristol, UK. one-story.co.uk · IG @pippaonestory

Rachel Glueck is a recovering nomad rooting down in Scotland. She's the author of the award-winning, philosophical cookbook, *The Native Mexican Kitchen*. Her greatest loves are walking alone through Scotland's forests and her wise and joyful six-year-old daughter. She currently works as a content manager for a Scottish distillery. rachelglueck.com · IG @reroot_rewild

Raven S Hunter is an artist, songwriter, astrologer and writer living in the mountains of New Mexico, Land of Enchantment. Raven weaves nature's beauty and the sacred feminine into her art, music and writing. Samples of her work can be seen on her Facebook page using her mundane name, Peg Edmister. ravendreams55@yahoo.com

Rebecca Lowe is a poet, singer and freelance writer from Swansea, South Wales. She has two published collections, *Blood and Water* (The Seventh Quarry) and *Our Father Eclipse* (Culture Matters). She enjoys playing Celtic music on the hammered dulcimer. You can find her music on YouTube @BeckyLoweSwansea.

Rev Jo Royle is an Interfaith Minister and Creatrix of ceremony. She's passionate about healing the patriarchal wounds of the feminine and our beautiful earth. She LOVES to craft meaningful and magical ceremonies, for herself and others, especially nature based, in the wilds of the Isle of Skye, her home. revjoroyle.co.uk · IG @revjoroyle

Rosalie Kohler is a nature-inspired artist, writer and yoga nidra facilitator who dreams into the stories of the Living Earth singing beneath our feet. Passionate about rest, wild swimming, cyclical wisdom and rewilding the Feminine, she lives with her family in the Black Forest. spiralshores.com · IG @spiralshores

Ruth Everson is a published poet, life coach and international speaker who weaves these threads together to help people live into the most powerful versions of themselves. Poetry is the mirror that reflects who we are. It is a path through inner landscapes. IG @everson.ruth

Sayra Pinto, is the chief practitioner for Moon Jaguar Strategies LLC. In a thirty-year career devoted to cross-sectoral social transformation, Sayra has worked with numerous human service organizations, colleges and universities, public schools, and philanthropic organizations. She founded and is board chair of For a Loving Future, the board chair for the Center for Cooperative Development and Solidarity in East Boston, and a board member for the Peacemakers Lodge. Sayra holds an undergraduate degree from Middlebury College, an MFA from Goddard College, and a PhD in Interdisciplinary Studies from the Union Institute and University. She has published two chapbooks and a doctoral dissertation to date: *Pinol : Poems* (2012), *Vatolandia* (2012), and the dissertation *The Ontology of Love: A Framework for Re-Indigenizing Communities of Color in the U.S* (2015) among other ancillary publications.

Shannon Cotterill is a Level 2 Sister Circle facilitator, professional ceramicist and hand poke tattoo artist, passionate about guiding others to tap into their innate spirit, wisdom and creativity through ceremony and ritual. She regularly holds circles, Wheel of the Year events and pagan inspired pottery workshops within her Central Coast studio space, Asha Moon. Shannon is also co-host of 'Turns Out She's a Witch' podcast, and the artist and author 'Of Earth & Ether Oracle' and 'The Sacred Stones' divination tools.
  ashamoon.squarespace.com · IG @ashamoondesigns

Sharon Ann Rose is a poet and ceremonialist who liberates feminine wisdom. She helps woman walk through transitions into their native body's medicine. She's the author and co-author of three books that explore a woman's heart and sacred earth-connection. She lives in Portland, Oregon, on an urban farm with her three boys and life partner. sharonannrose.com · IG @sharonann.rose

Siobhán McGuire is an eco-somatic visual artist and poet working in paint and woodcut mediums. Originally from Manchester, Siobhán has been living in Co. Mayo since 2001. Her work explores the female body, mind and soul and the deep healing connection she has to her ancestral Irish land. IG @wildanuart.

Sophie Messager seamlessly blends science and spirituality. With a PhD in reproductive physiology, Sophie transitioned from the lab to holistic practices after experiencing an empowered birth. With over a decade of experience as a doula, educator, healer and workshop facilitator, and author of *Why Postnatal*

Recovery Matters, she offers rituals and bodywork, including the transformative Closing the Bones ritual, and integrates energy healing and shamanic drumming into her work. A holistic life transition mentor, Sophie supports women through pivotal moments like childbirth, postpartum, and perimenopause, combining her scientific knowledge with ancestral wisdom to help women to tune into their inner wisdom and reconcile their analytical and intuitive selves.

Sophie is author of *The Beat of Your Own Drum*, 2025, Womancraft Publishing. sophiemessager.com

Stella Tomlinson is an author, poet and priestess of Brigid sharing a healing path honouring life's sacred cycles. Currently she's sharing words to nourish your soul through the messy midlife chrysalis that is the peri/menopause transition.

Her offerings are based on almost twenty-five years' experience in personal and spiritual development through meditation, yoga, mindfulness, energy healing, menstrual cycle awareness, and Goddess and nature spirituality. She's been writing and teaching since 2011.

Connect with Stella on Instagram @stellatomlinson.author, read her Substack 'The Midlife Spirit' at stellatomlinson.substack.com or visit her website stellatomlinson.com

Sue Johnson is a poet, novelist and playwright. She also creates books aimed at helping other writers. She lives in Evesham, Worcestershire, UK and enjoys walking in the local countryside. Her other interests include yoga, reading and cooking. For further details see writers-toolkit.co.uk

Suzanne West lives in Durham, North Carolina, USA. She love sharing wisdom through her writing; diving deeply into the imaginal realms of metaphor, symbols, dreams, the Akashic Records, and poetry. She feels a deep calling to embody the Crone archetype as a healing balm for a troubled world.

Terry Youmell, Aragon Studio's resident artist, specializes in pencil and ink drawings as well as pastel paintings. Terry is currently writing and illustrating a children's book (maybe a series!) set in the Adirondack Mountains.

'Celestial Mother'

Terry Youmell

About the Charities

10% of the proceeds from this title are shared between the following causes.

For a Loving Future

For a Loving Future/Por un Futuro Amoroso was founded in 2021 as a home for a community of practitioners committed to a world of belonging, connection and abundance.

Beyond being a home, we have become a grassroots practice-based think tank bringing together grassroots leaders to articulate and share new practice theories emerging from their lifelong community work with a focus on the role of love in creating and sustaining long term multisectoral change in complex adaptive systems. We engage leaders to serve as advisors for our organization through the sharing of resources, relationships, tools, ideas and skills. We nurture emerging leaders to strengthen grassroots movements and build power throughout their lives.

The HOPE Foundation

The HOPE Foundation is dedicated to promoting the protection of street-dwelling and slum-connected children in Kolkata, work to free children and poor families from lives of pain, abuse, poverty and darkness.

Living on the streets, children are exposed to horrendous physical and sexual abuse. Those who survive are left to fend for themselves, with no promise of a safe future. They are forced to work from as young as five years of age to earn money for food and so cannot go to school. HOPE works to free them from child labour, funding and operating fifty-eight projects.

About Womancraft Publishing

Womancraft Publishing was founded on the revolutionary vision that women and words can change the world. We act as midwife to transformational women's words that have the power to challenge, inspire, heal and speak to the silenced aspects of ourselves.

We share powerful new voices with new visionary ideas, empowering our readers to actively co-create cultures that value and support the female and feminine. This to us is deeply exciting and powerful work.

Womancraft Publishing is a small, independent publisher, founded in 2014 by Amazon-bestselling author, Lucy H. Pearce, and is based in East Cork, Ireland. Our authors are based in the US and Europe, and several of our titles are in multiple languages – nine so far, from Polish to Chinese.

Our books have been endorsed by many of our heroines...and heroes: Oriah Mountain Dreamer, Glennie Kindred, Dr Jean Shinoda Bolen, ALisa Starkweather, Naomi Lowinsky, Steve Biddulph, Dr Michel Odent, Lynne Franks, Phyllis Curott, Thomas Moore, Jeanine Cummins...and treasured as "life-changing" by women around the world.

What sets our books apart is their focus on women's lived experience. We value Feminine ways of knowing – the intuitive, the sensory and sensual, the embodied and personal revelation – as valid and valuable ways of knowing the world and ourselves. Our books centre the personal voice of the author as woman, grounded in her research and intellectual knowing – modelling woman as an authority in her own life, something so often dismissed, belittled or silenced in our culture.

To support this, we offer many free online communities connected to our titles, so that you can continue the journey of discovery in the company of like-minded women, long after you have closed the covers of the book.

As we find ourselves in a time where old stories, old answers and ways of being are losing their authority and relevance, we at Womancraft are actively looking for new ways forward. Our books ask important questions. They are not a wholesale refusal of our current cultural authorities – science, organised religion, academia – but rather saying, "yes and…" What is missing from these perspectives? Who is missing? How partial are these current ways of knowing? What else is needed to ensure we have a more holistic understanding? What lies beneath which has been silenced or ignored? The answer to most of these questions is the female and the Feminine. This is what our books centre.

We aim to share a diverse range of voices, of different ages, backgrounds, sexual orientations and neurotypes, seeking ever greater diversity, whilst acknowledging our limitations as a very small press. Each of our books is chosen personally by Lucy, and is hand-crafted through a creative and collaborative midwifery process.

At the heart of our Womancraft philosophy is fairness and integrity. Creatives and women have always been underpaid: not on our watch! We split royalties 50:50 with our authors. We offer support and mentoring throughout the publishing process as standard. We use almost exclusively female artists on our covers, and as well as paying fairly for these cover images, offer a royalty share and promote the artists both in the books and online. We pay above the living wage to our employees and provide flexible working practices that centre family, menstrual and health needs. We pride ourselves on being fair, open and accountable. Our books have been #1 Amazon bestsellers in many categories, Nautilus and Women's Spirituality Award winners.

Whilst far from perfect, we are proud that in our small way, Womancraft is walking its talk, living the new paradigm in the crumbling heart of the old: through financially empowering creative people, through words that honour the Feminine, through healthy working practices, and through integrating business with our lives, and rooting our economic decisions in what supports and sustains our natural environment. We are learning and improving all the time. I hope that one day soon, what we do is seen as nothing remarkable, just the norm.

We work on a full circle model of giving and receiving: reaching backwards, supporting Treesisters' reforestation projects and the UNHCR girls' education fund, and forwards via Worldreader, providing e-books at no-cost to education projects for girls and women in developing countries – over half a million readers so far. We donate many paperback copies to menstrual education projects, red tents, women's groups and women's libraries around the world including: India, South Africa, Haiti, USA, Canada, UK, Ireland and France… As we grow, we can give more back.

We build alliances with independent, women-run media outlets in order to share our books and help promote and support these important publications. We speak from our place within the circle of women, sharing our vision, and encouraging them to share it onwards, in ever-widening circles.

We are honoured that the Womancraft community is growing internationally year on year, seeding red tents, book groups, women's circles, ceremonies and classes into the fabric of our world.

We are the change we want to see in this world. Thank you for your presence in making this dream a reality.

We invite you to join our Womancraft Facebook Community Group…to connect with other readers and our authors…as well as dedicated Facebook groups for readers of: *Creatrix; Yoga for Witches; Medicine Woman; Burning Woman; The Way of the Seabhean; She of the Sea* and many more.

Do join our mailing list to receive our free digital care package, as well as exclusive pre-order offers and discounts.

womancraftpublishing.com

Also from Womancraft Publishing

Weaving Our Way Beyond Patriarchy

— A Womancraft Publishing Compendium

Compiled, edited and with an introduction by
Womancraft Publishing founder Lucy H. Pearce.

If what we are experiencing right now are the death throes of patriarchy…how did we get here…and what comes next?

Taking the ancient women's work of weaving as its framework, *Weaving Our Way Beyond Patriarchy* is a collaborative text of voices woven from the Womancraft community – our own authors, both established and upcoming, aligned authors published elsewhere, and readers, ranging in age from twelve to over seventy. Through poetry, prose, letters, articles and artwork, more than eighty women – authors, activists, artists, community builders, doctors, doulas, priestesses, poets, permaculturalists, professors, teachers, witches, yoga teachers, mothers, grandmothers – reflect on what it might look like beyond patriarchy and how we might get there, from the big picture to the domestic details.

This diverse and inclusive compendium of contemporary women's wisdom is bound to become a much-loved handbook to carry us forward through these strange and uncertain times, with words to encourage and inspire us and our sisters, daughters, granddaughters, friends and communities.

Celebrating the ten-year anniversary of Womancraft Publishing.

Wild & Wise

— sacred feminine meditations for women's circles & personal awakening

Amy Wilding

Wild & Wise is not merely a collection of guided meditations, but a potent tool for personal and global transformation. The compelling meditations within beckon you to explore the powerful realm of symbolism and archetypes, inviting you to access your wild and wise inner knowing. Suitable for reflective reading, or to facilitate healing and empowerment for women who gather in red tents, moon lodges, women's circles and ceremonies.

Full Circle Health

— integrated health charting for women

Lucy H. Pearce

Welcome to *Full Circle Health*: a creative approach to holistic health for all who love planners, trackers and bullet journals to guide and support you in a greater understanding of your physical, mental and emotional health. Whether you are menstruating or not, pregnant or post-partum, Full Circle Health provides a highly flexible, deeply supportive way of tracking your health, whatever your current health conditions.

Dirty & Divine
— *a transformative journey through tarot*

Alice Grist

There is something sacred within you, in all that you are and all that you do. In a mix of you that is everyday dirty, and spiritually divine, there is something so perfect, something more. Welcome to your journey back home; to your dirty, divine passage back to you.

Wherever you are, whether beginner or seasoned tarot practitioner, *Dirty & Divine* is written for you, to accompany you on a powerful personal intuitive journey to plumb the depths of your existence and encompass the spectrum of wisdom that the cards can offer.

Dirty & Divine is a tarot-led vision quest to reclaiming your femininity in all its lucid and colourful depths.

The Beat of Your Own Drum
— *the history, science and contemporary use of drumming as a path for women's wisdom, health, and transformation*

Sophie Messager

Part practical guide, part scholarly exploration, and part inspirational journey, *The Beat of your own Drum* invites women to reclaim their rhythmic heritage and harness the healing power of percussion for personal and collective transformation.

Weaving together science and sacred wisdom, Sophie Messager explores the transformative power of drumming for women's wellbeing. Written by a former biological research scientist turned holistic women mentor, this ground-breaking text bridges the gap between evidence-based research and ancient feminine wisdom.

Digging for Mother's Bones
— a guide to unearthing true feminine nature

Coco Oya Cienna-Rey

Do you hear Her calling? Softly, oh so sweetly, edging you home.

Digging for Mother's Bones is a clarion call, an awakening for women who are ready for a new evolutionary edge of growth. This is a powerful guidebook to bring us home to The Great Mother – the regenerative force of creation, She who is the cosmic womb, the feminine aspect of the divine; so that we may unearth the wisdom of our bodies as living libraries and remember how to be the wisdom-keepers that can resurrect Her bones.

Cycles of Belonging
— Honouring ourselves through the sacred cycles of life

Stella Tomlinson

Cycles of Belonging is a guide to unlocking the powers of cyclic living to lead a more fulfilling, meaningful, and wholehearted life. It offers an embodied feminine and feminist psycho-spiritual path for women to reclaim their inner wisdom, follow the callings of their soul, and come home to a profound sense of belonging to the seasons and cycles of life.

Stella Tomlinson guides you through six sacred temples of belonging, each of which explores the energies of each cycle, their healing gifts and shadows/challenges, together with practical suggestions on how to work with the cycles, including journal prompts, rituals and blessings, as well as magical words of poetry and soul guidance.

Walking with Persephone
— A Journey of Midlife Descent and Renewal

Molly Remer

Midlife can be a time of great change – inner and outer. How do we journey through this… and what can we learn in the process? Molly Remer is our personal guide to the unraveling and reweaving required in midlife. She invites us to take a walk with the goddess Persephone, whose story of descent into the Underworld has much to teach us. This book is a journey of soul-rebuilding, of putting the pieces of oneself back together.

Walking with Persephone weaves together personal insights and reflections with experiences in practical priestessing, family life, and explorations of the natural world. It advocates opening our eyes to the wonder around us, encouraging the reader to both look within themselves for truths about living, but also to the earth, the air, the animals, and plants we share our lives with.

Descent & Rising
— Women's Stories & the Embodiment of the Inanna Myth

Carly Mountain

Descent & Rising explores real stories of women's descents into the underworld of the psyche – journeys of dissolution, grief and breakdown precipitated by trauma, fertility issues, loss of loved ones, mental health struggles, FGM, sexual abuse, birthing experiences, illness, war, burnout…

This is territory that Carly Mountain, psychotherapist and women's initiatory guide, knows intimately, and guides us through with exquisite care and insight, using the ancient Sumerian myth of the goddess Inanna as a blueprint. She maps not only the descent but the rising and familiarises us with a process of female psycho-spiritual growth overlooked in patriarchal culture.

Red Tents

— Unravelling our Past and Weaving a Shared Future

Aisha Hannibal and Mary Ann Clements

When women come together, magic happens. We know this to be true from our own experience. And we have also seen that something else happens too when these communities grow: they can become a beacon to others.

Full of inspiration and practical learning, along with questions and practices to support and stimulate discussion about some of the challenges Red Tents face.

Written by the founders of the Red Tent Directory, including interviews with over seventy women from diverse backgrounds who run Red Tents, this book provides the practical support women need to establish and sustain a Red Tent in their own community. With a foreword by ALisa Starkweather.

The Heroines Club

— a Mother-Daughter Empowerment Circle

Melia Keeton-Digby

The Heroines Club offers nourishing guidance and a creative approach for mothers and daughters, aged 7+, to learn and grow together through the study of women's history. Each month focuses on a different heroine, featuring athletes, inventors, artists, and revolutionaries from around the world ? including Frida Kahlo, Rosalind Franklin, Amelia Earhart, Anne Frank, Maya Angelou and Malala Yousafzai as strong role models for young girls to learn about, look up to, and be inspired by. Offering thought-provoking discussion, powerful rituals, and engaging creative activities, Melia Keeton-Digby fortifies our daughters' self-esteem, invigorates mothers' spirits, and nourishes the mother-daughter relationship. In a culture that can make mothering daughters seem intimidating and isolating, it offers an antidote: a revolutionary model for empowering your daughter and strengthening your mother-daughter relationship.

Sisters of the Solstice Moon

— Book 1 of the When She Wakes trilogy

Gina Martin

On the Winter Solstice, thirteen women across the world see the same terrifying vision. Their world is about to experience ravaging destruction. All that is now sacred will be destroyed. Each answers the call, to journey to Egypt, and save the wisdom of the Goddess:

She who is Kali Ma from the jungles of Arya, Tiamet from the Roof of the World, Badh of the Cailleach from the land of Eiru, Awa from the Land of Yemaya, Uxua of Ix Chel from the Yucatan, Parasfahe from the Land of Inanna all racing against time and history to bring us their story.

This is the history before history. This is herstory, as it emerged.

Mother in the Mother

— looking back, looking forward – women's
reflections on maternal lineage

Pippa Grace

When a woman becomes a mother, it is often a time she reflects back upon the way she herself was mothered. Our maternal inheritance from our mother, grandmother, great-grandmother and beyond can have a great influence upon the ways in which we choose to bring up our own children.

Whilst much has been written about the complexity of the mother/daughter relationship, *Mother in the Mother* explores new territory by looking at the three-way relationship between grandmother, mother and child. Featuring the voices of over fifty mothers from a diverse range of ages, cultural backgrounds and experiences exploring themes of: love, stress, loss, healing, belonging, infertility, mental and physical health issues, twin pregnancy, adoption, pre-maturity, sexuality, single motherhood, young motherhood, abortion, maternal ambiguity and long-distance relationships with families of birth.

Use of Womancraft Publishing work

Often women contact us asking if and how they may use our work. We love seeing our work out in the world. We love you sharing our words further. And we ask that you respect our hard work by acknowledging the source of the words.

We are delighted for short quotes from our books – up to 200 words – to be shared as memes or in your own articles or books, provided they are clearly accompanied by the author's name and the book's title.

We are also very happy for the materials in our books to be shared amongst women's communities: to be studied by book groups, discussed in classes, read from in ceremony, quoted on social media… with the following provisos:

- If content from the book is shared in written or spoken form, the book's author and title must be referenced clearly.

- The only person fully qualified to teach the material from any of our titles is the author of the book itself. There are no accredited teachers of this work. Please do not make claims of this sort.

- If you are creating a course devoted to the content of one of our books, its title and author must be clearly acknowledged on all promotional material (posters, websites, social media posts).

- The book's cover may be used in promotional materials or social media posts. The cover art is copyright of the artist and has been licensed exclusively for this book. Any element of the book's cover or font may not be used in branding your own marketing materials when teaching the content of the book, or content very similar to the original book.

- No more than two double page spreads, or four single pages of any book may be photocopied as teaching materials.

We are delighted to offer a 20% discount of over five copies going to one address. You can order these on our webshop, or email us at info@womancraftpublishing.com